Dear Al,

Here is my newly published book. I hope you enjoy it. Thanks for your support for my research!

— Roseanne

Statements of Resolve

Statements of resolve – in which leaders indicate that their country is committed to a position and will not back down – are a fixture of international conflict. However, scholars have not agreed on how much these statements affect conflict outcomes or which conditions give them coercive credibility. *Statements of Resolve* argues that an important and underappreciated factor influencing the impact of resolved statements is the ability to follow through. Roseanne W. McManus explains how adversaries analyze a leader's ability to follow through on statements and shows that perceptions of the ability to follow through are influenced not only by military capabilities, but also by less obvious domestic political conditions. Through rigorous statistical tests based on quantitative coding of US presidential statements and case studies of three Cold War conflicts, this book shows that resolved statements can effectively coerce adversaries, but only when a sufficient physical and political ability to follow through is present.

Roseanne W. McManus is an Assistant Professor at Baruch College, The City University of New York. Before earning her PhD at the University of Wisconsin–Madison, she worked for four years at the US Defense Intelligence Agency, eventually rising to the position of Senior Analyst. Her dissertation, on which this book was based, was runner-up for the Kenneth Waltz Dissertation Prize from the APSA International Security and Arms Control section. She has articles published or forthcoming in *International Organization*, the *Journal of Conflict Resolution*, the *Journal of Peace Research*, and *International Interactions*.

Statements of Resolve

Achieving Coercive Credibility in International Conflict

ROSEANNE W. MCMANUS

Baruch College, The City University of New York

CAMBRIDGE
UNIVERSITY PRESS

CAMBRIDGE
UNIVERSITY PRESS

University Printing House, Cambridge CB2 8BS, United Kingdom

One Liberty Plaza, 20th Floor, New York, NY 10006, USA

477 Williamstown Road, Port Melbourne, VIC 3207, Australia

4843/24, 2nd Floor, Ansari Road, Daryaganj, Delhi – 110002, India

79 Anson Road, #06–04/06, Singapore 079906

Cambridge University Press is part of the University of Cambridge.

It furthers the University's mission by disseminating knowledge in the pursuit of education, learning, and research at the highest international levels of excellence.

www.cambridge.org
Information on this title: www.cambridge.org/9781107170346
DOI: 10.1017/9781316756263

First published 2017

Printed in the United States of America by Sheridan Books, Inc.

A catalogue record for this publication is available from the British Library.

ISBN 978-1-107-17034-6 Hardback

To my parents, John and Peggy McManus

Contents

Figures

Tables

Acknowledgments

I am grateful for the help and support of many individuals in completing this book. The first version of it took shape as my dissertation at the University of Wisconsin–Madison, and I owe the greatest debt to my two dissertation advisors: Andrew Kydd and Jon Pevehouse. Andy provided keen theoretical insights, helping me to identify gaps in my argument and strengthen it. He also worked with me patiently on improving my formal models. Jon played a critical role in the development of the statistical analysis and also provided important feedback on the theory and the application of the theory to US foreign policy. Lisa Martin was also actively involved at all stages of the dissertation process, and she helped me greatly with identifying what was most interesting about my theory and findings. My other committee members – Mark Copelovitch and Katja Favretto – also provided valuable suggestions at various stages of the project.

This project has also benefited from the advice and support of other people at the University of Wisconsin–Madison. Among the other faculty members who provided me with advice and feedback are Scott Gehlbach, Yoshiko Herrera, Daniel Kapust, Kenneth Mayer, Ryan Owens, Margaret Peters, Jonathan Renshon, Alexander Tahk, Jessica Weeks, and David Weimer. I also received valuable input from many of my friends and colleagues in the PhD program, including Jason Ardanowski, Inken von Borzyskowski, Jessica Clayton, Mert Kartal, Patrick Kearney, Richard Loeza, Kira Langoussis Mochal, Ryan Powers, Mark Toukan, and especially David Ohls. In addition, I am grateful to Nicholas Barnes, Jessica Clayton, Brandon Lamson, Rebecca LeMoine, Jennifer Peterson, Matthew Scharf, and Steven Wilson for consultation on the content analysis dictionary used in this project. I am also grateful to Hong Ding, an undergraduate student, for his assistance with reformatting my statement text files.

I converted my dissertation to a book manuscript as an assistant professor at Baruch College. At Baruch, I would like to thank my department chair, David

Jones, for creating a supportive environment for research and giving me advice on the book publication process. I would also like to thank my colleague Till Weber for statistical advice and camaraderie. In addition, I am grateful to Maria Smirnova, my undergraduate research assistant, for her work on my statement text files. Finally, I thank the Weissman School of Arts and Sciences at Baruch College for funding Maria's work and the indexing of the book.

I have also received helpful advice and feedback from many colleagues outside my institutions, including (but not limited to) Allan Dafoe, Raymond Kuo, Eleonora Mattiacci, Henry Nau, Glenn Palmer, Mark Schafer, Todd Sechser, Mark Souva, Robert Trager, Joshua Wu, and Keren Yarhi-Milo. I am also particularly grateful to the two anonymous reviewers of the book manuscript, whose comments helped me to clarify important aspects of the argument and improve the presentation of the theory and empirical results. In addition, I would like to thank B. Dan Wood and James Golby for generously sharing their research materials. I would also like to thank Gerhard Peters and John Woolley for making US presidential statements available online and answering my questions about their search engine.

At Cambridge University Press, I would like to thank Robert Dreesen for supporting the publication of the manuscript. I would also like to thank Adam Hooper, Brianda Reyes, and Meera Seth at Cambridge for guiding the manuscript through the publication process. I am also grateful to Sage Publications for allowing parts of my 2014 article in the *Journal of Peace Research* to reappear here.

I am very lucky to have had the love and support of many family members and friends. My parents, John and Peggy McManus, have always believed in me, encouraged me to excel, and supported my dreams in whatever ways they could. My mother, Peggy, deserves particular thanks for her help with proofreading the first full draft of the book manuscript. Finally, I am always deeply grateful to God for everything He has given me.

Introduction

In a speech to the nation on September 10, 2014 President Barack Obama declared that the United States would "degrade and ultimately destroy the terrorist group known as ISIL [aka the Islamic State or ISIS]." In a subsequent national address on December 6, 2015, Obama reiterated, "We will destroy ISIL and any other organization that tries to harm us." The theme of ISIL's destruction also appeared frequently in many of Obama's other remarks from 2014 onward. Although Obama sometimes included the caveat that the destruction of ISIL would take time, he emphasized that the United States was "not going to stop until we destroy this terrorist organization" (December 19, 2015, quoted in Peters and Woolley 2016). For the Islamic State, an organization estimated to consist of no more than about 30,000 fighters in 2015 (Sciutto, Starr, and Liptak 2016), being targeted for destruction by the world's most powerful country might be intimidating. Thus, a rationalist theory of conflict bargaining might predict that ISIL would seek an accommodation with the United States or modify its behavior to prevent its destruction. Yet, ISIL only increased its aggression, carrying out prominent terrorist attacks in Europe, and Islamic State leader Abu Bakr al-Baghdadi gave a defiant speech in late 2014, calling the United States "terrified, weak and powerless" and saying that ISIL would keeping fighting down to the last man (BBC 2014).

There are various possible explanations for the Islamic State's defiant response. The simplest explanation might be that the leaders of the Islamic State are irrational, but this explanation is not helpful because it precludes any logical analysis of how ISIL responds to incentives. It is also not clear that this explanation is valid, since having extreme or even depraved goals does not preclude behaving rationally to achieve them. One alternate explanation within the realm of rationality might be that ISIL leaders believe any appearance of backing down or moderation would damage their recruitment efforts. However, this explanation by itself is insufficient because recruiting more fighters would ultimately be fruitless if the United States carried out its stated commitment to destroying the organization. Therefore, it seems that ISIL leaders must have been skeptical of the US commitment to ISIL's ultimate destruction.

Why did leaders of the Islamic State not believe President Obama's statements that the United States was committed to destroying them? We can answer this question by analyzing Obama's statements as part of a larger category of leadership statements which I refer to as "statements of resolve." Statements of resolve are generally defined as public statements that leaders make in the context of international conflict to indicate that their country is committed to a position and will not back down from it. Statements of resolve sometimes include explicit military threats, as in Obama's statements about ISIL, but other times the possibility of using force is merely implied or even ambiguous. This book aims to explore the effect of these statements on the outcome of international conflicts, including both conflicts in which military force is used and conflicts that have the potential to escalate to the use of force but have not yet done so.

In theory, statements of resolve have great potential to prevent misunderstandings, promote peace, and achieve better conflict outcomes for countries that employ them skillfully. If these statements can convince adversaries that the country issuing them is truly resolved to stand firm on an issue, this may prompt the adversaries to back down in order to avoid the escalation or continuation of conflict over the issue. When an adversary backs down, this means that the costs of military conflict can be avoided or curtailed, while the country that effectively conveyed its resolve through statements emerges victorious. However, as seen in the case of the Islamic State, this type of outcome does not always occur. Even though ISIL might justifiably be viewed as a new type of international actor, its failure to be intimidated by statements of resolve is far from unprecedented. For example, the United States also failed to convince a much weaker adversary of its resolve to continue fighting during the Vietnam War. This caused President Johnson to lament the ineffectiveness of his own resolved statements, saying "I so much wish that it were within my power to assure that all those in Hanoi could hear one simple message–America is committed to the defense of South Vietnam" (March 15, 1967, quoted in Peters and Woolley 2016).

In order to understand why statements of resolve may sometimes be successful at persuading adversaries to back down and other times not, this book develops and tests a theory of the conditions that allow statements of resolve to be effective at influencing adversary behavior and international conflict outcomes. Specifically, the book will argue that statements of resolve are most effective when leaders have a clear ability to *follow through* on them. Although it is intuitive that statements of resolve will be ineffective when leaders lack an ability to follow through, previous research has not carefully considered exactly what it means to have the ability to follow through or the conditions that give a leader the ability to follow through. I argue that the ability to follow through includes both military and *political* components.

When President Obama made resolved statements targeted at the Islamic State, the political ability to follow through was particularly in doubt. Divisions among elites and the public over the best course of action and a contentious political environment would make it difficult for Obama or his successor to obtain sufficient political support to carry out a costly long-term plan to completely destroy ISIL, and ISIL's leaders probably realized this. At the time of writing in early 2017, the United States has begun to make progress in reversing ISIL's territorial gains and President Trump has vowed to take stronger action against ISIL, but the ultimate destruction of ISIL still remains in doubt. The case of ISIL is therefore an example of how an uncertain ability to follow through can harm the effectiveness of resolved statements.[1] This book will explore other examples of effective and ineffective statements of resolve, both statistically and using historical case study research, in order to better understand the role of these statements in international conflicts and under what specific conditions they can be used successfully.

IMPORTANCE OF UNDERSTANDING THE EFFECT OF RESOLVED STATEMENTS

Statements of resolve have a long history. According to the account of Thucydides, prior to the outbreak of the Peloponnesian War in 431 BC, Athenian envoys defended the imperial policies of Athens to an assembly of Spartans and warned, "[W]e bid you not to dissolve the treaty, or to break your oaths.... Or else we take the gods who heard the oaths to witness, and if you begin hostilities, whatever line of action you choose, we will try not to be behindhand in repelling you" (Thucydides, *Peloponnesian War* 1.78 [2006]). Another classic example of a resolved statement is Lloyd George's Mansion House speech during the 1911 Agadir Crisis. During this crisis, Britain supported France in a confrontation with Germany over interests in Morocco. George (1911), the British Chancellor of the Exchequer, stated, "[I]f a situation were to be forced upon us in which peace could only be preserved by the surrender of the great and beneficent position Britain has won by centuries of heroism and achievement ... then I say emphatically that peace at that price would be a humiliation intolerable for a great country like ours to endure." He thus strongly implied that Britain was willing to use force to defend its interests.

In the modern era, in which public statements can be heard around the world instantaneously, statements of resolve have become even more of a fixture of international conflict. According to my coding, US presidents made at least one resolved statement in 72 percent of all militarized disputes in which the United States was involved between 1950 and 2010. Out of more serious disputes that lasted over 30 days and involved use of force by the United States, presidential

---

[1] Of course, this may not be the only reason why Obama's statements of resolve were ineffective. More details about this example will be discussed in the concluding chapter.

statements of resolve were made in 91 percent.[2] The fact that leaders issue such a large number of resolved statements indicates that they believe the statements are important and can potentially affect conflict outcomes.

Another indication that government officials view statements of resolve as important is the amount of time and effort that they put into crafting them. As one example, journalist Bob Woodward describes the lengthy discussions within the George W. Bush administration that produced the famous "axis of evil" phrase in Bush's 2002 State of the Union address. The originally proposed phrase was "axis of hatred," but Bush's head speechwriter changed it to "axis of evil" (Woodward 2004, 87). There was also debate about which countries to include in the "axis of evil." Only Iraq was included originally, but Iran and North Korea were added later, and Iran was almost removed again (Woodward 2004, 87–88). In the end, Bush's advisors liked the phrase because it signaled a new tougher foreign policy toward these countries without committing to specific action (Woodward 2004, 90–94). Therefore, this phrase is a classic example of a statement of resolve which signals commitment to address a problem without explicitly threatening force. The careful crafting of the phrase shows that high-level policymakers believed that the words used would have an effect. Of course, part of the intended effect of a phrase such as "axis of evil" might have been to shape the US domestic debate (Krebs 2015), but the phrase was clearly intended for an international audience as well. Bush himself even said, "And the fact that the president of the United States would stand up and say Iran is just like Iraq and North Korea … and the president is willing to call it, is part of how you deal with Iran. And that will inspire those who love freedom inside the country" (Woodward 2004, 88).

Another example that illustrates the importance that leaders place on resolved statements is a case in which a specific statement was not made. In September 2012, as Israeli concern over Iran's uranium enrichment program grew, the Israeli government urged the Obama administration to issue a "red line" statement regarding Iran's uranium enrichment program. Demonstrating the importance they placed on such a US statement, Prime Minister Netanyahu and other Israeli officials repeatedly made the case for it in public, including to US news outlets and the United Nations General Assembly. Netanyahu (2012) said, "[T]here's only one way to peacefully prevent Iran from getting atomic bombs, and that's by placing a clear red line on Iran's nuclear weapons program." Although President Obama (2012) had previously stated that preventing Iran from getting a nuclear weapon was "a profound national security interest of the United States," he declined to issue a more specific statement about the level of nuclear capabilities Iran could be allowed to achieve or to set deadlines for Iranian cooperation. Knowledgeable observers speculated that the reason for reluctance to issue a red line statement was fear that such a statement could tie the hands of the US president and force

---

[2] Details on my coding of resolved statements will be provided in Chapter 2.

the United States into military action (Gearan 2012; Ignatius 2012; Zakaria 2012). Thus, while US and Israeli leaders disagreed on whether a red line statement was desirable, both sides viewed the decision to make a statement of resolve as important.

These examples show that officials in the United States and other governments face dilemmas in the decision to issue statements of resolve. In general, leaders will be inclined to make statements of resolve if they believe that they will be effective at influencing adversary behavior. Unfortunately, leaders are not always good at predicting this. In the case of the "axis of evil" speech, Bush administration officials expected the tough wording to persuade Iraq, Iran, and North Korea to cooperate more with US demands, but this did not happen, and it is possible that the speech actually made Iran and North Korea more eager to make progress toward obtaining nuclear weapons. Knowing that statements of resolve are not always effective, leaders might sometimes hold back from making them for fear of being boxed in, as in the case of Obama's refusal to draw a specific red line for Iran. While this approach might be viewed as more prudent, it can also be suboptimal if leaders are hesitant to make resolved statements in cases where they actually could be effective.

The United States is now entering an era in which the ability to use statements of resolve effectively is particularly crucial. The United States faces increasing challenges in the Middle East due to civil wars in many countries, the rise of the Islamic State, and an increasingly assertive Iran. It also faces a rising China that increasingly challenges US allies and interests in Asia and heightened concern about Russian aggression in Europe. While statements are not the only way that the United States can signal resolve in the face of these threats, statements have an advantage over other signals, such as military exercises or deployments, in that they can convey more nuanced levels of resolve and more specific demands for less cost. Due to fatigue from the Iraq and Afghanistan Wars as well as the growing US government debt, US military spending has been reduced, and some have called for the United States to scale back its forward deployments and power projection capabilities (for example, Parent and MacDonald 2011). During the Cold War, the United States relied on the worldwide deployment of its forces as well as statements to signal its resolve. If the United States is less willing or able to project its military power widely in the future, then it will become increasingly important for US government officials to be able to signal with their words which interests are truly important to the United States.

Thus, particularly in current times, understanding and being able to predict when statements of resolve will be effective at influencing adversary behavior and conflict outcomes is crucial. Policymakers must be able to not only correctly analyze the likely effect of statements that they hear but also make accurate determinations about when their own statements are likely to be effective or counterproductive. Unfortunately, such determinations can be difficult to make because the historical evidence regarding the effectiveness of resolved statements is mixed.

EFFECTIVE AND INEFFECTIVE STATEMENTS

This book seeks to explore what makes statements of resolve effective or ineffective. History provides numerous examples of statements of resolve that appear to have been effective at influencing conflict outcomes. The United States, as a superpower and one of the most active countries on the world stage, has issued many statements that seem to have caused adversaries to believe in US resolve and back down. During the 1961 Berlin Crisis, President Kennedy made many public statements expressing commitment to West Berlin, such as "We cannot and will not permit the Communists to drive us out of Berlin, either gradually or by force" (July 25, 1961, quoted in Peters and Woolley 2016). The Soviet Union believed that the United States was resolved and backed away from its ultimatum over the city. The next year, during the Cuban Missile Crisis, Kennedy publicly demanded that the Soviet Union reverse its deployment of nuclear missiles to Cuba, which he called "a deliberately provocative and unjustified change in the status quo which cannot be accepted by this country" (October 22, 1962, quoted in Peters and Woolley 2016). Based on Kennedy's public statements, as well as private negotiations and a naval blockade, Soviet leaders became convinced that the Kennedy administration was resolved enough to attack Cuba and agreed to withdraw the missiles several days later to avoid a war.

The United States issued a variety of nuclear deterrent threats, which are a strong form of statements of resolve, to defend its interests around the world during the Cold War. Although we cannot know for sure what would have happened in the absence of these threats, they appear to have been successful, as no major US allies were attacked. Some observers have argued that the reason South Korea was attacked in 1950 was that US secretary of state Dean Acheson had declared earlier that year that the United States would defend Japan and the Philippines but neglected to mention South Korea (Byman 2013; Matray 2002). Of course, the United States came to South Korea's aid anyway. In current times, the United States continually makes clear its resolve to defend South Korea, and this is arguably responsible for the fact that peace remains on the Korean Peninsula, despite clear North Korean dissatisfaction with the status quo.

In more recent years, President Obama's off-the-cuff remark that "a red line for us is we start seeing a whole bunch of chemical weapons moving around or being utilized" (August 20, 2012, quoted in Peters and Woolley 2016) initially failed to deter the Syrian government from using chemical weapons in its civil war. Yet, when Obama began to make more explicit threats of military action and asked Congress to authorize such action (August 31, 2013, Peters and Woolley 2016), the Syrian government agreed to give up its stockpile of chemical weapons and did not carry out any other attacks with banned chemicals during the remainder of Obama's time in office. Therefore, this could also be viewed as at least a partially successful case of compellence using statements of resolve, although the statements were not successful until they were accompanied by some moves toward military action.[3]

---

[3] However, recent evidence of a nerve agent attack in Syria in April 2017 suggests that the Syrian government deceived the United States by failing to give up its full chemical weapons' stockpile.

Despite these examples of successful statements of resolve, it is also not hard to find examples where statements have failed to make an impact. At the outset of the Vietnam War, President Johnson said, "It is and it will remain the policy of the United States to furnish assistance to support South Viet-Nam for as long as is required to bring communist aggression and terrorism under control" (March 20, 1965, quoted in Peters and Woolley 2016). Despite hearing this and other such statements, North Vietnamese leaders continued to believe that the United States would not remain involved in Vietnam indefinitely and that their own forces could outlast the United States in fighting. The United States never convinced the North Vietnamese that it was resolved throughout the long course of the war and was therefore unable to achieve its war aim of securing the sovereignty of South Vietnam.

Almost two decades later, when Iraq invaded and annexed Kuwait, President George H.W. Bush immediately declared, "This will not stand" (August 5, 1990, quoted in Peters and Woolley 2016). Over the next several months, Bush continued to make resolved statements, eventually giving Iraq an explicit ultimatum to withdraw by a certain date to avoid a US attack. However, Iraq's dictator Saddam Hussein was unmoved by Bush's threats, and his forces remained in Kuwait until a US-led military coalition forcefully drove them out. In 2003, the second President Bush was equally unable to influence Saddam Hussein with his statements of resolve. Despite Bush's threats and other signs that a US invasion was imminent, the Iraqi regime dragged its feet on complying with US demands to cooperate with weapons inspectors, and Saddam refused to step down as president. Bush followed through on his statements of resolve and launched a US invasion of Iraq.

In other cases, US statements of resolve have failed to influence adversaries, and the United States has also failed to follow through on its statements with military action. North Korea has developed and tested nuclear weapons despite repeated US statements declaring this unacceptable. The United States has responded with sanctions and diplomatic isolation, but not with the military force which would be necessary to actually eliminate North Korea's nuclear weapons. As another example, even before President Obama made statements of resolve about Syria's chemical weapons, he condemned Syrian president Assad's human rights violations and declared that "the time has come for President Assad to step aside" (August 18, 2011, quoted in Peters and Woolley 2016). However, despite the escalation of the Syrian civil war and US airstrikes on Islamic State targets within Syria, the United States has not attacked the Assad government or its forces directly.

The preceding examples show that the record of success for statements of resolve in international conflict situations is mixed. This raises the question of why statements of resolve are effective at influencing the behavior of adversaries and leading to successful conflict outcomes in some situations, but not in others. Why do the countries that hear resolved statements sometimes take them at face value and modify their behavior accordingly, yet other times seem to ignore them or even scoff at them? Clearly, each situation has certain unique characteristics to which we might point in explaining the effectiveness or ineffectiveness of statements. However, it would be more useful to develop a more systematic understanding of the conditions for the effectiveness of resolved statements. This is a key contribution that academic research can make to foreign policy.

CURRENT ACADEMIC UNDERSTANDING OF RESOLVED STATEMENTS

Despite the importance of understanding statements of resolve, academic knowledge of this topic is still somewhat limited. Some scholars believe that talk is cheap and that statements of resolve are therefore unlikely to have any impact in international conflict. After all, resolved statements do not carry any direct physical cost, so it might seem that there is nothing to stop leaders from making them constantly, regardless of whether they are truly resolved or not. If these statements were made equally frequently by both resolved and unresolved leaders, then the statements would not convey any information about the actual level of resolve and would be dismissed by adversaries as empty words. Snyder and Borghard (2011) take this perspective, arguing that leaders will typically make vague statements that allow them flexibility on whether or not to follow through and that there are often no negative consequences for backing down from a stated commitment.

On the other hand, many scholars do believe that statements of resolve have an impact in international conflict. Several theories have been put forward to explain how statements can be informative signals of resolve and thus help persuade adversaries to back down. Contrary to the previous argument that statements are costless, these theories argue that there are costs associated with making or backing down from statements.[4] These costs are not monetary, but they do represent real potential harm to a leader's or a country's position. The existence of these costs should deter leaders from making statements lightly or constantly, which in turn should allow the statements that are issued despite these costs to be truly informative about the issuer's resolve. However, although quite a few scholars have speculated that resolved statements are costly, there is no agreement on exactly what the costs associated with making statements are.

One possible explanation for how resolved statements can be costly is domestic audience cost theory. This theory holds that backing down from statements is politically costly for leaders because domestic publics or elites will disapprove of and possibly remove leaders who back down. Fearon (1994a) began the recent trend of interest in domestic audience costs with a formal model in which leaders face domestic punishment if they take escalating actions, such as threats or mobilization, in public view and subsequently back down.

---

[4] These costs are direct in costly signaling models and indirect in cheap talk models, but the intuitive logic is similar. See Trager (2010, 348–349) for an explanation of this distinction.

Escalating under these circumstances effectively signals a leader's resolve, while raising the risk that the leader will become locked into fighting by the cost of backing down.

Other scholars have built on Fearon's audience cost theory. Some have attempted to explain *why* the domestic audience punishes leaders who back down. For example, Guisinger and Smith (2002) show that when a country's reputation for credibility resides with its leader, it is rational for the domestic audience to remove a leader who backs down. Other scholars, such as Smith (1996) and Slantchev (2006), argue that voters punish leaders who back down because this is a sign of incompetence. Weeks (2008) also expands on Fearon's theory by explaining how it might apply not only in democracies but also in some types of autocracies. A related theory put forward by Schultz (1998) argues that a domestic opposition can also contribute to the effectiveness of resolved statements by deterring leaders from bluffing and by supporting honest statements. All of these variants of domestic audience cost theory would suggest that an important condition which promotes the effectiveness of resolved statements is domestic political vulnerability of the leader issuing statements, either to being removed in democratic elections or being forced from office by a circle of elites.

Other explanations for the effectiveness of resolved statements exist at the international level. Sartori (2005) has advanced the concept of international reputational costs. According to Sartori's model, if a country makes a statement and subsequently backs down, it will develop a reputation for bluffing. States should therefore be reluctant to bluff because losing the ability to communicate credibly makes a state less able to attain its future goals. This disincentive to bluff makes resolved statements credible and effective in bargaining among states with honest reputations. Sartori's theory would suggest that statements of resolve will be more effective when the country issuing them currently has a reputation for credibility and perhaps when there are higher stakes for credibility.

More recently, Trager has argued that statements of resolve can be informative and effective if a leader takes certain risks in making them. One possible risk of making a resolved statement is that the target of the statement will react hostilely, by building up arms, forming new alliances, or even attacking preemptively (Trager 2010). Another risk is that if a state makes too big a demand with a resolved statement, there is an increased chance that the demand will be rejected (Trager 2013). A third risk is that resolved statements may embolden protégés to take provocative actions (Trager 2015). These risks function as indirect potential costs for making statements. If a leader makes resolved statements despite these risks, this can be a credible demonstration of resolve. Based on Trager's perspective, it seems that the conditions that can make both public and private statements effective are fairly widespread.

There is currently no consensus among international relations scholars regarding which type of costs are produced by making resolved statements, and therefore there is no agreement on the precise theoretical mechanism that makes these statements effective. Because the various theories discussed point to different conditions that are likely to influence the effectiveness of statements, the lack of theoretical consensus on the causes of statements' effectiveness also means that international relations scholars do not have a good understanding of which conditions make statements most effective. Further complicating matters, other scholars have proposed that in addition to the costs associated with statements, there may also be other factors that influence their effectiveness, such as the level of national interests at stake (Danilovic 2002; Press 2005).

The problem of having so many different theories about resolved statements is exacerbated by the fact that these possible explanations for the effectiveness of statements have not been competed against each other empirically. Some analyses have attempted to test the mechanisms of individual theories. For example, some studies have tested whether the domestic public disapproves of backing down (Tomz 2007) and whether countries with regimes that make leaders more vulnerable to removal do better in international conflict (Schultz 1999; Weeks 2008), as predicted by audience cost theory. Others have tested whether countries that back down have worse conflict outcomes in the future (Sartori 2005), as predicted by the theory of international reputational costs. However, these empirical analyses have not compared the different theories against each other. Furthermore, these tests do not involve real-world data on statements of resolve.

There have been very few direct empirical tests of the effectiveness of resolved statements. In a case study analysis of a dozen great power crises, Trachtenberg (2012) finds a mixed record of success for public statements. Snyder and Borghard (2011) also find little evidence that public statements of resolve were effective in three out of the four cases they examine. In the only quantitative study of the impact of statements prior to my work, Wood (2012, 129–132) performs time series analysis of the relationship between US presidential "saber-rattling" statements and event data measuring adversary behavior. His results suggest that saber rattling either has no effect on adversary behavior or makes it more hostile.

These empirical findings that statements do not have much helpful impact in international conflict are surprising given the widespread belief among scholars and policymakers that statements are effective. However, these studies have limitations. The research designs based on qualitative case studies are naturally limited in scope, and even though Wood performs statistical analysis with many data points, he only examines the behavior of three US adversaries. In addition, Wood's analysis only shows that saber-rattling statements often precede hostile adversary behavior, not that they cause it. Furthermore, even if it is true that adversaries initially answer US saber rattling with saber rattling of their own, this fact tells us nothing about whether the United States ultimately wins conflicts in which it engages in saber rattling. Therefore, these existing studies do not conclusively answer the question of whether statements of resolve have an effect on international conflict outcomes.

In sum, the existing scholarly literature has not reached a theoretical consensus on which conditions are most helpful for promoting the effectiveness of resolved statements, and there has been no direct comparison of the impact of different conditions. Furthermore, due to limited empirical testing, there remains some uncertainty about whether or how often statements of resolve have any impact on international conflict outcomes at all. Therefore, academic research on statements of resolve to date can be of limited help to policymakers who seek to analyze the statements of resolve that they hear or predict whether their own statements will be effective.

CONTRIBUTIONS OF THIS BOOK

This book aims to provide a more thorough and definitive answer to the question of which conditions make statements of resolve effective at influencing international conflict outcomes. It offers a new theory that analyzes a crucial, but previously neglected, condition for the effectiveness of these statements, namely, the military and political ability to follow through on them. It also presents a new quantitative measure of resolved statements that is used to test my theory as well as other existing theories in statistical analysis. Finally, it analyzes how adversaries interpreted and reacted to statements of resolve in three historical case studies.

The primary theoretical contribution of this book is to offer a new theory regarding the importance of the ability to follow through on resolved statements as a key condition for the statements' effectiveness. It is highly intuitive that statements of resolve are unlikely to be effective *without* any ability to follow through on them, and previous research has made some acknowledgment of this. However, most modern theories about the effectiveness of statements have focused *primarily* on the costs of making or backing down from the statements. Therefore, previous research has not fully considered exactly what the ability to follow through consists of or how it varies among leaders. As I define it, the ability to follow through on statements of resolve consists of both an absence of major obstacles to following through and an absence of unacceptable risks to following through.

Leaders often lack a clear ability to follow through on their resolved statements because the risks and obstacles to following through can be substantial. The military risks and obstacles to following through are most obvious and have received the most attention in previous academic work. However, political risks and obstacles can also create substantial uncertainty about the ability to follow through. First, leaders who are vulnerable to domestic punishment for backing down from statements are likely to be even more vulnerable to domestic punishment for following through and losing or incurring high casualties, since these things are likely to be more noticeable to the domestic audience. This might make following through on statements of resolve too risky for some leaders. Second, almost all leaders have some sort of domestic veto players who can restrain their ability to act in the international arena. Thus, other domestic actors may block a leader's ability to initiate or escalate conflict, making it difficult or even impossible to follow through on statements of resolve. If adversaries can observe these impediments to following through, statements of resolve are unlikely to be credible or effective.

This book proposes several factors that can mitigate these risks and obstacles and give a leader the ability to follow through on resolved statements. The first factor is military strength. Countries that have greater military capabilities relative to their adversary should face a lower risk of losing or suffering high casualties when following through on statements with military force. This gives more powerful countries a greater physical ability to follow through. The second factor is hawkish domestic veto players. While dovish veto players are likely to create obstacles to following through on statements, hawkish veto players are unlikely to stand in the leader's way. Therefore, if domestic veto players are more hawkish, there will be less doubt that the leader can follow through on statements. The third factor is security in office. Secure leaders face less personal risk from following through on statements because fighting a losing conflict is less likely to lead to their removal from office. Secure leaders are also likely to have more sources of leverage over other domestic actors to convince them to support conflict escalation. For both of these reasons, more secure leaders should have a greater ability to follow through on statements. While the beneficial effect of military strength on the effectiveness of threats has been acknowledged by previous theories, I am the first to identify a positive impact of hawkish veto players and security in office on the effectiveness of resolved statements.

This book also makes a substantial contribution to our empirical knowledge about the role of resolved statements in international conflict. The most unique empirical contribution is the introduction of new quantitative data which code the level of US presidential statements of resolve made during various international conflicts. I created these data using content analysis of full statements by US presidents. This unique dataset allows me to perform statistical analysis addressing questions such as when statements of resolve are made, whether they are effective, and what conditions make them most effective, based on a direct measure of statements. This is a major step forward from the indirect statistical tests and small numbers of case studies in the previous literature. Using this new data source, I not only test my theory regarding the importance of the ability to follow through on statements but also compare the explanatory power of my theory with other existing theories, including domestic audience cost theory and international reputational cost theory.

While the statistical analysis of my data on resolved presidential statements is the most systematic analysis of these statements to date and fills an important gap in the literature, there are certain inherent limitations of statistical methods. In particular, these methods cannot tell us for certain what causal mechanism underlies the statistical relationships that are observed. To analyze the causal mechanisms in more detail, I also present three case studies in which I examine historical evidence regarding how statements of resolve and the ability to follow through affected conflict outcomes. In two of the cases, the Cuban Missile Crisis and US-Soviet tensions under President Reagan, US presidents had the ability to follow through and their resolved statements were effective. In the third case, the Vietnam War, the lack of an ability to follow through rendered statements ineffective.

Although the theory developed in this book is intended to be applicable to different types of countries, both the statistical analysis and the case study analysis are focused on US statements of resolve. The decision to focus on the United States was driven in part by technical considerations, as will be described in Chapter 2. However, there are also broader reasons for this decision. The United States is the most powerful country in the international system, yet it is at a crossroads, facing new challenges throughout the world and lacking a domestic consensus on how assertively to confront these challenges. Whether or not the US government can signal its resolve effectively in the upcoming years will have implications for the whole world. Therefore, although it is certainly desirable to apply my theory of the ability to follow through and methods of empirical testing to other countries in the long term, developing a thorough understanding of the role of US statements of resolve in international conflict is the priority of this book.

Therefore, in addition to being an international security book, which speaks to classic theoretical debates about conflict bargaining, credible communication in the context of distrust, and the relationship between domestic and international politics, this is also a US foreign policy book. The book will shed light on why certain US presidential statements of resolve have been effective or ineffective in the past and draw out implications for how US presidents can make their statements more effective – or at least avoid making statements that are doomed to be ineffective – in the future. This could potentially allow the United States to communicate more credibly and effectively with current and possible future challengers, including the Islamic State and other international terrorist organizations, Iran, North Korea, Russia, and China. President Theodore Roosevelt (1901, 288) famously said that in managing its foreign policy, the United States should "speak softly and carry a big stick." The findings in this book confirm that the "big stick" of US military power is important to statement credibility, but it is insufficient by itself to ensure that US statements will always be taken seriously. Furthermore, the success of more strongly resolved public statements made by some presidents suggests that "louder" speech can also play an important role in US foreign policy.

PLAN FOR THE BOOK

Chapter 1 further develops my theory regarding the importance of the ability to follow through on statements of resolve as a condition impacting statements' effectiveness. First, it explains in more detail how statements operate as a signaling mechanism. Next, it describes how the absence of the ability to follow through can undermine the effectiveness of statements. It then discusses in more detail how military strength, the hawkishness of veto players, and the security in office of the leader can impact the ability to follow through and thus make statements of resolve more or less effective. This discussion leads to the development of several hypotheses, which are tested in the subsequent chapters. The chapter also develops hypotheses based on domestic audience cost theory and international reputational cost theory, for purposes of comparison.

Chapter 2 describes the original data on US presidential statements of resolve used in the book and gives details regarding how the data were created. In this chapter, I define statements of resolve in more detail, explain my decision to focus on US presidential statements, describe how relevant presidential statements were identified, and discuss how these statements were coded using content analysis software. The chapter also includes some initial analysis of the data, with a focus on when resolved statements are made. The analysis indicates that the decision to make statements is affected more by the international situation than by domestic political factors and that statements are primarily made in times of heightened tension.

Chapter 3 uses the data on US statements of resolve to test the effectiveness of statements in militarized interstate disputes (MIDs). I find that a higher level of resolved statements is associated with a greater chance of a favorable MID outcome, suggesting that statements are indeed effective at influencing adversaries to back down. This finding is highly significant and robust, and it represents the first attempt to date to systematically test the effectiveness of statements across a large number of cases. Chapter 3 also employs several tests to reduce concerns that the result might be driven by reverse causality, a confounding effect of the president's underlying level of resolve, or other confounding factors. The statistical analysis in this chapter serves as a basis for the analysis in the next two chapters.

In Chapter 4, I use the same dataset of US presidential statements of resolve to test the impact of the factors predicted to influence the effectiveness of statements under my theory of the ability to follow through. I also test hypotheses derived from domestic audience cost theory and international reputational cost theory. In keeping with my theory, I find that US presidential statements of resolve are more effective when the United States has greater military capabilities relative to its adversary, when the president is more secure in office, and when there are more hawks in Congress. I also find evidence in support of international reputational cost theory, but no evidence of support for domestic audience cost theory.

Chapter 5 advances the theory and statistical analysis further by examining how the conditions that make statements effective interact with each other. I find that the lack of any one factor associated with the ability to follow through can be enough by itself to undermine the effectiveness of statements, which makes the other factors irrelevant. Therefore, for the most part, the factors associated with the ability to follow through mutually enhance each other's impact on the effectiveness of statements. However, when the ability to follow through is high, the various factors can begin to crowd out each other's impact. I also find that having a credible international reputation enhances the impacts of the factors related to the ability to follow through.

The next three chapters present historical case studies as another method of testing my theory of the ability to follow through. Chapter 6 begins by explaining the rationale for the case studies and describing the case selection method. It then moves on to discuss the Cuban Missile Crisis. It describes how Soviet leaders were worried, though initially reluctant to back down, after hearing President Kennedy's public speech demanding the removal of the missiles. As the crisis developed, Soviet leaders placed great importance on information received about the hawkishness of veto players surrounding Kennedy. As it became clear that veto players would be more likely to encourage Kennedy to follow through on his statements than block him, the Soviets decided to comply with Kennedy's statement of resolve.

Chapter 7 describes how President Reagan's resolved and highly critical statements about the Soviet Union caused genuine fear among Soviet officials. Initially, the Soviet leadership hoped that the US domestic public would restrain Reagan's ability to take a tough line against the Soviet Union, but they became increasingly alarmed by Reagan's rhetoric as he maintained widespread public support and security in office. Immediately after Reagan won reelection, the Soviets became more willing to participate in arms control negotiations and eventually offered concessions in keeping with Reagan's demands.

Chapter 8 discusses how the absence of both hawkish veto players and presidential security in office throughout most of the Vietnam War undermined the effectiveness of resolved statements by Presidents Johnson and Nixon. There is evidence that the North Vietnamese leadership paid attention to US statements of resolve but remained unmoved by them. The North Vietnamese believed that presidential insecurity in office due to the unpopularity of the war and opposition from an increasingly dovish Congress would make the United States unable to follow through on its stated commitments to continue fighting.

Chapter 8 concludes by summarizing the findings of the book and discusses their implications for international relations theory as well as foreign policy. The three appendices at the end of the book contain the most important supporting information, including game theoretic models that illustrate the theory laid out in Chapter 1 more formally and my content analysis dictionary for coding resolve in US presidential statements. Additional supporting information, including full results for the robustness checks, the data and commands that were used to produce the results, and the statement text files that I coded, will be posted on my website. The website is currently located at http://faculty.baruch.cuny.edu/rmcmanus/ and can always be found by searching for my name.

PART I

THEORY

I

The Ability to Follow Through and Other Conditions for Statements' Effectiveness

The introductory chapter established that while statements of resolve are a fixture of international politics and are believed by most scholars and policymakers to serve a useful purpose, important unanswered questions remain regarding their role in international conflict. Chief among these is the question of under which conditions statements of resolve can be effective at influencing adversary beliefs and behavior. Although the Introduction presented several explanations that have previously been offered for the effectiveness of statements, including domestic audience costs and international reputational costs, there is no consensus or clear empirical evidence regarding which theory offers the strongest explanation. This leaves a gap not only in our theoretical understanding but in our practical ability to predict when statements of resolve are likely to be effective versus when they are a waste of breath.

In this chapter, I argue that despite all of this theorizing about what makes statements of resolve effective, one important condition has not been fully explored. This condition is the ability to follow through on statements of resolve. While the importance of having an ability to follow through has been acknowledged by some previous research, most recent theories do not treat the ability to follow through as very interesting or analyze it very deeply. In contrast, I argue that it is important to develop a better understanding of what the ability to follow through consists of and how various observable factors can influence it. This chapter will explain why analyzing the ability to follow through is so crucial and then lay out my theory regarding factors that contribute to the ability to follow through in more detail. It will also compare the implications of my theory to the implications of other existing theories.

STATEMENTS AS A SIGNALING MECHANISM

Before discussing the ability to follow through, I will begin by providing a deeper overview of what we know so far about how statements of resolve operate in international conflict. The key question to answer is, why should statements of resolve be important? After all, in many cases, countries that are involved in international conflict are already aware of each other's general preferences. For example, even without any public statements from the United States, the government of Iran could probably infer based on past history that the United States would prefer for Iran to not have nuclear weapons. Perhaps, this expectation of US opposition and the knowledge that the United States is a powerful country could be enough to deter Iran. If this were the case, statements of resolve might be unnecessary. In reality, however, it can be difficult to determine exactly how vital a country considers a particular issue to be to its interests. History is full of examples of miscalculations about how much an adversary cared about an issue, such as the Soviet view that the United States would grudgingly accept its nuclear missiles in Cuba (Dobbs 2008, 113) and the US view that China would not intervene in the Korean War (Roe 2000).

I define resolve as the value that a country or leader places on a particular issue, which determines how far the country will go to achieve its preferred outcome on that issue. A country's exact level of resolve regarding a particular issue is an example of what game theorists refer to as "private information" (Fearon 1995). The fact that this information is private can lead to potentially inefficient outcomes. Rationalist logic suggests that states involved in bargaining in the context of international conflict could benefit from being able to honestly share information about their respective resolve and capabilities with each other. This would allow them (barring other complications) to reach a settlement reflecting the likely outcome of a military conflict without actually having to fight a costly conflict. However, a major obstacle to such an efficient outcome is that states have private information about their capabilities and resolve, and they have the incentive to make exaggerated claims about these things in order to obtain a better settlement (Fearon 1995). Given that leaders have this incentive to claim they are more resolved than they truly are, we might be tempted to dismiss statements of resolve as a waste of breath.

Yet, as mentioned in the Introduction, several scholars have put forward theories regarding how statements might be able to effectively convey resolve to adversaries and thus influence the outcomes of international disputes. Each of these theories relies on some sort of consequence or "cost" associated with making statements as an explanation for their effectiveness. The cost may be a decline in domestic support, as in domestic audience cost theory (Fearon 1994a), or harm to the state's international position, as in Sartori's (2005) and Trager's (2010) theories. Regardless of the nature of the cost, it has a similar effect and plays a crucial role in conflict bargaining. If resolved statements carried no cost, then all leaders could and would make these statements freely, and it would be impossible to determine which statements were genuine. Thus, statements would convey no useful information about resolve.

Fortunately for leaders seeking to convey resolve, the presence of a domestic and/or international cost associated with statements allows the statements to be genuinely informative about the issuer's resolve. Specifically, this happens through a signaling mechanism, which differentiates the behavior of resolved and unresolved leaders, and/or through a commitment mechanism, which commits a leader to follow through on statements because of the added cost that statements create for backing down. In simpler terms, leaders who are genuinely more resolved are more likely to make statements of resolve because less resolved leaders are deterred from making statements by the potential cost. Furthermore, the act of making a statement itself can actually make a leader more resolved by creating a new cost for backing down. Thus, if statements of resolve are costly, then leaders who choose to make statements can be expected to be more resolved on average than leaders who choose not to make statements.

If statements are informative due to their costs, then an adversary who hears statements of resolve should be more likely to believe that the issuer of the statements is actually resolved to stand firm. As the adversary's belief that the issuer of statements is resolved increases, the adversary itself should become more likely to back down. This is because any adversary that underestimated the issuer's resolve should have its belief corrected by the statements, and once an adversary is convinced that the issuer of statements is fully resolved to fight or continue fighting, the adversary must back down unless it is willing to do the same. If the adversary is more likely to back down, then the issuer of resolved statements should be more likely to obtain a favorable outcome. Therefore, there is reason to expect that resolved statements will increase the probability of a favorable conflict outcome.

Resolved statements can be expected to increase the probability of a successful outcome both in international conflicts that have not yet escalated to force and in conflicts in which the use of force is already ongoing. Although most formal models used to derive theories about statements' effectiveness focus on pre-force bargaining, leaders can and do make statements while force is being used in order to express resolve to stay the course or escalate. From the perspective of the country hearing the statements, the calculations involved in making the initial decision to fight and making the decision to continue fighting are very similar. The main difference between pre-conflict bargaining and bargaining while fighting is that information can be learned from battle outcomes while fighting (Powell 2004; Slantchev 2003; Wagner 2000). However, battle outcomes mostly convey information about capabilities and do not negate the role of statements in conveying resolve. For example, Taliban fighters in Afghanistan probably know that the United States has high military capabilities, but they may doubt US resolve to bear the costs of fighting them over the long term. Therefore, the Taliban arguably learns at least as much from US statements as from US military operations. It is true that the coupling of statements with military operations probably increases the informational value of the statements because it establishes that the United States has at least some willingness to follow through on tough talk. However, without any resolved statements by US officials, military operations alone would tell the Taliban very little about long-term US intentions.

It should be noted that there are some theories which suggest that making statements of resolve is not always desirable. Levantoglu and Tarar (2005) and Kurizaki (2007) argue that public threats might be less efficient than private threats because of the potential to create audience costs on both sides. Their models are supported by some empirical evidence that resolved statements made by the leader of one country can cause citizens in another country to have greater disapproval for backing down (Gottfried and Trager 2016). However, their models do not indicate that public statements are ineffective, but just that they are less efficient under some circumstances. A bigger challenge is raised by Slantchev (2010) and Trager (2010), who each argue that signaling resolve to an adversary can sometimes be counterproductive because it can prompt the adversary to make military preparations that decrease the signaler's chance of victory. However, it is not clear that this would be the case very often, and Slantchev and Trager predict that countries are more likely to refrain from signaling resolve when this risk exists. Therefore, we should still expect resolved statements that are actually issued to have a generally beneficial effect on conflict outcomes.

This section has laid out the basic logic of why we might expect statements to be able to function as effective signals of resolve in a variety of different types of conflicts. The crucial question for this book, however, is when statements of resolve are *most likely* to be effective. To answer this question, we must understand which factors create variation in the effectiveness of statements. As explained earlier, recent theories have argued that statements of resolve are effective due to the costs associated with making or backing down from them. Scholars working in the tradition of these theories have focused on using variation in these costs to explain variation in effectiveness (Fearon 1994a; Schultz 1999; Weeks 2008). I agree that variation in these costs should be considered when seeking to explain statements' effectiveness, and at the end of this chapter I develop hypotheses related to this. However, I argue that by focusing so much on the costs of backing down, recent literature has neglected to fully explore another important condition for statements' effectiveness, namely the ability to follow through. This book shows that a crucial factor influencing the effectiveness of resolved statements is whether the leader has the ability to follow through on the statements by carrying out the implicit or explicit threats contained within them.

IMPORTANCE OF THE ABILITY TO FOLLOW THROUGH

Although several theories have previously been put forward to explain what makes statements of resolve effective, there is one important condition that has not been fully considered. This condition is the ability to follow through on resolved statements by carrying out the implicit or explicit threats contained within them. While the importance of having an ability to follow through has been acknowledged by some previous research (for example, Debs and Weiss 2015; Zagare and Kilgour 2000), exactly what the ability to follow through consists of has never been explored in depth. Thus, previous research does not provide a comprehensive method of assessing whether a leader has the ability to follow through or not. In this book, I seek to define the ability to follow through more clearly by considering how both physical factors and political factors contribute to the ability to follow through in a parallel manner. As I define it, the ability to follow through consists of both an absence of major obstacles to following through and an absence of unacceptable risks to following through. If adversaries believe a leader lacks the ability to follow through on resolved statements because the risks and obstacles are too high, the statements are unlikely to be effective. There are various situations in which a leader may lack the ability to follow through.

In some situations, following through on statements of resolve may be literally impossible for leaders. The existing literature largely ignores this possibility, typically assuming that leaders can automatically follow through on their statements of resolve if they want to do so. One exception is Zagare and Kilgour (2000), who note that having the capability to hurt an opponent is an important component of any successful deterrent threat. However, Zagare and Kilgour treat this condition as uninteresting. If the impossibility of following through on a threat is extremely obvious, then it is true that the failure of the threat is unsurprising and not greatly interesting. For example, when North Korea threatens to strike Manhattan with nuclear missiles, but has never successfully tested a missile capable of hitting Manhattan, it is not puzzling that this threat is unsuccessful.

In other situations, however, observers might be uncertain about whether following through on a statement of resolve is possible. One reason for this is domestic political constraints. In almost all types of regimes, leaders face some constraints on their ability to act. In democracies, these constraints are usually institutionalized. However, even most authoritarian leaders have at least a small circle of supporters on whom they rely to remain in power (Weeks 2012), and this group is likely to have some formal or informal ability to constrain the leader's actions. If leaders face domestic political constraints on their ability to carry out threats, this can make their ability to follow through on statements of resolve ambiguous to outside observers. If it looks likely that other domestic actors will block the ability to follow through on statements, this will undermine the credibility of the statements and make them less effective.

Another situation in which the ability to follow through might be ambiguous is when following through is perceived as too risky for the leader. It has long been known that the risk of overly high costs can prevent an actor from following through. For example, in discussions of nuclear deterrence, the risk of mutually assured destruction is often considered an obstacle to credible threats (Schelling 1960; Schelling 1966). Furthermore, in any formal model of conflict bargaining, actors will take into account the expected costs and outcome of fighting when considering whether to fight or back down. Still, most existing theories related to statements of resolve do not devote much attention to what the costs and consequences of fighting are and fail to consider how they might vary among leaders. This is important to consider because, in addition to whatever losses or gains accrue to the country as a whole, leaders may also face personal consequences due to the outcome of a dispute.

Leaders who take the risk of fighting and leave their country worse off are likely to be punished. Quantitative evidence shows that domestic audiences will often remove leaders who lose conflicts (Bueno de Mesquita and Siverson 1995; Chiozza and Goemans 2004; Debs and Goemans 2010; Miller 2015), particularly if the leader is deemed culpable for the conflict (Croco 2011; Croco and Weeks 2015). Even before a conflict is won or lost, domestic publics may disapprove of leaders if there are unacceptably high causalities (Aldrich et al. 2006). Wood (2012, 113) lists examples of US presidents who have suffered from reduced domestic popularity for standing firm and carrying out their threats, including Johnson's experience with Vietnam and George W. Bush's experience with Iraq. Thus, leaders may have reason to fear the consequences of following through on statements with force. If adversaries perceive that the risks of following through are too high, either for the country as a whole or for the leader personally, this could make statements of resolve less effective.

In sum, there are several reasons – both physical and political – why leaders may lack the ability to follow through or why this ability might be ambiguous to adversaries. If adversaries doubt the ability to follow through, statements of resolve are likely to be less effective. In contrast, if adversaries can see that a leader faces no substantial risks or obstacles to following through on resolved statements, they are more likely to take the statements seriously.[1] Therefore, although we already have a variety of theories that explain how statements can function as signaling mechanisms, it is important to analyze the ability to follow through as well to obtain a better understanding of variation in the effectiveness of statements.

It is important to note that by taking into account both obstacles and risks to following through, my definition of the ability to follow through encompasses both pure ability and also willingness to follow through. If there are physical or political obstacles that make it absolutely impossible for a leader to follow through, then this is a clear case of lack of ability to follow through.

---

[1] An adversary's perception of a leader's ability to follow through may also be influenced by the characteristics of the adversary itself, such as how its government processes information. However, I assume that adversaries' perceptions will generally have a basis in reality.

If instead, it is overly high risks that prevent a leader from following through, then this might arguably be more of a case of lack of willingness to follow through. While this is a valid distinction, I still opt to use the umbrella term "ability to follow through" to refer to both situations. I do so for brevity and also to emphasize how risks and obstacles both have a similar impact on the effectiveness of statements in practice. In using this umbrella term, I seek to emphasize my focus on a range of different considerations associated with following through on statements, in contrast to previous research that has focused on considerations associated with backing down.

It is also important to note that the ability to follow through is distinct from resolve itself, even though some previous research has blurred this distinction by defining resolve in terms of the cost of fighting. Again, I define resolve as how much a country or leader cares about an issue. Thus, there might be situations in which a leader cares a lot about an issue and therefore could personally be considered resolved, but lacks the ability to follow through. There might also be situations in which a leader can easily follow through on any statement, but is unresolved because he or she simply does not care about a particular issue. Furthermore, resolve and the ability to follow through differ in terms of observability. Whereas resolve is an internal characteristic of individuals that cannot be observed directly, the ability to follow through consists of external factors that can usually be observed without great difficulty.

Finally, it should also be noted that there is one theoretical perspective that might argue against the importance of the ability to follow through. Fearon's (1994b) game theoretic analysis of the role of signaling compared to the balance of power and interests predicts that observable factors should be taken into account when an adversary is considering initiating a crisis and therefore should not matter during the crisis itself. If it was assumed that factors related to the ability to follow through were fully observable before a conflict, then Fearon's analysis might argue against the ability to follow through having any impact on the effectiveness of statements made in times of conflict. However, while my theory does rest on the assumption that adversaries can make reasonably good inferences about the ability to follow through, their inferences are not always perfect. In all three of the historical cases that I examine in Chapters 6–8, I find that adversaries updated their beliefs about the ability to follow through as the conflict progressed. This is one reason why Fearon's analysis might not be applicable. Furthermore, Fearon's assumption that crisis initiation is a strategic choice is a strong one. While some confrontations between states do result from a deliberate decision of one to challenge the other, it is also common for disputes between countries to arise in an unplanned manner or as an inevitable result of broader policies. This is another reason why Fearon's predictions may not always be relevant. Therefore, Fearon's argument should not be seen as ruling out the importance of the ability to follow through in most real-world instances of international conflict.

Having established the importance of the ability to follow through, I will now move on to analyzing what it consists of in more detail. In the upcoming sections, I will discuss specific factors that can reduce the risks and obstacles to following through, make a leader's ability to follow through on statements more obvious to adversaries, and therefore make statements of resolve more effective. Although my theory is intended to be general in nature, I will often turn to examples from the United States to illustrate concepts, since the United States is the focus of my empirical chapters.

MILITARY STRENGTH

The most obvious factor impacting the ability to follow through on resolved statements is military strength. Inadequate military capabilities relative to the adversary can undermine the effectiveness of resolved statements in several ways. First, if military strength is too low, following through on resolved statements might be literally impossible. If following through on resolved statements is entirely beyond a nation's military capabilities, then there is no reason to take the statements seriously. As noted previously, this is the case for North Korea's threats to attack the United States, which have been unsuccessful at changing US policy. As a White House spokesperson said, "The DPRK will achieve nothing by threats or provocation, which will only further isolate North Korea" (MacAskill 2013).

Second, even if following through is not impossible, lower military strength relative to the adversary typically means a higher expected cost of fighting and a lower probability of winning. This means that leaders will generally be more reluctant to follow through on statements of resolve when their country is relatively weaker. Knowing this, adversaries are more likely to regard statements of resolve by weaker countries as bluffs, even if following through is technically possible. One well-known case that might represent this situation is the US dismissal of Chinese threats to intervene in the Korean War. China warned the United States that it would enter the war if US forces came too close to its border. However, the Central Intelligence Agency (CIA) assessed that China would probably not follow through on its threats for a variety of reasons, including that China feared fighting the United States, that the best opportunity for intervention had already passed, that there was a risk of high casualties for China, and that intervention would make the Chinese regime more vulnerable to attacks by domestic anti-communist forces (Roe 2000, 107–108). Thus, the military impediments that China faced contributed to US skepticism of its threats, despite the fact that China did ultimately intervene.

Third, even if a country with relatively low capabilities has enough resolve to be willing to attack despite the risks, its lower capabilities will mean that it can probably impose less pain upon its adversary. Therefore, even if the first country successfully conveys its resolve with statements, the adversary may not back down if it does not view fighting as prohibitively costly. For example, although Ukraine has expressed resolve to fight to maintain its territorial integrity (Besheer 2014; Brumfield 2014), Russia has not altered its policy of providing military support to Ukraine's separatists. Because the Ukrainian military is smaller and weaker than the Russian military, Russia probably has little to fear in fighting Ukraine.

In sum, if a country has greater military strength relative to its adversary, not only will there be lower physical obstacles to following through, but the risk of losing or incurring high casualties will be lower. Therefore, adversaries should understand that militarily stronger countries will be more likely to follow through. Furthermore, since stronger countries can impose more pain when following through, adversaries should be less willing to tolerate the risk of fighting them. For all of these reasons, an adversary is more likely to back down in response to a statement of resolve from a stronger country.

This argument is in keeping with previous work. Mearsheimer (1983) argued that the success of deterrent threats depends upon a potential challenger's perception of the likelihood and cost of winning a military conflict with the state attempting deterrence, which in turn depends in large part upon relative military strength. Early statistical analysis of deterrence theory found some support for predictions that threats are more credible when military capabilities are greater in cases of immediate deterrence (Huth 1988; Huth and Russett 1984). In more recent work testing the effectiveness of general deterrence threats, Johnson, Leeds, and Wu (2015) find statistical evidence that military alliances with greater capabilities and higher levels of military coordination are more effective at deterring attacks against member states. In addition, Press (2005) includes the balance of power as a factor affecting threat credibility in his "current calculus" theory and argues that this played a role in the "Appeasement" Crises prior to World War II, the Berlin Crises during the Cold War, and the Cuban Missile Crisis.

Military capabilities are also a standard component of formal models of signaling and conflict bargaining. For example, Kydd (2015, 172–173) presents a simple costly signaling model which shows that the probability that an adversary will back down in response to a state's threat is increasing in the threatener's probability of winning a military conflict, decreasing in the threatener's cost of fighting, and increasing in the threat recipient's cost of fighting. All of these predictions imply that threats by countries with greater military capabilities are more likely to be successful. Therefore, my prediction that greater military strength will increase the effectiveness of statements of resolve is not unique, but it is such an obvious and important implication of my broader argument about the ability to follow through that it is worth testing. Therefore, this book will test the following hypothesis:

Hypothesis 1: *Statements of resolve will be more effective when the country issuing them has greater military strength relative to the target of the statements.*

Military strength is an obvious component of the ability to follow through, but it is not necessarily the most interesting component. Because they are based on a concrete physical reality, military capabilities are relatively easy to observe. There are, of course, some components of military capabilities that are hard to measure, such as morale and training, and some military equipment may be hidden. Because of this, countries do sometimes disagree about their military strength in relation to each other. Still, the room for disagreement is limited. For example, there can be no reasonable disagreement with the fact that the United States is currently the most militarily powerful country in the world. Despite this unambiguous power advantage, this book will show that there are sometimes doubts about the US ability to follow through. Therefore, I now turn to the discussion of two domestic political factors that can inhibit or render ambiguous the ability to follow through, even for powerful countries.

HAWKISHNESS OF VETO PLAYERS

Having discussed the physical capability to follow through, I now turn to the political ability to follow through, which is often more ambiguous and has received less attention in previous work. One domestic political condition that might affect the level of obstacles to following through is the biases or preferences of other individual or institutional actors in the government who have the power to provide a check on the leader's ability to initiate or continue conflict. I refer to these actors as "veto players," a term which I define *broadly* to include those that lack explicit institutional veto power but whose concurrence a leader would want before initiating military conflict. Almost all leaders, except for a few personalistic dictators, are likely to have some veto players.

In democracies, the most obvious veto player is the legislature. For example, Congress is the most prominent institutional veto player in the United States. Certain individual members or committees of Congress might also be powerful enough to be considered veto players by themselves, under some circumstances. Howell and Pevehouse (2007) discuss how Congress prevented intervention in Indochina in 1954, blocked aid to the Contras in Nicaragua in the 1980s, and delayed intervention in Bosnia in the 1990s. In parliamentary democracies, the legislature can also function as a veto player, although it may be less likely to oppose the leader in practice. In addition to the legislature, there are also likely to be actors in the executive branch who can constrain a leader (Saunders 2015). In particular, leaders are often dependent upon experts in the security establishment when making military decisions. For example, President Kennedy was reliant on military officials for evaluating the feasibility of military options during the Cuban Missile Crisis (Allison 1969). In nondemocratic regimes, the checks on the leader are often less obvious, but there are still likely to be some regime insiders who are veto players. Like democratic leaders, all but the most powerful dictators would be reluctant to go to war without the support of top military and foreign policy officials. Looking at the Cuban Missile Crisis from the other perspective, Khrushchev requested approval from other Politburo members at every stage (Fursenko and Naftali 1997). He arguably could have done a better job of listening to advice, but he did at least get other officials to sign off on his decisions.

Thus, almost all world leaders have some veto players who have influence on the decision to follow through on statements of resolve. The importance of these veto players goes beyond a leader's desire for domestic support. Veto players have the power to directly hinder the ability to follow through, using either legal methods or more informal means. Under my broad definition of veto players, I do not necessarily assume that the opposition of any single veto player alone (such as a single member of Congress or the White House staff) can absolutely block the decision to follow through, but I do expect that more veto player opposition will make following through more difficult and that sufficient veto player obstruction (particularly from the most important veto players) can make following through impossible. Therefore, a leader can only be said to have the ability to follow through on statements of resolve with military force in the absence of significant veto player opposition to following through.

For this reason, the preferences of veto players regarding the use of military force are important. Several previous theories have focused on the self-interested political incentives of domestic actors to support or oppose the use of force (Levy and Mabe 2004; Ramsay 2004; Schultz 1998). However, I argue that in addition to self-interested incentives, most veto players will also have policy preferences. It is often in the interest of political actors to pursue certain policy preferences consistently, both because they may believe that their policy preferences are genuinely good for the country and because inconsistency on policy preferences can result in a reputation for being indecisive or insincere. I therefore argue that policy preferences will often override short-term political interests when it comes to the use of military force. This means that veto players who are political allies of the leader will not always approve of the decision to follow through on statements of resolve with force, and veto players who are political opponents of the leader will not necessarily seek to block following through with force. In Chapter 5, I further consider the self-interested incentives of a leader's domestic political opponents to oppose the use of force, but for now I focus on the policy preferences that I expect to dominate veto players' decision-making.

Regarding how veto players' policy preferences for allowing or blocking the ability to follow through on statements are determined, I argue that rather than considering each international dispute from a fresh perspective, most veto players will have preexisting biases either in favor of or against conflict.

In keeping with common parlance, I refer to people with a bias toward conflict and tough foreign policy as "hawks" and to people with the opposite bias as "doves." I assume that hawkishness and dovishness exist on a single continuum, so that saying an actor is "more hawkish" is equivalent to saying the actor is "less dovish." How do these biases affect the ability to follow through on resolved statements?

Based on their preferences, dovish veto players are more likely to create obstacles to attempts by the leader to follow through on resolved statements. Again, I do not assume that a single dovish veto player can absolutely block the decision to follow through, but I expect that more dovish veto players will make following through more difficult. For example, when Democrats gained control of Congress in 2007, they took a more skeptical view of the Iraq War than the previous Republican leadership of Congress, and this created doubt about whether the 2007 Iraq troop surge that President Bush had announced would be allowed to occur. Similarly, when the more dovish Labor Party joined hawkish Israeli prime minister Benjamin Netanyahu's coalition government in 2009 (Kershner 2009), it led to speculation that Israel might be less likely to rely on military force in dealing with adversaries, despite Netanyahu's personal history of resolved statements and policies. These examples illustrate that if veto players are too dovish, adversaries may believe that the leader is unable to follow through on resolved statements. However, if an adversary can observe that veto players are hawkish, it is likely to believe that the leader will face few political obstacles to following through.[2] Therefore, resolved statements should be more effective when veto players are more hawkish.

Appendix 1 contains a game theoretic model that proves this logic formally. The game portrays a scenario in which the leaders of two countries (player 1 and player 2) are bargaining over some good, in a dispute that has not yet escalated to full-scale war. The crucial assumption in the game is that a veto player who is more hawkish is less likely to block a leader's decision to follow through on a statement of resolve. Based on this assumption, player 2 raises his or her estimate of the probability that player 1 will follow through on a statement when player 1's veto player is more hawkish.[3] Player 2, who faces a choice between backing down and standing firm in response to player 1's statement, thus recognizes that there is a higher risk of full-scale war associated with standing firm when player 1's veto player is more hawkish. This recognition makes player 2 less likely to stand firm and more likely to back down.

The model shows that player 2's probability of backing down or standing firm in response to a statement is also affected by a variety of other factors, including the cost of fighting a war for both sides, the expectation about which

---

[2] Having few or no veto players at all would have a similar effect as having all or mostly hawkish veto players, but I argued above that most leaders do have a substantial number of veto players. I will consider the situation of leaders with no veto players in more detail in the Conclusion.

[3] For simplicity, the game assumes that only player 1 has a veto player.

side would win, and the size of the audience cost that player 1 is assumed to pay for backing down. However, the presence of a more hawkish veto player consistently increases the probability that player 2 will back down in response to a statement, regardless of the values of the other factors. Therefore, the game helps to confirm that the effect of hawkish veto players is not confounded by any other factors or unforeseen strategic behavior. More generally, the game theoretic model uses more rigorous formal logic to verify the expectation developed above using intuitive logic that having more hawkish veto players gives leaders a greater ability to persuade adversaries to back down using statements of resolve. Based on both the formal and informal versions of this logic, we obtain Hypothesis 2:

Hypothesis 2: *Statements of resolve will be more effective when domestic veto players are more hawkish.*

This hypothesis is unique from previous literature, although there is some other literature that is related. As noted previously, Howell and Pevehouse (2007) have already pointed out the ability of Congress to hamper presidential use of force, but they focus more on the role of party politics, and they do not directly explore the implications of Congress's role as a veto player for the effectiveness of presidential statements. As discussed in more detail in Chapter 5, several other scholars have explored how the electoral incentives of opposition parties affect threat credibility (Ramsay 2004; Schultz's 1998), but the concept of domestic opposition only partially overlaps with the concept of veto players, and again this work does not consider hawkish or dovish preferences. There is another strand of research that does consider how the hawkish or dovish preferences of certain actors influence foreign policy outcomes, although none of this work has investigated how hawkish or dovish veto players influence threat credibility. For example, Schultz (2005) explores whether hawkish or dovish leaders are in a better position to make peace, and Clare (2014) discusses how the danger that a dovish leader will be replaced by a more hawkish opposition can influence an adversary to make concessions. Other research has found that more hawkish right-wing governments have more and longer military conflicts (Arena and Palmer 2009; Koch and Sullivan 2010; Palmer, London, and Regan 2004). While much of this previous research is complementary to my theory, my theory is the first to explore how hawkish or dovish veto players (who may or may not be part of the opposition or the legislature) impact the effectiveness of resolved statements.

One final thing to note regarding the hypothesis about hawkish veto players is that in addition to reducing obstacles to following through, hawkish veto players could also increase domestic audience costs by criticizing decisions to back down. This mechanism would have a complementary effect with the mechanism posited by my theory of the ability to follow through. However, this effect of hawkish veto players on audience costs is not likely to play an equally large role because it is more likely to be confounded by party politics. For example, while evidence presented later in the book suggests that Republicans in Congress are not likely to block either a Republican or a Democratic president's ability to follow through on statements, Republicans in Congress would probably be less likely to criticize a Republican president for backing down. The relationship between hawkish veto players and domestic audience costs will be explored further in Chapter 6, which finds that Soviet fears about the hawkishness of Kennedy's veto players during the Cuban Missile Crisis had little to do with audience costs.

SECURITY IN OFFICE

An additional domestic factor that is likely to have an impact on the ability to follow through on statements of resolve is the security in office of the leader issuing the statements. I define security in office broadly as meaning that a leader is very unlikely to be removed from office in the near future, for any reason except constitutionally imposed term limits. There are various ways in which a leader can be considered to have security in office. In some autocracies, security in office could mean that there is no domestic group powerful enough to remove the leader. This would be the case for personalistic dictators, such as Iraq's Saddam Hussein. In democracies, the extent to which leaders are secure in office is likely to depend on their popularity and on election laws. In parliamentary systems in which elections could be called at any time, security in office will depend very heavily on the leader's public support. In presidential systems, in contrast, a president who is not facing another election for at least a few years might be considered secure in office regardless of public support. Presidents who will not run for election again due to term limits can also be considered secure because even though their remaining time in office is limited, they need not worry about being removed before their designated time in office is up.

One reason why resolved statements by secure leaders should be more effective is that secure leaders are likely to face fewer obstacles to initiating or continuing a conflict from other domestic actors. The previous section established that almost all leaders face at least some veto players with the power to restrain their actions. However, if veto players oppose conflict, a leader may sometimes be able to persuade them to change their position. Leaders will need to use political capital for this type of persuasion, and leaders who are more secure in office should be able to do this more successfully for several reasons.

First, a leader who is expected to remain in office longer is likely to have more bargaining power. Turning to the example of American politics, classic scholarly work by Neustadt (1976) argues that a president's most important power is his ability to persuade other actors in the government that going along with the president's agenda is in their own interest. An important part of this persuasion is bargaining, and part of the bargaining process is based on expectations about the future. Even if the president cannot offer other government actors something that they want in the present, they might still go along with him based on the implicit or explicit promise that they will get something from him in return in the future. This is related to security in office because more secure leaders are more likely to be around in the future and thus should be better able to bargain based on future trade-offs.[4] Although Neustadt's argument is made in the US context, the idea that leaders who are expected to be around longer will have a greater domestic bargaining ability should apply to almost any country.

In addition, in democracies in particular, security in office is closely related to popularity with the public, and popularity may also assist leaders in overcoming domestic obstacles to military action. Neustadt (1976) identified prestige with the public as one factor which allows US presidents to be successful in persuading other government actors to go along with their agenda. Edwards (2003) lays out more detailed reasons why popularity might benefit the president in gaining support from Congress. First, if the president is popular, members of Congress might interpret this to mean that voters support his agenda. Second, popular presidents can threaten to campaign against those who oppose their agenda. Third, a popular president can provide cover for voting against constituent preferences by allowing Congress members to frame their votes as supporting the president. There is some empirical support for the assertion that more popular presidents are better able to persuade Congress to support their agenda (Brace and Hinckley 1992; Canes-Wrone and De Marchi 2002; Ostrom and Simon 1985; Rivers and Rose 1985). After the September 11 terrorist attacks, for example, the climate of patriotism and elevated approval for President Bush led to near unanimous Congressional passage of the Authorization to Use Military Force resolution, giving Bush wide latitude to combat terrorism. Therefore, in the United States and most likely in other countries as well, a leader's popularity may also be associated with a less restricted ability to follow through on statements with military action.

Another reason why security in office might make it easier to follow through on statements of resolve is that leaders who are secure in office may feel they have more flexibility to take risks. As noted earlier in this chapter, there is substantial evidence that leaders who initiate conflicts that go poorly face an increased danger of losing office. Even though the initiation of force might produce a boost to a leader's popularity, such boosts are generally short-lived (James and Rioux 1998) and easily overwhelmed by public backlash against unsuccessful military operations. However, the danger of losing office due to the unsuccessful use of force is not constant among all leaders (Croco and Weeks 2015). Leaders who are sufficiently secure in office are unlikely to lose power

---

[4] The only exception to this would be leaders approaching the end of their term limit.

even if a conflict goes poorly. Therefore, secure leaders might feel they have more freedom to take a risk by initiating or continuing military conflict.

As noted earlier, there are several different ways in which a leader can have security in office, but each of these can engender a similar freedom to take risks. Weeks (2012) finds that personalistic dictators are particularly prone to take risks because no domestic actors are empowered to remove them for making bad decisions. Within democracies, leaders who are very popular are likely to feel more freedom to run risks because even if their popularity declined somewhat, it would not be likely to put them in danger of losing office. Leaders who will not face elections for a long time might also feel they have more flexibility to run risks because the outcome, whether popular or unpopular, is likely to be overshadowed by more recent events and concerns by the time elections occur. For example, although President Obama's first term was marked by several significant foreign policy events, including the withdrawal of troops from Iraq, a troop surge in Afghanistan, a military intervention in Libya, and the killing of Osama bin Laden, exit polls from the 2012 elections indicated that voters were more influenced by domestic concerns, including the government response to the recent Hurricane Sandy (CNN 2012). In all of these situations, the leader is essentially insulated from the consequences of disapproval from his or her domestic audience, meaning that the personal cost of following through on a statement of resolve with the use of force and losing the resulting conflict is lower.

The Costs of Following Through versus Backing Down

It is important to note, however, that this insulation from public opinion is also likely to mean that the personal cost of backing down from a statement of resolve is lower. Therefore, secure leaders should face fewer costs associated with backing down from statements of resolve *as well as* fewer costs associated with following through on them. Domestic audience cost theory focuses exclusively on the cost of backing down and thus claims that statements by secure leaders should be less effective (Fearon 1994a). However, in order to truly understand how security in office impacts the effectiveness of resolved statements, it is important to consider how security in office simultaneously affects *both* the costs associated with backing down and the costs associated with following through. Because these two types of costs can interact with each other in complex ways, I explore this using a game theoretic model, shown in Appendix 2.

The model discussed in Appendix 2 is in most respects a standard conflict bargaining model in which the leader of a country, referred to as player 1, has the option to make a statement of resolve and pays an audience cost for backing down from the statement. However, unlike other models of conflict bargaining, it also includes a separate audience cost that player 1 pays if he or she follows through on the statement of resolve by fighting and loses the resulting conflict.

The audience cost for backing down is linked to the audience cost for following through and losing through the parameter v_1, which represents player 1's vulnerability to removal from office. v_1 is multiplied by both audience costs, meaning that when player 1 is more vulnerable to removal (i.e., less secure in office), the expected punishment for both backing down and losing will be higher. Therefore, in comparison to previous game theoretic models, this model more accurately captures the dilemma faced by insecure leaders, for whom both backing down and following through after making a statement of resolve can be domestically risky.

The model confirms the earlier argument developed intuitively that greater security in office for a leader will have two competing effects – making it easier to back down after a statement, but also making it easier to follow through and fight a military conflict. But which of these two effects dominates in influencing the adversary's estimation of the probability that the leader will follow through after making a statement? In other words, does greater security in office make statements of resolve more credible and effective because of the lower risk of domestic punishment for following through, or does greater security in office make statements less effective because of the lower risk of domestic punishment for backing down? The game theoretic model tells us that conditions which make security in office beneficial to the effectiveness of statements *and* conditions which make it detrimental to the effectiveness of statements can both exist. The model also identifies the specific conditions under which security in office is most likely to be beneficial. Here I will discuss some of the key conditions identified in an intuitive way.

The model indicates that security in office is more likely to have a beneficial impact on the effectiveness of resolved statements when the domestic political cost for losing is high relative to the domestic political cost for backing down and when the probability of losing is high. This is intuitively plausible because under these conditions, the cost of losing is likely to dominate a leader's calculations, meaning that leaders will be more sensitive to a change in the cost of losing than a change in the cost of backing down. Thus, an increase in security in office under these conditions is likely to increase the probability that a leader will follow through on statements of resolve because it will reduce the leader's fear of losing more than the leader's fear of backing down. If adversaries understand this, then they will treat statements of resolve by more secure leaders as more credible.

Now that we have identified some conditions under which greater security in office makes leaders more likely to follow through on statements and increases the effectiveness of statements, the key question is how often these conditions exist in the real world. I argue that these conditions exist in the majority of international disputes. First, it is reasonable to expect that the domestic political cost for losing will usually be much higher than the cost for backing down. Despite the findings of survey experiments that the public strongly disapproves of backing down (Trager and Vavreck 2011), in the real world, losing is likely to be much more noticeable to domestic audiences than backing down. In the case of the United States, research has shown that the public does not pay much attention to presidential statements (Edwards 2003). Thus, when the domestic audience is large and not highly engaged, many audience members may not even notice that a leader backed down from a statement of resolve. In contrast, following through on a resolved statement by fighting and then ultimately losing would be much more noticeable. Even less engaged members of the domestic public would probably be aware of losing in an armed conflict because the conflict would garner substantial media attention and might impose direct costs upon the audience in the form of casualties or economic costs.

Second, the probability of losing will be high enough in most disputes that the cost of losing must be given serious consideration. International conflict is unpredictable, and clear victories are rare. Even the United States has failed to achieve clear victories in some major conflicts, such as the Vietnam War and Iraq War, and Presidents Johnson and Bush suffered reduced popularity as a result. Based on this logic, I argue that in most situations, leaders will view following through on statements of resolve with military action as an option that is riskier for their security in office than backing down. Therefore, adversaries will only expect more secure leaders to take this risk, meaning that the resolved statements of more secure leaders are more likely to persuade adversaries to back down.

The discussion thus far has assumed that leaders are risk-neutral, i.e., they have neutral preferences between a gamble and a certain outcome if the expected payoff is the same. Another possibility is that some leaders are risk-loving and may prefer to gamble. Leaders with such preferences would be more likely to prefer following through on statements over backing down, despite the risks. However, while there are undoubtedly some leaders with risk-loving preferences, there is no reason to think they are in a majority. To reach the position of leadership of a country, individuals usually must be patient and calculating rather than rash. Therefore, there are unlikely to be many leaders who are risk-loving enough to undermine the logic of my theory.

An additional possibility is that leaders may choose to gamble not because they love risks, but because they have nothing left to lose. This may be the case for the most insecure leaders, who know that they will certainly lose office if they back down from a statement. If there is even a slim chance of a military victory that could revive their political fortunes, it would be rational for these leaders to "gamble for resurrection" by following through on their statements with force (Downs and Rocke 1994). However, this situation is also unlikely to be common. Given the rules about election timing in democracies and the difficulties of organizing to remove a leader in nondemocracies, situations in which leaders can expect to immediately be removed for backing down are likely to be rare. Most leaders, even if insecure, can hope to remain in office long enough that it makes sense to think in a longer-term way about the impact of backing down versus following through on their popularity. I do, however, test whether leaders gamble for resurrection in Chapter 4.

In the preceding paragraphs, I have identified conditions under which greater security in office is most likely to have a beneficial impact on the effectiveness of statements, according to my game theoretic model. I have also made the argument that these conditions are widespread, and ruled out some possible objections. Based on all of this, I argue that greater security in office will *most typically* increase the effectiveness of resolved statements due to the greater freedom from worry about removal that secure leaders have. As discussed earlier in this section, secure leaders should also face fewer obstacles in persuading veto players to support following through on statements. Therefore, there are at least two reasons to expect that security in office will generally improve the effectiveness of resolved statements by reducing the risks and obstacles to following through. This leads us to Hypothesis 3:

Hypothesis 3: *Statements of resolve will be more effective when the leader issuing them is more secure in office.*

This hypothesis is also unique from previous literature. There has been a substantial amount of research on how security in office affects conflict behavior, including the democratic peace literature (for example, Bueno de Mesquita et al. 1999; Doyle 1983), literature about how security in office affects signaling decisions and decisions to back down in conflict (for example, Chiozza 2015; Croco 2011; Goemans 2000), and literature about how adversaries can seek to support or undermine the security in office of a sitting leader by granting or withholding bargaining concessions (for example, Clare 2014; Wolford 2012). Some of this literature complements my theory by assuming or asserting that engaging in international conflict can be risky to a leader's security in office. However, within the smaller subset of literature that specifically discusses how security in office impacts the effectiveness of resolved statements or threats (discussed in the next section), there is almost universal agreement that security in office makes statements and other threats *less* effective. Thus, my theory breaks new ground in understanding the relationship between security in office and the effectiveness of statements of resolve.

OTHER THEORIES

The previous sections laid out my theory of the importance of the ability to follow through for the effectiveness of resolved statements and developed three hypotheses regarding the observable implications of my theory. In subsequent chapters, I will test whether these hypotheses are supported by empirical evidence. However, the goal of this book is not only to test my own theory but also to compare it to other theories regarding the effectiveness of resolved statements. Therefore, this section will consider two previously existing theories regarding the effectiveness of statements and generate testable hypotheses regarding which conditions they would predict to be influential.

The previous theories considered in this section are focused on the consequences associated with backing down from statements. These theories are not fundamentally in opposition to mine because the ability to follow through and the consequences of backing down can simultaneously impact the effectiveness of statements. Indeed, I agree with the logic of these theories that it is necessary for there to be some potential negative consequence for making or backing down from statements in order for statements to be at all effective at communicating resolve. However, my theory emphasizes that the consequences of backing down are not necessarily the most important thing causing variation in effectiveness.

The first existing theory to consider is domestic audience cost theory, which argues that statements are effective because of domestic political punishment for backing down from them (Fearon 1994a). The theory of audience costs has been very influential, but the empirical support for it is uncertain. Several survey experiments have found evidence of audience costs for backing down from resolved statements (Tomz 2007; Trager and Vavreck 2011), but it is not entirely clear if the domestic public pays as much attention to leadership statements in the real world as in these experiments. Furthermore, in other survey experiments, Chaudoin (2014) finds that only respondents without strong policy preferences seem to care significantly if a leader backs down from a commitment, and Levendusky and Horowitz (2012) find that leaders can substantially reduce disapproval for backing down by explaining their reasons for doing so. Kertzer and Brutger (2015) further argue that many survey experiments overestimate the number of domestic audience members who disapprove of backing down from statements because some of the observed disapproval actually results from the decision to make a statement in the first place. Meanwhile, historical case study research has raised doubts about the existence of audience costs (Snyder and Borghard 2011; Trachtenberg 2012). It may be difficult to directly observe the existence of audience costs because leaders have the incentive to avoid invoking audience costs when they are most likely to be paid (Schultz 2001).

However, domestic audience cost theory has another testable implication. In contrast to my theory, audience cost theory suggests that more secure leaders should be *less* able to issue effective statements because they are less vulnerable to punishment for backing down. Fearon (1994a) and scholars who have built on his work have used this logic to argue that leaders of regimes in which the leader is more vulnerable to removal can generate more audience costs and should therefore be able to convey resolve more effectively (Eyerman and Hart 1996; Gelpi and Griesdorf 2001; Partell and

Palmer 1999; Schultz 1999; Weeks 2008). The same logic would imply that within democratic regimes, leaders who are unpopular or facing imminent elections should be able to generate greater audience costs. Contrary to my Hypothesis 3, audience cost theory would therefore suggest the following hypothesis:

Hypothesis 4: *Statements of resolve will be less effective when the leader issuing them is more secure in office.*

The contrast between the prediction of audience cost theory and my theory does not mean that the theories cannot both be correct, but because the theoretical mechanisms push in opposite directions, the question is which one dominates.

At the international level, another explanation for variation in the effectiveness of resolved statements is the theory of international reputational costs, which has been most prominently advanced by Sartori (2005). Sartori argues that if a country makes a statement and backs down, it will develop a reputation for bluffing, causing other countries to view its future statements as less credible. This creates a disincentive to bluff and makes statements more credible among states with honest reputations. Empirical evidence regarding international reputations is mixed, and its interpretation is complicated by the fact that there are different types of reputation. Most scholars who have studied the relationship between reputation and conflict have focused on reputation for resolve, i.e., a reputation for being willing to fight or having a low cost of war. Some scholars have found evidence that reputations for resolve do develop (Huth 1997; Miller 2015; Weisiger and Yarhi-Milo 2015), while others have expressed skepticism (Mercer 1996).

Although some of these findings may be relevant, the specific question for determining the costliness of statements is whether states develop reputations for *honesty*, i.e., keeping commitments and actually fighting after they say they are resolved. There has been less research on this question, and the results are mixed. Press (2005) finds no evidence that countries develop reputations for honesty in several case studies. On the other hand, Sartori's (2005) statistical analysis shows that defenders who have a history of bluffing are less able to deter attacks, although she measures bluffing indirectly based on conflict reciprocation and hostility levels. Miller's (2011) historical research also finds that countries with a greater reputation for following through on threats find it easier to form alliances. Relatedly, Gelpi (1997) finds that states' history of abiding by international agreements, as well as their history of toughness in previous disputes, affects future dispute outcomes through reputational mechanisms.

My dataset of resolved statements provides a new way to measure bluffing and test the theory of international reputational costs. If this theory is correct, we should expect to see that states which have backed down from more resolved statements in the recent past should be less able to make effective statements in the present. This logic gives us Hypothesis 5:

Hypothesis 5: *Statements of resolve will be less effective if the country issuing them recently backed down from a large number of previous statements of resolve.*

Unfortunately, this book is unable to test all explanations for variation in the effectiveness of statements. Trager's (2010; 2013; 2015) theories about the inherent risks associated with making statements of resolve do not suggest any readily observable conditions that would create much variation in the effectiveness of statements. Theoretical arguments by Danilovic (2002) and Press (2005) also predict that the effectiveness of resolved statements will vary with the level of national interests at stake, but national interests are very difficult to measure.[5] Indeed, I argued at the beginning of this chapter that even adversaries often have difficulty making accurate inferences about which issues a country considers vital to its interests and that this is why resolved statements can convey useful information. The difficultly in observing national interests might be reason for skepticism that they greatly impact the effectiveness of resolved statements, but it also makes their impact quite difficult to test. For these reasons, this book is unable to offer any new tests of Trager's theoretical arguments or of the impact of national interests on the effectiveness of statements. Nonetheless, by comparing my theory of the ability to follow through to the widely cited theories of domestic audience costs and international reputational costs, I hope to significantly improve the understanding of what conditions make statements of resolve most effective.

SUMMING UP

In this chapter, I have argued that the ability to follow through on statements of resolve is an important condition determining statements' effectiveness. This is because adversaries are aware that there are risks and obstacles associated with following through on statements of resolve and will be skeptical of a statement's credibility if these risks and obstacles are too great. Despite the importance of the ability to follow through on statements, previous scholarly work has devoted little systematic attention to studying exactly what the ability to follow through includes and how it varies among leaders.

I discussed three specific factors that can help mitigate the risks and obstacles to following through and make resolved statements more effective. The first factor is higher military capabilities relative to the adversary, which helps to

---

[5] Danilovic (2002) performs statistical analysis of deterrence attempts and creates a regional measure of the interests that major powers have in protégés based on factors such as alliance ties and trade. However, this measure cannot be applied to most of the military disputes that I use in my statistical analysis because they do not involve defense of a protégé.

improve the physical ability to follow through on statements. The second factor is hawkish domestic veto players, who are less likely than dovish veto players to create domestic political roadblocks to military action. The final factor is security in office of the leader, which gives the leader more leverage over veto players and more freedom to take military risks without danger of losing office. In the following chapters, I will test the importance of these factors to the effectiveness of statements using both quantitative data and historical case studies.

PART II

DATA ON STATEMENTS AND STATISTICAL ANALYSIS

2

Data on Statements and When They Are Made

As established in the previous chapters, existing scholarly work regarding the impact of statements of resolve includes many theories but few strong empirical tests. A major reason for this situation is the lack of appropriate data for testing the theories. Without data on statements of resolve, it is very difficult to prove any of the theories wrong or compete them against each other. While it can be valuable to test the theories with historical case studies, such studies are naturally limited to only a few cases and are therefore unlikely to definitively settle the theoretical debates over statements of resolve. Experiments also hold some promise for studying the effect of resolved statements, but experimental research designs often suffer from concerns about external validity, i.e., whether the experimental conditions accurately reflect the real world. Likewise, statistical tests using measures such as regime type (Schultz 1999; Weeks 2008) or escalation levels (Sartori 2005) have offered some suggestive evidence about the impact of statements, but the indirect nature of these tests makes it difficult to rule out alternate explanations. Therefore, it seems that a dataset directly measuring statements of resolve is necessary to provide a more satisfying answer to the questions of whether and under what conditions statements are effective.

It is understandable that data on statements of resolve has so far been lacking because it is challenging to measure these types of statements in a systematic way. Nonetheless, this type of measurement is necessary to address the unanswered questions regarding statements of resolve and move the study of this issue forward. In recent years, social scientists have increasingly utilized content analysis techniques to measure abstract concepts in written and spoken words (Grimmer and Stewart 2013; Neuendorf 2002; Schwartz and Ungar 2015). Building upon this tradition, I develop a simple and transparent method of counting resolved words and phrases in US presidential statements. This allows me to systematically code how resolved US presidential statements were across a wide variety of conflict situations.

This chapter describes my process for measuring statements of resolve and explains some of the important decisions that I made regarding the data collection process. It also describes the resulting data and analyzes when statements of resolve are most likely to be made. There are two particularly important findings regarding when statements are made, which have implications for testing the effectiveness of statements in the upcoming chapters. First, I find that statements of resolve are rarely made in calm times for the sole purpose of general deterrence and are much more commonly made during active disputes or tensions. This suggests that it is most appropriate to study the effectiveness of statements in the context of active disputes. Second, I find that the level of presidential statements of resolve is not significantly influenced by the president's ability to follow through. While this finding is somewhat surprising, it does not undermine the causal mechanisms in my theory and reduces concerns about selection effects.

DEFINITION OF RESOLVE STATEMENTS

I define statements of resolve as public statements which indicate that a country is committed to a position. Once a leader of a country indicates a commitment, any deviation from that commitment can be viewed as backing down. The statements which indicate the strongest level of resolve are those which make an explicit threat. This type of statement clearly establishes the country's position and creates specific expectations about what will happen if the adversary fails to comply. Threats are the most commonly studied type of resolved statement, but they are far from the only type of statement that can convey resolve. A slightly lower level of resolve can be conveyed by statements which express a concrete demand or concrete refusal without a threat. Even though these statements do not promise specific action, they still create specific expectations about a state's position on an issue. For example, when President George H.W. Bush said that Iraq's occupation of Kuwait would "not stand" (August 5, 1990, quoted in Peters and Woolley 2016), he was creating the expectation that the United States would force Iraq out of Kuwait, even without directly mentioning the use of force.[1] Any backing down from this type of statement is easy to observe, meaning that it also conveys substantial resolve.

Although explicit threats, demands, and refusals are important in creating strong expectations and therefore conveying strong resolve, they are not the only type of statement which can convey resolve. More implicit statements can also convey a certain measure of resolve. Any public statement by a country which characterizes the status quo or another state's behavior negatively can raise expectations that the country is committed to changing the situation or the

---

[1] As the occupation of Kuwait dragged on, Bush increasingly made more explicit threats of force as well.

other state's behavior. For example, when Reagan called the Soviet Union an "evil empire" (March 8, 1983, quoted in Peters and Woolley 2016), this contributed to the impression that Reagan intended to stand firm against the Soviet Union and oppose its policies. If a leader failed to make any firm response to a country or situation after issuing such a statement, it could be viewed as backing down from the statement. On the other hand, because such negative characterizations do not promise any specific action or outcome, they allow leaders some flexibility in how to respond to a situation without being viewed as backing down. Therefore, statements which complain, denounce, or make other negative characterizations about a country or situation can also be viewed as statements of resolve, but because of the flexibility associated with them, they do not convey as strong a level of resolve as explicit threats or demands.

Even though negative characterizations convey a weaker level of resolve and less specific goals, I include them in my main analysis along with explicit threats, demand, and refusals. The reason is that negative characterizations appear frequently in presidential statements as well as the statements of other world leaders. Making negative characterizations seems to be attractive to leaders, both because of the flexibility it allows them and because of norms with regard to politeness and diplomatic speech. Thus, leaving negative characterizations out of the analysis would leave the majority of statements made in the context of international conflict unaddressed. Therefore, my primary measure of statements of resolve includes threats, demands and refusals, and negative characterizations, but gives more weight to the more strongly resolved types of statements.

PUBLIC VERSUS PRIVATE STATEMENTS

The definition of statements of resolve given in the previous section refers only to public statements. It should be noted, however, that resolved private statements can also be made in confidential diplomatic channels. There is some debate in the academic literature over whether it is necessary or even desirable for statements to be public in order to be effective (Kurizaki 2007). Some of the existing theories discussed in Chapter 1 could apply to either public or private statements because they do not rely on imposition of costs by the public. These include Trager's (2010; 2013; 2015) argument about the inherent risks associated with making statements and Sartori's (2005) concept of international reputational costs. In contrast, theories about domestic audience costs (Fearon 1994a) or the role of the opposition (Schultz 1998) are applicable only to public threats. My own theory of the ability to follow through could apply to either public or private threats.

This book focuses on public statements for multiple reasons. First, public statements are much easier to obtain. Records of most private statements are available only in government archives, and the time and expense associated with archival research would limit the number of crises covered. In addition, the fact that more recent information is likely to be classified would limit the temporal scope of any effort to collect private statements. Furthermore, even the most thorough archival research could not obtain exact quotes of all relevant private statements issued because often these would not be recorded verbatim. In addition to these logistical reasons to focus on public statements, public statements are also more theoretically interesting than private statements because they have been theorized to be successful through a greater number of mechanisms.

In sum, because my theory of the ability to follow through could also apply to private statements, the results in this book are probably also relevant for those who seek to understand the effectiveness of statements made through confidential diplomatic channels. However, the focus of the book is on public statements, and the empirical findings are based solely on the coding of public statements. Thus, inferences about the effectiveness of private statements should be drawn with some caution.

FOCUS ON US PRESIDENTIAL STATEMENTS

My measure of statements of resolve was created based on content analysis of full statements by US presidents. The decision to use statements by US presidents and not other world leaders was primarily driven by the fact that a searchable archive of US presidential statements was readily available and posed no language or cultural barriers to identifying resolved words in US statements. However, focusing on the United States is also desirable for the first test of my theory because the United States is an important country in the international system and because the US political system is relatively transparent, allowing adversaries to observe the hawkishness of veto players and security in office of the president without great difficulty. For example, Soviet officials understood that US veto players were hawkish during the Cuban Missile Crisis (Dobrynin 1995, 87), and North Vietnamese officials were able to correctly interpret changes in Nixon's security in office during the Vietnam War (Ang 2004, 102–110).

A potential downside of the focus on the United States is that the results for US statements might not necessarily be applicable to other countries in the world since the United States has some unique characteristics, most notably its superpower status. US military capabilities could arguably make US statements of resolve more convincing. However, because the United States is not always willing to use force to enforce its will, it still faces the same basic challenge as other countries in conveying when it is truly resolved to fight. Furthermore, establishing whether or not statements are effective at conveying resolve for even just one country is an important empirical step forward given that this has never before been clearly demonstrated.

Another concern might be whether statements by additional US officials should be included. Unfortunately, no equally comprehensive source of statements by other US officials is available. However, since most administrations try to stay "on message," the president's statements should be somewhat representative of statements by other officials. Furthermore, if a lower-level official makes a particularly hawkish statement, the press is likely to ask the president about it, ensuring that the president will reiterate or refute most controversial statements by other officials. Finally, while statements by all officials may play a role, presidential statements will usually carry the most weight since the president has the sole authority to authorize force.

COLLECTION AND CODING PROCESS

I now turn to discussing how the measure of statements of resolve was created. All public presidential statements and remarks released by the Office of the Press Secretary since 1929 are available in the *Public Papers of the Presidents of the United States*, made available online by the American Presidency Project (Peters and Woolley 2016). This resource is a comprehensive archive of all types of presidential statements, ranging from major speeches, to remarks at ceremonies and other events with narrower audiences, to brief impromptu exchanges with reporters. I searched this resource to obtain the set of presidential statements that I use for content analysis. I engaged in two main statement collection efforts. The first involved collecting statements directed at long-term US rivals over a period of decades, while the second involved collecting statements targeted at US adversaries in the context of shorter-term militarized interstate disputes (MIDs). I will explain more about the rationale and parameters for these collection efforts in the subsequent sections, as I discuss the data produced by each.

The method of processing the text was the same in both collection efforts. I began by searching the *Public Papers* for rival or MID adversary names within the relevant time frames (described below). In a manual review of the search results, I excluded statements that were not spoken by the president personally and paragraphs about topics other than the rival or adversary. I considered a paragraph to be about a particular country if the country was the subject or object of any sentences in the paragraph, if the paragraph made demands of the country, or if the paragraph stated US policy toward the country or regarding a dispute with the country. After following this procedure, I was left with only relevant portions of statements.

I coded these remaining statement portions using the *Yoshikoder* content analysis program and a content analysis dictionary which I created to measure resolve in presidential statements. I developed the content analysis dictionary through an inductive process. I read the statements I collected, identified words or phrases which indicated resolve, and added these items to the dictionary. This process was not biased by my knowledge of MID outcomes because most

MIDs in the dataset were too obscure for me to have historical knowledge of the outcome before reading about them for the first time. After gathering most of the dictionary items in this manner, I also added a few words from Wood's (2012) dictionary measuring presidential "saber rattling" and words recommended by colleagues. I then used the *Yoshikoder* program to find instances in which the dictionary items appeared in the statements. I examined the *Yoshikoder* output to identify dictionary items which appeared to have inflated tallies, investigated the instances in which these suspicious words or phrases appeared in the statements, and edited the dictionary as necessary. The final dictionary, which is available in Appendix 3, includes 264 words and phrases. Table 2.1 provides some examples of dictionary words in context.

The primary weighting scheme that I used for the dictionary has three tiers, corresponding to the conceptualization of the relative strength of different types of statements given in the definition of statements of resolve above. Words and

TABLE 2.1 *Examples of Statement Types*

Statement Category	Examples
Negative Characterizations	"I refer to the problem of military conflicts in regions of the developing world, where the facts of Soviet action are **brutal**, a **danger** to peace and our future relations." Ronald Reagan, April 10, 1987
	"[W]e **condemn** the Taliban regime. It is not only **repressing** its own people; it is **threatening** people everywhere by sponsoring and **sheltering** and supplying terrorists. By aiding and **abetting murder**, the Taliban regime is committing **murder**." George W. Bush, September 20, 2001
Demands or Refusals	"And so, the bottom line for us is that Iraqi *aggression* will **not be allowed** to **stand**." George H.W. Bush, October 16, 1990
	"That's why we joined with more than a hundred other nations in the United Nations to *condemn* this *aggression* and to **demand** withdrawal of the Soviet invasion forces from Afghanistan." Jimmy Carter, February 19, 1980
Threats	"Any *hostile* move anywhere in the world against the safety and freedom of peoples to whom we *are committed*–including in particular the brave people of West Berlin–will be met by **whatever action** is needed." John F. Kennedy, October 22, 1962
	"America protects its own. Anyone, anyone, who takes on our troops will suffer the **consequences**. We **will fight** fire with fire and then some." Bill Clinton, November 27, 1995

Note: Words and phrases that appear in the dictionary in the relevant category are in bold. Dictionary words and phrases from other categories are in italics.

phrases that are commonly associated with explicit threats, for example, "take action" or "whatever is necessary," were weighted as three. Words and phrases commonly associated with demands or refusals, such as "unwavering" or "not negotiable," were weighted as two. Finally, words and phrases typically associated with negative characterizations, for example, "dangerous" or "barbaric," were weighted as one. The most appropriate category for each dictionary item was determined based on consultation with seven colleagues. The categorization of most dictionary items was not controversial.

Based on the dictionary, I obtained scores totaling the number of dictionary words and phrases used by the president in each MID and in each month of each rivalry. I refer to these as "statement scores." Later in the book, I perform robustness checks involving different ways of creating the statement scores. For example, I vary the statement collection time periods, I utilize different dictionary weighting schemes, and I split out different types of statements. The fact that the results stand up to all of these changes indicates that they are not driven by some random quirk of the primary measurement method.

COMPARISON TO PREVIOUS MEASURES

My quantitative coding of resolved statements represents a major step forward in studying these statements because no one has previously attempted to define and code the full universe of statements that signal resolve. Much of the existing work that has studied signals of resolve empirically has focused on measuring actions rather than statements. For example, Sartori (2005) interprets actions taken in MIDs as signals of resolve, while Huth and Allee (2002) have interpreted refusals to make concessions in negotiations as signals of resolve. Far fewer studies have attempted to measure verbal signals of resolve. A few scholars, including Huth (1988) and Sechser (2011), have coded deterrent or compellent threats. Because such clear and specific threats are rare, these data collection efforts have been undertaken using human coding. In contrast, my research design uses computer content analysis to code a much wider range of statements that can be considered resolved.

A more similar data collection effort to mine has been undertaken by Wood (2012, 35–36), who uses computer content analysis to identity US presidential statements which constitute "saber rattling," defined as "hostile foreign policy rhetoric of all styles and contexts" and "threats of either a general or specific nature." Wood's definition of saber rattling is somewhat narrower than my definition of statements of resolve, but it is undeniable that we are measuring similar concepts. Nonetheless, substantial differences exist between our coding methods, and I argue that my method improves upon Wood's in some ways.

One key difference is that my method relies more on human input at the beginning, while Wood's method relies more on human input at the end. Wood began his content analysis of presidential statements by using computer code to obtain word frequencies, whereas I began the coding process by actually reading through the statements I collected. This had the advantage of allowing me to identify dictionary terms by looking at words in context and resulted in a dictionary more than twice as large as Wood's.[2] At the end of Wood's coding process, human coders reviewed the results and discarded results that were determined to be false positives. In contrast, after creating the best possible dictionary, I made no adjustment to the results produced by the content analysis software, leading to coding that is more transparent and replicable.

My coding method also captures more relevant statements and more nuances in language than Wood's method. I code every paragraph about an adversary in its entirety, even if the adversary is not mentioned by name.[3] In contrast, Wood only analyzes sentences that include certain words relevant to foreign policy. Additionally, I count all resolved words within each relevant paragraph and give them different weights. Wood, on the other hand, gives each word equal weight and does not even weight sentences differently based on how many saber-rattling words they contain. Thus, Wood's measure is essentially an unweighted count of sentences, whereas mine is a weighted count of words. Therefore, my measure captures considerably more variation in presidential statements than Wood's.

Despite the differences in our coding methods, Wood and I find fairly similar results when using time series analysis to examine the relationship between presidential statements and adversary behavior, as discussed later in this chapter. Otherwise, there is little overlap between Wood's analysis and mine because Wood is primarily interested in the motivations of presidents for making statements, whereas this book focuses on the international effectiveness of statements. Wood's book makes important contributions to the literature on the US presidency, but is less focused on contributing to the international security and US foreign policy literatures in which this book is situated.

DESCRIPTION OF THE RIVALRY STATEMENT DATA

Having explained how my data on resolved statements were created and compared my data collection process to the efforts of other scholars, I now turn to describing the data and performing some preliminary analysis of the patterns observed, particularly with regard to when statements of resolve are made. I will begin by discussing the data on statements of resolve made in rivalries. The goal of collecting these data was to

---

[2] I am very grateful to Dan Wood for sharing his PERL code, including his list of saber-rattling words, with me.

[3] In my manual review of the search results, I was able to identify paragraphs that were about an adversary, despite not mentioning it by name. I found these by reading the paragraphs before and after those that did mention an adversary by name. It is quite common for the president to speak about an adversary without mentioning its name in every paragraph.

examine how the level of resolved statements goes up and down over the long term, in times of both tension and relative peace. Coding statements aimed at rivals is more manageable than attempting to code all presidential statements issued over a period of decades, and it is also more logical because rivalries are where statements of resolve are most likely to be observed.

The general time frame that I selected for analyzing statements made in rivalries was 1975–2000. This period is fertile ground for rivalries because it spans Cold War rivalries as well as newer rivalries in the Middle East. Within this time period, I selected five countries about which to collect statements: Iran, Iraq, Libya, North Korea, and the Soviet Union. These are all countries with which the United States had serious long-standing disputes over policies and systems of government, and therefore I expected the president to make many resolved statements directed at them. The US relationship with these countries is not representative of the US relationship with most other countries in the international system, but statements of resolve directed at most countries in the international system are too rare to create a time series with a sufficient number of non-zero observations for statistical analysis. I consider Libya and North Korea to be rivals throughout the whole 1975–2000 time period, but I consider the Soviet rivalry to end with the fall of the Berlin Wall in 1989, and I consider the Iranian rivalry to start in 1979, the year of the Iranian Revolution. It could be argued that Iraq did not become a major rival until the Gulf War, but I extended the statement collection back to the 1984 "Tanker War," which included some minor US-Iraqi tensions.

The statement data for each US-rival relationship are coded on a monthly basis. I choose to aggregate the statements by month to reduce the impact of random noise and possible reporting delays. Figure 2.1 shows the level of statements of resolve over time for all five rivalries. The level of statements is shown in relation to a measure of the hostility of rival behavior, which I will discuss shortly. Focusing for now on the level of statements made in each rivalry, we see considerable variation. All of the graphs show that the level of resolved statements directed toward each rival spikes up and down a great deal between months. It is also clear to see that some rivals were the target of more resolved statements than others.

The Soviet Union and Iraq clearly dominate as recipients of resolved statements. The Soviet Union has the highest mean and median statement scores, being a frequent target of resolved statements throughout the entire collection period. The most resolved statements targeting the Soviet Union were made under President Reagan, in keeping with his reputation as a leader who took a tough line against the Soviet Union. Even though the USSR was the top target of US statements overall, the absolute highest monthly score belongs to Iraq during the Gulf War, and there are also some significant spikes in statements directed at Iraq during the later crises over weapons inspections. Iran is the target of a fairly large amount of statements of resolve during the

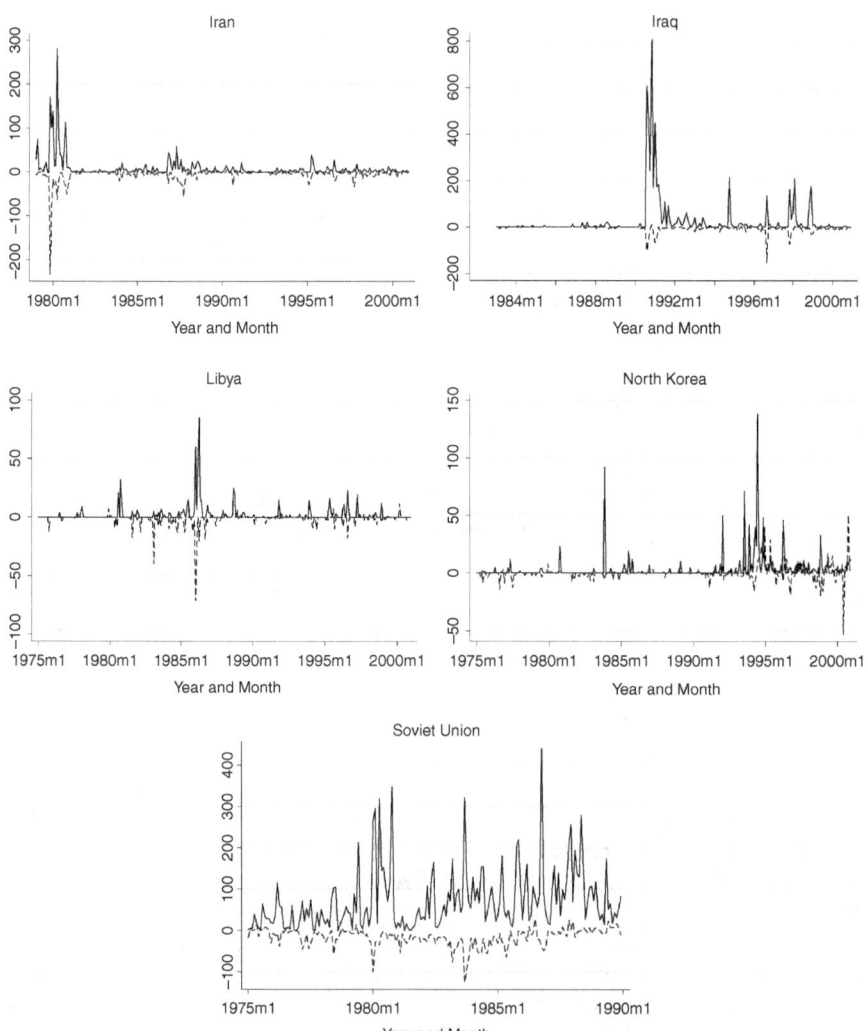

FIGURE 2.1 Statements of Resolve and Rival Hostility over Time
Note: The solid, positive line is the statement score. The dotted line, which is usually negative, represents rival behavior. The graphs have different scales.

Iranian hostage crisis, although this spike is not as large as some of the other spikes on the graph, probably reflecting President Carter's desire to avoid rhetoric that would endanger the hostages. After the hostage crisis, statements of resolve directed at Iran are fairly infrequent. Libya and North Korea are targets of the fewest statements. There are some moderately high spikes for North Korea in the mid-1990s due to concerns over its nuclear weapons program, and Libya experienced a spike in statements in 1986 in response to Libya's bombing of a Berlin nightclub and in conjunction with US airstrikes.

WHEN RESOLVED STATEMENTS ARE MADE IN RIVALRIES

The aforementioned observation that spikes in resolved statements seem to correspond with memorable real-world events is reassuring because it suggests that the measure of resolved statements has some face validity. However, it is possible to test the correspondence between resolved statements and real-world events more systematically. In order to do this, I utilize a measure of the hostility of rival behavior, which is based on event data. Event data code international interactions based on news reports. I obtained event data on rival behavior toward the United States from two sources. The first, known as the World Event/Interaction Survey (WEIS), contains events from 1966 through 1993 and was created using human coding of the *New York Times* (McClelland 1978; Tomlinson 1993). The second, known as Integrated Data for Events Analysis (IDEA), contains events from 1990 onward and was created using computer coding of Reuters reports (King and Lowe 2003). I weighted the event observations from these sources using a popular scheme developed by Goldstein (1992), in which negative scores denote hostile behavior and positive scores denote cooperative behavior. I aggregated the Goldstein scores representing each rival's behavior toward the United States by month, to match the statement data. Since the WEIS and IDEA datasets use the same basic event codings, I followed Thyne (2010) and combined the aggregated Goldstein scores from both datasets into a single series by simply averaging them where they overlapped. This yields a monthly measure of rival behavior toward the United States, in which more negative values indicate greater hostility.

Based on Figure 2.1, it is clear to see that there is a very close correspondence between statements of resolve and rival behavior. In general, when the rival's event score indicates more hostile behavior, the US president makes more statements of resolve directed at the rival. The Iran and Libya graphs show a close relationship between the two variables, with most large spikes in one being mirrored by a large spike in the other. The Iraq graph likewise shows that most large spikes are mirrored, but the spikes in statements are larger relative to the spikes in behavior. The North Korea graph shows less of a close relationship between statements and rival behavior, but there are still many instances in which spikes in one variable are mirrored by spikes in the other. In the Soviet graph, spikes in statements and Soviet behavior mirror each other to some extent, but this relationship weakens in the late 1980s as Soviet behavior becomes more cooperative.

It is reassuring that my measure of resolved statements has such a close relationship with this independent measure of rival behavior because it is another indication of face validity. However, the close relationship between statements of resolve and rival behavior also raises the question of causation. Is hostile rival behavior causing resolved statements to be made, or are resolved statements causing rivals to behave more hostilely? A theoretical argument could be made for either direction of causation. On one hand, hostile rival behavior may create an incentive for the president to make statements of resolve in order to convey that the behavior is not acceptable and that the United States will stand firm against it. On the other hand, it is possible that US statements of resolve might make the rival behave more hostilely, at least in the short term, in an effort to competitively signal its own resolve. This could be true even if the ultimate impact of the statements is to persuade the rival to back down.

It is impossible to tell from Figure 2.1 whether US statements are causing rival behavior, rival behavior is causing US statements, or both. One method that has potential to shed some light on this matter is vector autoregression (VAR). A VAR model is a system of equations in which each variable is regressed on its own past values and the past values of all other variables in the system. Having multiple equations means that all variables in the system can be treated as potentially endogenous. Thus, for each rival, I estimate a VAR model in which the US statement score is regressed on lagged US statement score values and lagged rival hostility score values, while the rival hostility score is simultaneously regressed on the same variables.[4]

In addition to the lagged values of the US statement score and rival hostility, I also include several variables related to the ability to follow through on statements in the VAR models. There is logical reason to expect that more statements of resolve might be made when the ability to follow through is greater. My theory asserts that if the ability to follow through is greater, then statements of resolve are more likely to be successful, and naturally a greater probability of success makes issuing statements more attractive. I do not include any measure of the military ability to follow through in the models because it has little variation within rivalries.[5] I do include a variety of political factors that might affect the ability to follow through, including the percentage of Republicans in Congress (US House 2014; US Senate 2014) as a measure of hawkish veto players, the president's net approval rating (Peters and Woolley 2016) as a measure of security in office, and an indicator variable equal to 1 in each month during the year before a presidential election as another measure of security in office.[6] I treat net approval as a potentially endogenous variable and

---

[4] The number of lags in each model was determined based on a variety of lag order selection statistics and adjusted as necessary to produce white noise residuals. The Soviet model requires only two lags, but the others require six to eighteen lags.

[5] If capabilities are included, the other results remain essentially unchanged, and the capability variable is not significant, except for predicting North Korean behavior, which is more hostile when North Korea is weaker relative to the United States. See the Online Appendix for details.

[6] When I test my hypotheses related to the impact of the ability to follow through on statements' effectiveness in Chapter 4, I provide more detail and justification regarding my measurement of factors related to the ability to follow through.

TABLE 2.2 *Effect of the Ability to Follow Through on US Statements*

Variable	Iran	Iraq	Libya	North Korea	USSR
Republicans in Congress	−6.109	−90.936	1.418	−1.010	316.121**
(Coefficient and Standard Error)	(8.742)	(95.278)	(5.310)	(11.946)	(129.393)
Election Indicator	−0.255	−6.502	1.311*	0.041	45.586***
(Coefficient and Standard Error)	(1.049)	(10.391)	(0.761)	(1.513)	(12.719)
Net Approval	13.602	10.537	1.973	7.585	0.139
(Granger χ^2 Statistic and Degrees of Freedom)	(18 df)	(6 df)	(6 df)	(11 df)	(2 df)
N	246	210	306	301	178

Note: * P <.10, ** P <.05, *** P <.01

lag it. In contrast, I treat the percentage of Republicans in Congress and the upcoming election indicator as exogenous and do not lag them because they have much less variation than the other variables in the system of equations.

The results for the effect of the factors related to the ability to follow through on the level of resolved statements directed at each rival are summarized in Table 2.2.[7] The first and second rows of the table show the coefficient and standard error for the percentage of Republicans in Congress and the upcoming election indicator. Because these variables do not have lags included in the regression, the significance of their effect can be interpreted by looking at their coefficients and standard errors alone. In the case of the president's net approval, however, the presence of lagged values creates multicollinearity and complicates the interpretation. Therefore, the impact of this variable on US statements is assessed using a Granger (1969) causality test, which evaluates the null hypothesis that all of the lags of one variable can be dropped from the equation predicting the other variable without a loss in explanatory power. The χ^2 statistics produced by this test are shown in the last row of the table.

The results indicate that there is little effect of the domestic political factors related to the ability to follow through on the level of resolved statements. The only result that is significant in the expected direction is the coefficient for the level of Republicans in Congress in the Soviet regression. In most regressions, all three of the domestic factors are insignificant. In two

[7] The full VAR results are available in the Online Appendix. I performed standard diagnostic tests, such as checking for unit roots, stationarity, and white noise residuals. If the variables are aggregated weekly instead of monthly, the pattern of significance is very similar, but many more lags are needed.

TABLE 2.3 *Effect of US Statements and Rival Behavior on Each Other*

	Iran	Iraq	Libya	North Korea	USSR
Granger χ^2 statistic for US statements predicting rival hostility	31.890**	15.361**	18.162***	58.296***	1.493
Granger χ^2 statistic for rival hostility predicting US statements	63.041***	7.644	116.37***	19.071*	0.775
Degrees of Freedom	18	6	6	11	2
N	246	210	306	301	178

Note: * P <.10, ** P <.05, *** P <.01

regressions, the election year indicator is at least weakly significant, but the coefficient indicates that presidents are more likely to make statements when they are more insecure during election season, contrary to my expectation.[8] The fact that a greater domestic ability to follow through does not seem to consistently encourage presidents to make more statements is somewhat surprising given the expectation of my theory that statements are more effective when the ability to follow through is higher. However, it appears that the reason the ability to follow through has so little effect is that the decision to make resolved statements is driven strongly by rival hostility.

The VAR model results for the effect of rival behavior on US statements and the effect of US statements on rival behavior are summarized in Table 2.3. Again, because multiple lagged values of these variables are included in the VAR, it is necessary to use Granger causality tests to evaluate the relationship between the variables. The results suggest that US statements and rival hostility are mutually causal. In four out of the five models, there is a significant Granger causality statistic indicating that the US statement score should not be excluded as a predictor of rival hostility. In three out of the five models, there is also evidence that rival hostility should not be excluded as a predictor of US statements.

The Soviet model is the only one in which neither Granger causality statistic is significant, which is not necessarily surprising given that Figure 2.1 shows much more variation in US presidential statements directed at the Soviet Union

---

[8] This finding is more in keeping with diversionary war theory, which asserts that leaders behave more aggressively in the international arena when they are domestically insecure and want to divert attention from domestic problems (Levy 1989). However, this theory does not have a great deal of support either, since the election year indicator is insignificant in the majority of models, and the president's net approval is never significant.

than in Soviet behavior. This result appears to be a peculiarity of the Reagan era because when the Reagan years are dropped from the dataset, the Granger test statistic for Soviet behavior predicting US statements becomes significant at the 99 percent confidence level. Based on the data, it appears that Reagan continued to express resolve toward the Soviet Union on a frequent basis even when Soviet behavior was relatively accommodating. Meanwhile, the Soviets pursued an increasingly cooperative strategy toward the United States over time, with little variation in response to Reagan's statements. The case of US-Soviet relations under Reagan is discussed in much more detail in Chapter 7, but it appears that both sides were primarily following long-term strategies rather than engaging in monthly tit for tat. The uniquely long-term nature of US and Soviet strategies in this era may reflect the particular visions of Reagan and Gorbachev, and it may also partially reflect the enduring and high-stakes nature of the US-Soviet rivalry.

Thus, the results suggest that resolved statements by US presidents do lead to more hostile rival behavior, at least in the near future. This is similar to what Wood (2012) finds using his "saber rattling" data. Does this mean that statements of resolve are ineffective or even counterproductive at persuading rivals to back down? In fact, there is not enough evidence to conclude this. One reason is that despite the name of the Granger causality test, it cannot actually prove causation. The test really only tells us that US statements help to predict hostile rival behavior. It is possible that this is because US presidents make more statements when they anticipate that hostile behavior is likely. Second, even if US statements do cause an upsurge in rival hostility, this does not necessarily mean they are ineffective. The scholarly literature has long recognized that countries may engage in a prolonged competition to signal resolve before either one country backs down or war occurs (Fearon 1994a). Therefore, it is quite possible that the ultimate outcome of making resolved statements can be to persuade a rival to back down, even if the intermediate effect is more hostile behavior as part of a competition to demonstrate resolve. To answer the question of what the ultimate impact of making resolved statements is, it is necessary to use different data that contain information on the *outcome* of conflicts.

In addition to rival behavior responding to US presidential statements, it also appears that US presidential statements are responsive to rival behavior. When rivals behave more hostilely, presidents respond with more resolved statements. In contrast, when rivals are not being provocative, presidents usually make very few resolved statements. This means that there are some long periods in which very few statements are made about particular rivals. For all countries except the Soviet Union, there are periods of many consecutive months in which almost no resolved statements are made. An implication of this is that US presidents make statements of resolve primarily in response to specific situations and rarely make statements in calm times solely for purposes of general deterrence. For example, although the United States has made a formal treaty commitment to defend South Korea if it is attacked, the US president generally does not feel the need to reiterate this commitment verbally on a regular basis. Instead, it is usually only reiterated in response to aggressive behavior from North Korea.

In sum, while this time series analysis of the rivalry statement data has been informative, it also reveals some inherent limitations to the ability to draw conclusions from this type of data. First, without recording the ultimate outcome of crises, we cannot know if statements are effective. Second, many of the monthly observations do not actually provide much informational value because of the sparsity of presidential statements during periods of calm. Third, it is not feasible to do this type of analysis for countries that are less serious rivals because of an even greater sparsity of statements, and therefore, some uncertainty about the generalizability of the results remains. I turn to the MID data to remedy these shortcomings of the rivalry data.

DESCRIPTION OF THE MID STATEMENT DATA

My second statement collection effort involved collecting statements of resolve made in the context of MIDs involving the United States between 1950 and 2010. A MID is defined as any event in which a state threatens, displays, or uses force against another state (Palmer et al. 2015). For purposes of this analysis, MIDs, many of which are multilateral, are broken down into dyadic MIDs, which are pairs of countries on opposite sides of a MID. Only dyads which actually interacted during a MID are included, and I use conflict start and end dates which were adjusted to be correct for each individual dyad (Maoz 2005; Palmer et al. 2015). The MID dataset has been the most commonly used dataset in the quantitative analysis of international conflict over the last 20 years, and because it includes a variety of different types of conflicts, it allows me to analyze the role of resolved statements in the largest possible set of relevant observations. There were 272 dyadic MIDs involving the United States between 1950 and 2010.

For purposes of collecting statements, I considered a statement to be relevant to a dyadic MID if (1) it was made at any point during the dyadic MID or within 30 days before, and (2) it was about the dyadic MID adversary. I began the statement collection slightly before the recorded start date because I assume that the tensions associated with most disputes begin slightly before they meet the official criteria for being a MID. To make sure that the choice of 30 days is not driving the result, I vary the pre-MID statement collection period in the robustness checks in later chapters. Because the MIDs in my dataset vary greatly in length, ranging from one day to nearly ten years, I divided the statement scores produced by my content analysis by the number of days over which statements were collected in order to normalize them. Otherwise, my measure would be more likely to pick up the effect of conflict duration than the intensity of resolved statements. My normalized statement score has only a 0.02 correlation with

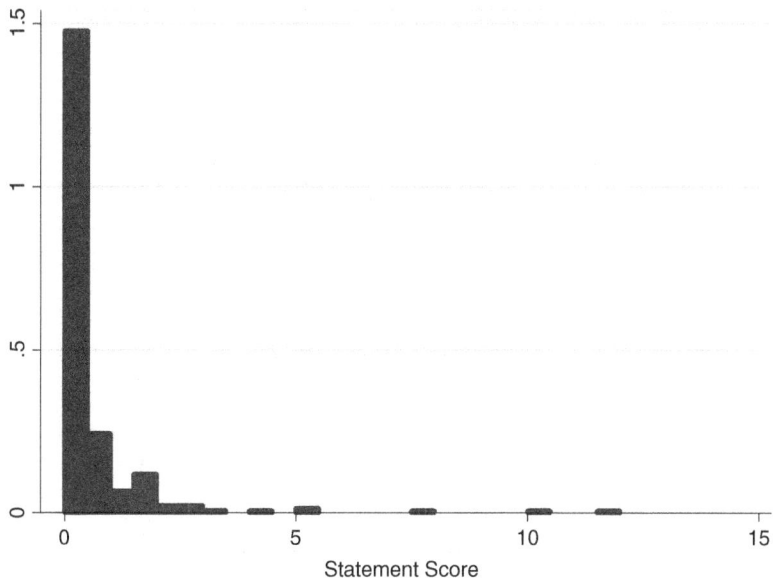

FIGURE 2.2 Histogram of US Dyadic MID Statement Scores
Note: The bin width is 0.5.

the MID duration, whereas the unnormalized score had a 0.59 correlation. Given the normalization, the MID statement score can be thought of as representing the average amount of resolve conveyed per day during the MID time frame, although it cannot be equated to a particular number of resolved words per day because different words have different weights.

Even after normalizing the statement score, its distribution is skewed, as shown in Figure 2.2. While 28 percent of observations have a score equal to zero and most other scores are less than 2, there are several high outliers. The ten highest outliers for MID statement scores are identified in Table 2.4. We see that some of these MIDs, including the Gulf War, the Afghanistan War, and the Kosovo conflict, involved significant use of US force. It is not surprising that these MIDs are associated with high statement scores. Other MIDs in the table, including the Yugoslavia–Macedonia border dispute and the five MIDs with the Soviet Union, were more minor incidents which experienced a high intensity of resolved statements because relations between the United States and the adversary were generally bad at the time the MID occurred. In general, it is reassuring that although the disputes listed in Table 2.4 vary in size, it fits with the historical record that all of them have high statement scores. Therefore, the quantitative coding of statements again appears to have face validity when compared to a more qualitative examination of historical events. The extent to which outliers drive the results is explored in later chapters. In general, I find that most results are not highly dependent on a few observations.

TABLE 2.4 *Dyadic MIDs with the Highest Statement Scores*

Rank	MID	Adversary	Start Year	Description
1	3957	Iraq	1990	Gulf War
2	2227	USSR	1980	US threat regarding Yugoslavia
3	2226	USSR	1980	US Baltic Sea maneuvers
4	4283	Afghanistan	2001	Afghanistan War
5	2233	USSR	1986	US ships violate Soviet maritime boundary in dispute over UN mission
6	4046	Serbia	1994	Yugoslavia–Macedonia border dispute
7	4137	Serbia	1998	Kosovo Conflict
8	2231	USSR	1983	Deployment of Soviet SS-22 missiles and US Pershing missiles
9	2957	Panama	1976	Panama seizes US boats in dispute over canal treaty
10	2217	USSR	1961	Covert US action to topple Castro

WHEN RESOLVED STATEMENTS ARE MADE IN MIDS

It is possible to use the dataset of MIDs to gain additional insight into the question of when resolved statements are made. The analysis of the rivalry data indicated that more statements of resolve are made in times of higher hostility or tension and that domestic political factors in the United States appear to have little impact on the decision to make statements. To see if I find similar results using the MID data, I estimate a statistical regression predicting the level of resolved statements made in each dyadic MID. The functional form of the regression is a tobit model, which is appropriate because the statement score cannot be less than zero. Similar to the previous analysis, I include a measure of the percentage of Republicans in Congress and the president's net approval, both captured at the midpoint of the dyadic MID. Also in keeping with the previous analysis, I include a measure of the percentage of the dyadic MID which took place within a year before a presidential election.

Because the MID dataset contains a greater variety of adversaries and covers a longer time period than the rivalry data, I am also able to include some new variables. As a way of measuring military strength and the physical capability to follow through, I include a measure of relative military capabilities, which is calculated as the percentage of total capabilities in the MID dyad held by the United States (Singer, Bremer, and Stuckey 1972). Since the previous analysis indicated that US presidents make more statements in response to more serious tensions, I also include several variables to capture the seriousness of MIDs. First, I include the highest hostility level reached by each side in the dyadic MID (Maoz 2005; Palmer et al. 2015). Possible hostility levels are no action (coded as 1), threat of force (2), show of force (3), use of force (4), and war (5). Second, I include an indicator for fatal MIDs, coded as 1 if either side experienced one or more fatalities. Third, I include indicator variables for the type of revision to the status quo sought in the MID: change in territory, change in government, or change in policy (Palmer et al. 2015). The omitted comparison category for these indicators consists of dyadic MIDs in which neither side sought to revise the status quo or the revision type is coded as "other."

I also consider it important to control for the relationship with the MID adversary because a president might make stronger statements in a MID against a long-standing rival compared to a MID that is an anomaly in a generally positive relationship. I therefore include an indicator for whether the United States had an ongoing rivalry with the adversary during the MID, according to the coding of rivalries by Thompson (2001). Finally, I include indicator variables for the identity of the president who was in power for the majority of the MID because certain presidents may be more inclined to make statements of resolve due to their personality or the norms at the time they were in office. Indicators for both Truman and Eisenhower are omitted as the comparison category because Truman alone is not president in enough observations to form the comparison category.

The tobit model results are given in Table 2.5. The first column gives the results for the entire sample of dyadic MIDs. In case there are different dynamics at work in more serious and less serious MIDs, I also split the sample into dyadic MIDs in which the United States used force and dyadic MIDs in which it did not. The second and third columns give the results for these subsamples. As in the previous time series analysis, the results generally show that the domestic political factors giving the president a greater ability to follow through do not increase the likelihood that resolved statements will be made. In most cases, the domestic political variables are not even close to significant. The indicator for an upcoming election is weakly significant in two of the regressions, but the positive coefficient is not in keeping with my expectation that more secure presidents would make more statements and less secure presidents would make fewer statements. The measure of relative capabilities is highly significant across all of the models, but its negative coefficient is also the opposite of what we would expect based on the ability to follow through. The negative coefficient is driven by the fact that presidents made a high level of statements directed at the Soviet Union, despite the fact that the USSR would be much more difficult to defeat militarily than any other adversary. Therefore, there is still no evidence that a greater ability to follow through increases the level of resolved statements.

Variables related to the characteristics of the dispute do a slightly better job of predicting when statements will be made. Presidents appear to make more resolved statements in MIDs with higher hostility levels and in MIDs that result

TABLE 2.5 *Tobit Models Predicting Statements in MIDs*

	All MIDs	MIDs with Force	MIDs without Force
Republicans in Congress	−1.443 (1.876)	−2.524 (1.997)	−3.042 (4.959)
Net Approval	0.204 (0.395)	0.349 (0.471)	0.102 (0.615)
Election Year	0.487* (0.274)	0.029 (0.203)	0.891* (0.489)
Relative Capabilities	−2.864*** (0.770)	−2.299*** (0.827)	−2.989*** (1.081)
US Hostility Level	0.319*** (0.115)	0.330*** (0.115)	0.005 (0.205)
Adversary Hostility Level	0.119 (0.090)	0.315*** (0.110)	−0.141 (0.171)
Fatal	0.464** (0.210)	0.321 (0.249)	0.396 (0.405)
Revision Sought to Territory	0.806* (0.480)	1.255 (0.887)	0.690 (0.545)
Revision Sought to Regime	0.311 (0.309)	−0.022 (0.370)	0.353 (0.492)
Revision Sought to Policy	0.313 (0.212)	0.144 (0.232)	0.383 (0.320)
Rivalry	0.534** (0.239)	0.266 (0.289)	0.999** (0.436)
Kennedy	0.693** (0.332)	0.853 (0.534)	0.435 (0.547)
Johnson	−0.017 (0.274)	0.530 (0.461)	−0.973* (0.567)
Nixon	−0.084 (0.371)	0.585 (0.490)	−0.856* (0.499)
Ford	1.117** (0.554)	1.576** (0.723)	0.344 (0.780)
Carter	2.306*** (0.757)	1.656** (0.642)	2.521** (1.180)

TABLE 2.5 *(continued)*

	All MIDs	MIDs with Force	MIDs without Force
Reagan	1.344***	1.390***	1.368**
	(0.322)	(0.473)	(0.528)
Bush, G.H.W.	2.541**	2.971**	1.476**
	(1.060)	(1.467)	(0.659)
Clinton	1.938***	2.497***	1.693**
	(0.407)	(0.631)	(0.689)
Bush, G.W.	1.676***	2.217***	1.392**
	(0.500)	(0.741)	(0.689)
Observations	262	161	101

Note: * P<0.10, ** P<0.05, *** P<0.01. Huber-White standard errors are in parentheses. MIDs after 2007 are excluded due to the unavailability of some variables.

in fatalities.[9] This fits with the previous results, which showed an association between greater rival hostility and higher levels of US statements. There is also evidence that presidents make more resolved statements when the MID adversary is a long-term rival, in keeping with expectations. Interestingly, the most significant predictors of the level of statements across all three models are the indicator variables for the identity of the president. Most of the president indicators are significant in a positive direction, indicating that most presidents made more statements of resolve than Truman and Eisenhower. The more recent presidents, including Carter, Reagan, George H.W. Bush, Clinton, and George W. Bush, have significant positive coefficients in all three models.

It is also possible to view the differences in the level of statements made by each president graphically. Figure 2.3 shows the average predicted statement score for each president, based on the first model in Table 2.5. The figure generally confirms the patterns seen in the coefficients. Presidents Truman, Eisenhower, Johnson, and Nixon have the lowest predicted statement scores, and the predictions for Presidents Kennedy and Ford are also fairly low. All of the more modern presidents have higher predicted statement scores. The predicted level of statements goes up dramatically under President Carter,

---

[9] There may be some uncertainty about the validity of the results for these variables because causality may flow in two directions – more resolved statements may raise the probability of higher hostility levels and more fatalities. There is no way to avoid the uncertainty surrounding these variables, but I did confirm that it is not biasing the other results by estimating alternate regressions without these variables. See the Online Appendix.

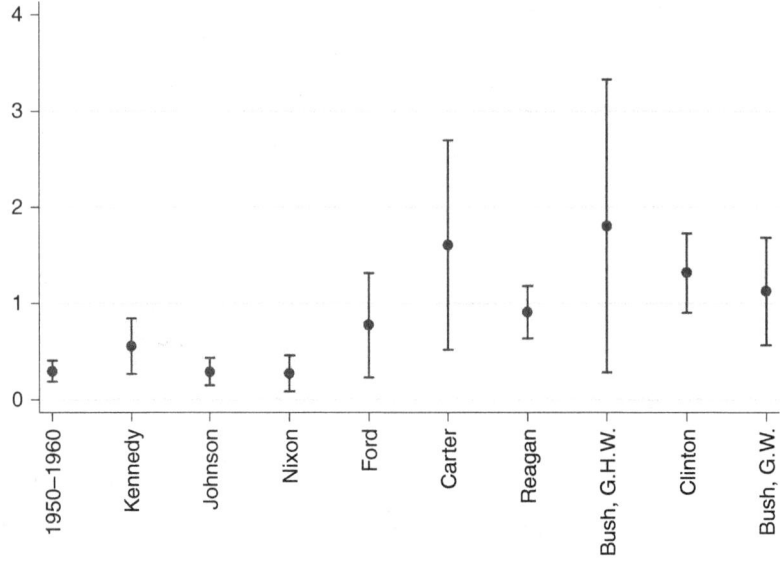

FIGURE 2.3 Predicted Statement Score by President
Note: This figure shows average predicted statement scores based on the first model in
Table 2.5. For each president, it predicts what the average statement score would be
across all MIDs if that president had been in power during every MID. The lines show
95 percent confidence bounds. Truman and Eisenhower are combined in the first
category, and there is no prediction for Obama because observations after 2007 were
excluded due to missing values of some variables.

whose prediction has wide confidence bounds because he dramatically
increased his level of resolved statements after the Soviet invasion of
Afghanistan. President Reagan's predicted score is lower than might be
expected based on his reputation for tough rhetoric, but most of his tough
statements were directed specifically at the Soviet Union, and he employed less
resolved statements in MIDs with other adversaries.

President George H.W. Bush has the widest confidence bounds around his
predicted statement score because of the unusually high level of resolved
statements that he made in the run-up to the Gulf War. His statement score
for the Gulf War MID against Iraq was more than five times higher than his next
highest statement score and more than 22 times higher than the average of his
other MID statement scores. Bush seems to have taken a particularly resolved
stance toward Iraq, possibly because it was the first challenger to the new US-led
world order that was emerging with the end of the Cold War. There were also
allegations that the Bush administration did not signal its resolve to protect
Kuwait's independence clearly enough prior to the invasion (Walt 2011), so
Bush may have sought to compensate for that.

In sum, the identity of the president seems to have substantial influence on the level of resolved statements. This makes sense because presidents have different personalities, and some of them enjoy public speaking more than others. For example, President Nixon hated the press and press conferences (Drew 2007). In contrast, President Clinton had a reputation for being naturally talkative and making particularly long public statements. Despite the variation by president, there is also a clear trend toward more statement-making over time. After President Carter began making a much higher level of resolved statements at the end of the 1970s, the average level of statements never returned to its previous level, despite several changes in president and many changes in the international situation. The trend toward more statements being made over time may be due to changing public expectations of the president or due to presidents learning from their predecessors that statements can be effective.

SUMMARY AND IMPLICATIONS FOR FURTHER ANALYSIS

This chapter has introduced new data on US presidential statements of resolve and described how the data are coded. The next three chapters will utilize these data to test whether statements of resolve are effective and under which conditions they are most effective. This chapter has also made some initial observations regarding when statements of resolve are made, which will have implications for the analysis in the forthcoming chapters.

One finding was that statements of resolve are rarely made in calm times for the sole purpose of general deterrence and are much more commonly made in response to the international situation and to other states' behavior. The scarcity of statements made in the absence of conflictual adversary behavior suggests that it is not likely to be fruitful to study the ability of statements to deter conflict initiation. Rather, studying the impact of statements within finite instances of international conflict is likely to be more informative because this is when statements are more likely to be made. Another advantage of studying finite conflicts rather than long-term rivalries is that they are more likely to have definitive outcomes. Although the most immediate effect of resolved statements often seems to be more hostile adversary behavior, it is important to determine the ultimate effect of statements by looking at the final outcomes of disputes. For these reasons, although the analysis of statements of resolve made in long-term rivalries has been useful for understanding the dynamics of how resolved statements are employed, the remainder of the book will utilize the MID data to analyze the effectiveness of statements.

Another notable finding in this chapter was that the level of resolved statements is not significantly influenced by the ability to follow through. Instead, the decision to make statements seems to be influenced much more by the international situation and specifically by the hostile behavior of other countries. This is probably in part because the international situation changes more rapidly and dramatically than the ability to follow through. Military strength changes slowly, veto players typically remain in their positions for years, and even security in office rarely changes overnight. In contrast, international crises often unfold rapidly, requiring a quick presidential reaction. Therefore, even though my theory holds that the ability to follow through promotes the effectiveness of statements, it is not necessarily contradictory to find that factors related to the ability to follow through are not significant predictors of when statements are made. This finding also has no effect on the predictions of my theory regarding how the ability to follow through impacts the effectiveness of statements because the causal mechanisms in my theory are unrelated to the propensity to make statements.[10]

For purposes of testing my theory, the fact that more statements do not appear to be made when the ability to follow through is greater may actually simplify matters. One potential concern about testing the effect of resolved statements on conflict outcomes is that leaders may select to make more statements when they expect victory, not because they expect the statements to help them achieve victory, but because they hope to use the statements to capitalize on the victory domestically. If this were true, it could confound the statistical analysis. I will address the merits of this concern in more detail in later chapters, but the fact that domestic political factors seem to have so little impact on the level of resolved statements suggests that making statements purely for domestic political gain is not common. Furthermore, the lack of a strong relationship between the level of statements and the indicators of the ability to follow through will reduce collinearity when all of these factors are used as independent variables in later regressions.

Therefore, this chapter has laid the groundwork for testing the effectiveness of resolved statements by establishing the most appropriate unit of analysis for this testing and by reducing concerns that political influences on the decision to make statements will confound statistical inference. I now move on to the analysis of statements' effectiveness.

---

[10] This can be proved based on the formal models in the appendices. In the formal model in Appendix 1, the hawkishness of veto players (h_3) affects player 2's probability of backing down (s_2^*) directly and also indirectly through player 1's probability of fighting (s_1^*). In the formal model in Appendix 2, player 1's vulnerability to removal due to losing ($a_{1L}v_1$) affects player 2's probability of backing down (s_2^*) only indirectly through player 1's probability of fighting (s_1^*). In neither model does the effect of these parameters on player 2's probability of backing down (s_2^*) depend upon player 1's probability of making a statement ($s_1^\dagger$). This is a difference between the causal mechanisms in my theory of the ability to follow through and the causal mechanism in audience cost theory, which does depend on the propensity to make statements.

3

The General Effectiveness of Resolved Statements

The previous chapter introduced new data coding US presidential statements of resolve. The next three chapters will use these data to analyze the effectiveness of resolved statements. This chapter will begin the analysis by asking whether statements of resolve are effective in general. That is, on average, is it helpful for US presidents to make statements of resolve during international conflicts? As discussed in the Introduction and Chapter 1, there are a variety of existing theories which predict that statements can effectively signal resolve and thus make adversaries more likely to back down in international conflict. These include audience cost theory (Fearon 1994a) and international reputational cost theory (Sartori 2005). The theory presented in this book builds on these existing theories by accepting the premise that statements can be effective and focusing on narrowing down the conditions that make them most effective. Yet despite the widespread belief among scholars in the effectiveness of statements, it has not yet been clearly proven with empirical evidence that statements do truly affect conflict outcomes.

As noted in the Introduction, only a few studies have attempted to examine the impact of statements of resolve in international conflict directly, and these studies have found a mixed record of success at best. Snyder and Borghard (2011) argue that there is little evidence that public statements of resolve were effective in the Suez Crisis, the Iranian Hostage Crisis, and the Sino-Indian War. Trachtenberg (2012) finds a mixed record of success for public statements in a dozen great power crises. In his analysis of time series data on US presidential saber-rattling statements, Wood (2012, 129–132) argues that saber rattling either has no effect on adversary behavior or makes it more hostile. However, all of these studies are limited in scope to a few adversaries or cases. In addition, Wood's analysis – like my analysis in Chapter 2 – does not tell us how often the United States ultimately wins conflicts in which it engages in saber rattling.

Given the lack of systematic analysis of the effectiveness of statements beyond a few cases, uncertainty remains regarding whether statements of resolve truly have an effect on international conflict outcomes. It is important to resolve this uncertainty before proceeding further to analyze the conditions for effectiveness of statements. This chapter attempts to present a more definitive answer to the question of statements' effectiveness by performing the first direct test of the relationship between resolved statements and conflict outcomes across a large body of observations. It finds that statements are indeed effective at influencing conflict outcomes.

UNIT OF ANALYSIS

The evidence in Chapter 2 showed that statements of resolve are most commonly made during episodes of tension or hostility. This suggests that the most appropriate context in which to test the statements' effectiveness is a sample of individual instances of international conflict. This chapter therefore analyzes the effectiveness of resolved statements in a dataset consisting of dyadic MIDs as the unit of observation. I introduced the MID dataset briefly in Chapter 2, but here I will provide more detail on the dataset and my rationale for using it.

Recall that a MID is defined as any event in which a state threatens, displays, or uses force against another state (Palmer et al. 2015). Some examples of MIDs, which include both serious conflicts and minor disputes, were previously shown in Table 2.4. For purposes of this analysis, MIDs, many of which are multilateral, are broken down into dyadic MIDs, which are pairs of countries on opposite sides of a MID. My dataset consists of all 272 dyadic MIDs in which the United States was involved between 1950 and 2010.[1] Most models are estimated based on slightly fewer observations because of limitations on the availability of some control variables in the most recent years. The dyadic MID observations are drawn from the MID 4.01 Dataset for the years 1993–2010 and the Maoz Dyadic MID Dataset for the years 1950–1992 (Maoz 2005; Palmer et al. 2015). Only dyads which actually interacted during a MID were included, and I use conflict start and end dates which were adjusted to be correct for each specific dyad.

The MID dataset has been used more than any other dataset to study international conflict, so utilizing it here will make it easy to compare the results in this book to previous research. Using the MID dataset also allows me to test my hypotheses on the largest possible set of relevant observations. The MID dataset includes tense situations in which force was never actually used, minor skirmishes, and more serious armed conflicts. This is appropriate because my theory of the ability to follow through is intended to be broadly applicable to both conflicts in which military force is used and conflicts that have the potential to escalate to the use of force but have not yet done so.

---

[1] These 272 dyadic MIDs represent 240 distinct MIDs. Using dyadic MIDs made it easier to code statements and other variables.

Bargaining does not end after fighting begins (Wagner 2000), and leaders can still express resolve to stay the course or even escalate. As in pre-force bargaining, these statements should be more effective if it is apparent that the leader has the ability to follow through. Furthermore, as argued by Dafoe, Renshon, and Huth (2014), most MIDs engage a state's reputation, so they should be good cases for testing expectations derived from domestic audience cost theory and international reputational cost theory as well.

One concern about this reasoning might be that statements will matter less after force is used because there are more sources of information. However, it is not always the case that battles convey more information than statements. In conflicts such as the Vietnam War and recent anti-insurgent campaigns in Iraq and Afghanistan, there was little doubt that the United States had dominant military capabilities, but there was uncertainty about US resolve to keep fighting over the long term. Therefore, adversaries in these conflicts arguably learned at least as much from US statements as from battle outcomes. For example, in 1971, the North Vietnamese updated their assessment of Nixon's resolve based on statements he had made, even though they had been engaged in military combat with the United States for years (Ang 2004, 84; Nguyen 2012, 226). Another concern might be that some MIDs are won solely by force and that statements therefore might have no room to make an impact. However, my investigation revealed that only 8 of the 272 dyadic MIDs in my dataset were won in this way.[2] Therefore, resolved statements should have the potential to play an important role in the vast majority of MIDs in the dataset.

A separate concern about the MID data might be whether it is appropriate to use MIDs as the unit of analysis for studying statements when, in some cases, the presence of a statement (i.e., a threat) is what defines the existence of a MID. The result of this research design is that clear threats are more likely to be captured because they constitute MIDs in themselves, while milder statements of resolve are not captured unless they were made in conjunction with other events that constitute MIDs. This should not bias the results for statements within MIDs, but it might suggest that the results in this book cannot necessarily speak to the effect of mildly resolved statements made in less tense situations. However, the analysis of the rivalry statement data in the previous chapter suggests that statements of resolve are rarely made in the absence of other tensions anyway.

DEPENDENT VARIABLE

This book aims to examine the impact of resolved statements on conflict outcomes. Specifically, this chapter asks whether making more resolved

---

[2] These are the invasion of Grenada (accounts for two dyadic MIDs with Grenada and Cuba), pressure on Libya over terrorism in 1986, the invasion of Panama, the Gulf War (accounts for two dyadic MIDs with Iraq and Jordan), the Iraq War, and the Afghanistan War. These MIDs were dropped in robustness testing.

statements improves conflict outcomes for the United States. Therefore, it is natural that the conflict outcome is the dependent variable in my statistical analysis. The conflict outcome variable that I use is a simplified version of the outcome variable in the MID 4.01 Dataset (Palmer et al. 2015). It is coded as 3 if the outcome clearly favors the United States, 2 if the outcome is neutral, and 1 if the outcome clearly favors the adversary. In creating this variable, I treated outcomes coded in the MID data as victory or yield as clearly favoring one side or the other, while I treated outcomes coded as compromise, stalemate, released, unclear, or missing as neutral. Some of the more ambiguous outcome categories are dropped in later robustness checks. I independently verified that the outcomes of 25 winning and losing MIDs were coded correctly.

Using alternate dependent variables, such as escalation to force or reciprocation, was considered but deemed infeasible because accurate escalation and reciprocation dates are not available for many dyadic MIDs. Using the wrong dates to collect statements to predict escalation or reciprocation could result in predicting these events with statements made *after* the events occurred or leaving out relevant statements made before the events. MID initiation is also not an appropriate dependent variable because, as shown in Chapter 2, statements of resolve are rarely made in the absence of conflict, and this would make it quite difficult to identify any deterrent effect of statements on the initiation of conflict.

INDEPENDENT VARIABLES

The crucial independent variable for this analysis is, of course, statements of resolve. The process for collecting relevant statements and coding them using a content analysis dictionary is described fully in Chapter 2. To summarize, I collected all presidential statements made about each MID adversary during the dyadic MID and within 30 days before from the *Public Papers of the Presidents of the United States* (Peters and Woolley 2016). It was not feasible to break down MIDs into phases and collect only statements made before force was used because, as noted previously, reliable information on the date of the first use of force is not available for all MIDs. Furthermore, as argued earlier, statements can influence MID outcomes even after force is used. After collecting the statements, I coded the resolved words within them using a content analysis dictionary with a three-tiered weighting scheme, and I normalized the resulting score by the duration of statement collection. This gave me the main variable used in the analysis in this chapter, referred to as the statement score.

Although this book is focused on statements of resolve, I do not claim or expect that they will be the only factor affecting conflict outcomes. Other factors, such as military power, are likely to matter as much or even more than statements. In order to correctly determine the impact of statements, it is important to control for other factors that might affect the conflict outcome as well. On the other hand, attempting to control for too many factors can lead to too much correlation among the independent variables and unstable results. Therefore, my main statistical model is parsimonious and controls for only three factors other than statements that I consider most likely to affect the conflict outcome.

The first control variable included is relative military capabilities, which is measured as the percentage of total military capabilities in the dyad held by the United States. This measure is calculated based on the widely utilized Composite Index of National Capabilities (CINC) scores for both countries in the dyad (Singer, Bremer, and Stuckey 1972).[3] It is important to control for capabilities because greater relative military power is also likely to contribute to more favorable conflict outcomes. The second factor that I control for is the adversary's regime type. Previous research has found that democracies are more difficult to defeat (Reiter and Stam 1998; Schultz 1999). I therefore include an indicator variable for a democratic adversary, which is coded as 1 if the adversary has a score equal to at least 7 on the Polity scale, a commonly used ranking of democracy and autocracy (Marshall, Jaggers, and Gurr 2010). Finally, I control for time. Because my dataset contains observations from a 60-year time period, there might be concern that the dynamics of US MIDs and probability of victory have changed over time. To control for this, I include a time trend consisting of the year at the midpoint of the dyadic MID and its square and cube. Alternative ways of controlling for time and additional control variables are explored in the robustness checks.

One control variable that is arguably missing is the US adversary's statements of resolve. It is not realistic to collect resolved statements for all MID adversaries, so the effect of the other side's statements is in the error term. However, this is unlikely to create an unacceptable level of bias because theory indicates that making more statements should improve the outcome for the United States regardless of what the other side does. Though the effect of statements may cancel out if both sides make them, the United States can still convey more resolve by making statements and letting them cancel out than by remaining silent and giving the other side a potential advantage. Thus, US statements should have a consistently positive effect regardless of the adversary's statements. This can be seen in the cases of the Cuban Missile Crisis and US-Soviet relations under President Reagan. During the Cuban Missile Crisis, Soviet premier Khrushchev issued a public statement demanding that the United States withdraw its missiles from Turkey in exchange for the withdrawal of Soviet missiles from Cuba (Fursenko and Naftali 1997, 275). In 1983, Soviet foreign minister Gromyko held a news conference in which he publicly rebutted Reagan's "evil empire" statement and rejected a US arms control proposal (Schmemann 1983). While such Soviet statements might have increased US perceptions of Soviet resolve, they

---

[3] The Online Appendix contains summary statistics for all variables. For control variables measured on a yearly basis, I use the value in the midpoint year of the dyadic MID.

certainly did not block the ability of US statements to influence Soviet beliefs, as shown in Chapters 6 and 7.

RESULTS

The results of the main statistical model regressing conflict outcome on the statement score and the control variables are given in Table 3.1. Because my coding of the conflict outcome is ordinal, the functional form of the statistical regression is an ordered probit model. Based on the P-value, we see that the score for statements of resolve is highly significant. The positive coefficient for the statement score indicates that a more favorable outcome is increasingly likely as the level of resolved statements increases. Specifically, this means that an increase in the statement score moves the expected conflict outcome closer toward the next threshold, either the threshold between a loss and a neutral outcome or the threshold between a neutral outcome and a win. Thus, the expectation that resolved statements should increase the probability of a more favorable conflict outcome is supported. Turning to the control variables, the results are unsurprising. It appears that the United States is likely to achieve a more favorable conflict outcome when it is more powerful relative to its adversary and is likely to receive a less favorable outcome when its adversary is a democracy, although the latter result is not significant. In addition, the time trend coefficients indicate that the United States has achieved better MID outcomes over time.

Although Table 3.1 shows that the effect of statements on conflict outcomes is statistically significant, it is also helpful to look at the substantive significance. The substantive effect of statements of resolve on the chance of a favorable conflict outcome can be seen by calculating predicted probabilities. As recommended by Hanmer and Kalkan (2013), I use average predicted

TABLE 3.1 *Effect of Statements on Conflict Outcome*

Variable	Coef.	SE	P-Value
Statement Score	0.226	0.071	0.001
Relative Military Capabilities	1.838	0.623	0.003
Adversary Democracy	−0.722	0.526	0.170
Year	0.034	0.015	0.028
Year Squared	0.001	0.0004	0.118
Year Cubed	0.0001	0.00003	0.013

Note: This is an ordered probit model predicting conflict outcome. $N=262$. Huber-White standard errors are used. The year was centered before squaring and cubing.

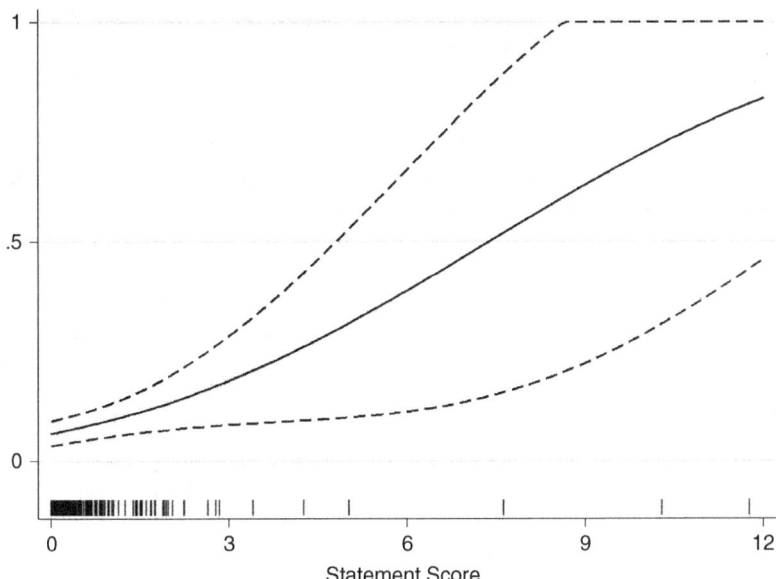

FIGURE 3.1 Predicted Probability of a Winning Outcome
Note: The dotted lines represent 95 percent confidence bounds. The rug plot along the bottom shows the distribution of the statement score variable. The MIDs with particularly high statement scores are listed in Table 2.4.

probabilities. This means that predicted probabilities for each observation in the sample were calculated and then averaged, providing a more realistic picture of the substantive effect than the alternate method of calculating the predicted probability for just one fictional "average" case.

Figure 3.1 shows how the predicted probability of a winning outcome (i.e., a conflict outcome coded as 3) increases with the statement score in the statistical model presented previously. We see a fairly dramatic increase in the predicted probability of a winning outcome as the level of resolved statements increases, going from near zero to around 80 percent. Of course, most observations lie between the statement score values of zero and 2, where the rate of change in the predicted probability is flatter. Even at these lower levels of statements, the model predicts some benefit from making statements. An increase in the statement score from zero to 2 raises the predicted probability of winning by 7 percentage points. Also, since the graph represents *average* predicted probabilities, there will be some situations in which making a small number of statements will change the predicted probability of winning by a larger amount.[4] On the whole, Figure 3.1 shows

---

[4] What these circumstances are will be considered in Chapter 4.

an impressive ability of statements to predict conflict outcomes. This is also verified by a Wald test, which shows with over 99 percent confidence that including statements of resolve in the regression improves the fit of the model for the data.

Since statements have such a large effect on the predicted probability of winning, and making more statements has a bigger effect, we might wonder why extremely high levels of statements are rarely observed in practice. This is most likely because making statements carries costs as well as benefits, and constantly making highly elevated statements might decrease the salience of statements. As seen in Chapter 2, presidents seem reluctant to make very high levels of statements unless an adversary is engaging in hostile behavior.

OBSERVATIONS WITH HIGHEST MARGINAL EFFECTS

We might also wonder which observations have the largest effect of resolved statements. Table 3.2 lists the dyadic MIDs with the largest predicted marginal effects of statements. Most of these MIDs are relatively serious disputes. Many of them also involved some use or display of force in conjunction with statements. However, only the Afghanistan War and the pressure on Libya over terrorism, which ended with US strikes on terrorist camps, were won primarily by force, and the tests discussed subsequently show that these incidents do not drive the results.

In many of the cases in Table 3.2, there is reason to believe that statements of resolve may have indeed played a role. In the case of MID 2227, the White House issued a statement on May 4, 1980, pledging to defend the independence of Yugoslavia after Tito's death (Peters and Woolley 2016). This statement implicitly targeted the Soviet Union, which was suspected of seeking to use Tito's death as an opportunity to strengthen its influence over Yugoslavia. This statement itself is not part of my statement coding because it was not spoken by the president personally, but it was issued in conjunction with many other tough statements toward the Soviet Union that President Carter was making personally around the same time. The Soviet Union appeared to comply with the US demand by not intervening strongly in Yugoslavia, resulting in a neutral status quo outcome. Of course, we cannot know for sure if the Soviet Union would have behaved differently in the absence of Carter's statements.

In MID 4046, the Serbian government of Yugoslavia disputed the location of its border with Macedonia, resulting in some clashes involving US peacekeepers. Eventually, however, Yugoslavia and Macedonia reached a border agreement that largely reflected the status quo (Milenkoski and Talevski 2001), leading to a neutral outcome. Given that the dispute took place during a time when the US president was already frequently condemning the Yugoslav government for its role in the Bosnian War, it is plausible that US statements might have influenced Yugoslavia not to further worsen US relations by pushing too hard on the border issue.

TABLE 3.2 *Observations with the Highest Predicted Marginal Effects of Statements*

MID	Adversary	Description	Start of US Involvement	Conflict Outcome	Marginal Effect
2227	USSR	US threat regarding Yugoslavia	1980	2	0.090
4046	Yugoslavia	Conflict on Yugoslavia–Macedonia border	1994	2	0.090
4283	Afghanistan	Afghanistan War	2001	3	0.090
4137	Yugoslavia	Kosovo conflict	1998	3	0.085
2226	USSR	Baltic Sea maneuvers	1980	2	0.076
3974	Iraq	Gulf War aftermath	1991	2	0.075
2353	Nicaragua	Show of force during Nicaraguan civil war	1986	2	0.075
3568	Iraq	Dispute over WMD inspections	1993	2	0.069
4271	Iraq	Response to Iraqi mobilization	1996	3	0.068
3636	Libya	Pressure on Libya over terrorism	1986	3	0.068

Note: Marginal effects are calculated for the probability of a winning outcome based on the model in Table 3.1.

The other case in Table 3.2 involving Yugoslavia was the Kosovo War. This case turned into a contest of wills between the US government and the Serbian-led Yugoslav government. The United States and NATO bombed Serbia for two and a half months before it finally agreed to NATO demands regarding Kosovo. There is evidence to suggest that statements of resolve played a role in this case because while the Serbs were willing to tolerate airstrikes for months, they finally acquiesced when President Clinton's statements began to indicate that he was resolved to do more. Whereas Clinton had initially ruled out a ground invasion when announcing the bombing of Kosovo, he said on May 18, 1999, that no options were "off the table" (Peters and Woolley 2016).[5]

A final case from the table that is worth mentioning is MID 4271, in which Iraq challenged the US commitment to protecting Kurds in northern Iraq by mobilizing troops and sending them into Kurdish territory. The United States responded with airstrikes on some Iraqi military targets as well as statements of resolve. For example, President Clinton said, "When you abuse your own people or threaten your neighbors, you must pay a price" (September 3, 1996, quoted in Peters and Woolley 2016). Iraq eventually backed down by withdrawing its troops from the area, making this a rare case of apparently successful US coercion against Iraq without the use of ground forces. We cannot know exactly how much of a role statements played versus airstrikes in this case, but since it was a contest of wills rather than an outright military victory, there was certainly room for US statements to play a role.

These examples have been intended to show how statements of resolve had room to play a role in some of the most influential observations in the data. These examples involve considerable speculation because information on the private thoughts of US adversaries in these cases is not available. The case studies in Chapters 6–8 will provide much stronger evidence of how resolved statements can directly influence adversary beliefs and behavior.

ADDRESSING THE POTENTIAL FOR REVERSE CAUSATION AND CONFOUNDING EFFECTS

The results presented earlier are statistically and substantively significant, and I have interpreted them as evidence that making more statements of resolve helps US presidents achieve better conflict outcomes. However, statistics cannot directly prove causation, only correlation. Therefore, it is important to consider whether there are alternate explanations for the close correlation between statements and favorable conflict outcomes that we observe and whether these alternate explanations are compelling. One alternate explanation for the relationship between higher levels of statements and better conflict outcomes could be that presidents make fewer resolved statements when they anticipate

---

[5] Public and private remarks by other US and NATO officials also indicated that NATO was considering a ground invasion.

losing and more resolved statements when they anticipate winning. This would mean that the direction of causality is the opposite of what I argue – instead of statements driving outcomes, anticipated outcomes would be driving the decision to make statements. This would make statements falsely appear to be effective.

This alternate view of the direction of causality seems less theoretically plausible. While it is plausible that presidents might make fewer statements when they expect to lose in order to avoid the costs of backing down, this perspective has difficulty explaining the positive incentive for presidents to make statements. If statements of resolve do not affect conflict outcomes, why make them? One possibility is that they are made to gain domestic credit for winning, but, as Baum (2004, 609–610) argues, foreign policy successes are much less likely than failures to affect the president's electoral prospects. It is also possible that presidents might seek to create a rally-around-the-flag effect by drawing attention to conflict, but such effects are typically small and short-lived and thus have limited benefits (James and Rioux 1998). Furthermore, if statements were made to boost the president's popularity, we would expect to see unpopular presidents making more statements, but Chapter 2 showed no evidence of this. Chapter 2 also showed no evidence that presidents make more statements of resolve when they have greater relative military strength and therefore should have higher hopes of winning. Thus, the argument that presidents make statements to gain domestic credit when they already expect to win has several weaknesses as an alternative to my interpretation of the results.

Another alternate explanation for the results might be that resolve itself – defined as how much the president cares about the issue at stake – is a confounding factor. Chapter 1 explained that because of the costliness of statements, presidents who are less resolved are reluctant to make them. Presidents who do make resolved statements are therefore more likely to be genuinely resolved, and this is what allows statements to be informative and to influence conflict outcomes. Therefore, a close relationship between the level of resolved statements and the president's genuine level of resolve must exist in order for my explanation of the statistical results to be valid. At the same time, the close relationship between statements of resolve and the president's genuine level of resolve could create problems for statistical inference.

Resolve itself cannot directly affect conflict outcomes because it is an unobservable characteristic, internal to individuals. However, there are at least two possible ways that the president's internal level of resolve could *indirectly* affect conflict outcomes and therefore confound the statistical results. One way is if the United States signals resolve through other methods in addition to presidential statements. If these other methods also influence adversaries' beliefs, then the statement score would be likely to pick up some of their effect. Another way in which resolve could have an indirect influence is if presidents who are genuinely resolved employ tougher or more skillful military and diplomatic strategies, leading to more winning outcomes. The statements variable could then also be picking up the effect of these superior strategies. It is important to note that this second alternate explanation, unlike the first, does not argue against the effectiveness of resolved statements. Indeed, it is entirely compatible with the belief that statements are effective. Nonetheless, it raises uncertainty about the results because it suggests that some of the observed effect of the statement score could be attributable to other signals and strategies rather than to statements of resolve themselves.

How much of the statement score effect then can actually be attributed to statements? There is an argument to be made that statements themselves are indeed driving most of the effect. The main reason is that a country's other signals of resolve, and even its military strategies and negotiating behavior, can be difficult to interpret without presidential statements. For example, if the United States made a show of military force without any explanation, the targeted country might not be sure exactly what the United States was demanding of it. Even if the United States accompanied the show of force with a private demand, the targeted country might view the demand as more malleable since the United States did not commit to it in public. Therefore, I argue that public statements of resolve are likely to be a crucial part of most signaling strategies, and that much of the effect picked up by the statement score can probably indeed be attributed to statements.

Thus far, I have considered the strengths and weaknesses of alternative explanations for the results at the theoretical level, but of course we also want to investigate these alternate explanations statistically to the extent that this is possible. With regard to a possible confounding effect of resolve itself, the simplest way to investigate this is by attempting to control for other signals of resolve and for other factors that might proxy for the president's genuine level of resolve. I therefore estimated a new model with several additional control variables. I controlled for additional signals of resolve by including the level of hostility (threat, show, or use of force) reached by the countries on each side of the MID (Maoz 2005; Palmer et al. 2015) and an indicator variable for whether the United States imposed sanctions upon its MID adversary (Morgan, Bapat, and Kobayashi 2013). I also controlled for several MID characteristics that might influence the president's underlying level of resolve, including whether the United States was on the initiating side of the MID (Palmer et al. 2015); whether the adversary had a defense pact with the United States (Gibler 2009); and the level of affinity between the adversary and the United States, measured based on UN General Assembly votes (Gartzke 2006; Voeten and Merdzanovic 2009). In addition, I added indicator variables for the primary type of revision to the status quo sought in the MID and for each of the seven most frequent MID adversaries: the Soviet Union/Russia, China, North Korea, Cuba, Libya, Iraq, and Iran.[6] The results indicate that several of the new control variables

---

[6] These seven countries combined account for 63 percent of the dyadic MIDs in the sample, whereas many other adversaries appear in the sample only once or twice.

TABLE 3.3 *Summary of Robustness Check Results*

Robustness Check	Coef.	SE	P-Value
Control for other signals/sources of resolve	0.276	0.065	<0.001
Control for *NYT* articles	0.141	0.070	0.044
Matched sample (original score)	0.552	0.160	0.001
Matched sample (binary score)	0.838	0.318	0.009
Control for a count of "the"	0.248	0.172	0.148
Control for a count of "that"	0.202	0.144	0.161
Multinomial logit (winning v. neutral)	0.478	0.157	0.002
Multinomial logit (losing v. neutral)	−0.010	0.220	0.964
Drop top 13 Cook's D values	0.320	0.172	0.063
Indicator for stat. score over 75th percentile	0.861	0.329	0.009
Natural log of statement score	0.865	0.252	0.001
10-day pre-MID collection period	0.224	0.074	0.003
60-day pre-MID collection period	0.231	0.083	0.005
Equal weight dictionary	0.353	0.112	0.002
1-to-10 dictionary	0.074	0.023	0.002
Threats only (drop top 13 Cook's D)	11.989	5.136	0.020
Demands/refusals only (drop top 13 Cook's D)	0.664	0.373	0.075
Negative char. only (drop top 13 Cook's D)	1.038	0.488	0.033
Drop MIDs won by force	0.173	0.086	0.045
Drop one-day MIDs	0.292	0.103	0.005
Drop non-revisionist MIDs	0.210	0.072	0.004
Drop unclear and missing outcomes	0.226	0.071	0.002
Drop overlapping MIDs	0.236	0.090	0.009
Retain only one dyad per MID	0.234	0.073	0.001
Linear time trend	0.239	0.070	0.001
President indicator variables	0.297	0.085	<0.001
Correct proportional odds violations	0.436	0.128	0.001
Drop capabilities to include 2008–2010	0.152	0.064	0.018

Note: All robustness checks are variations of the model in Table 3.1. Only results for the statement score are reported here. Full results are available in the Online Appendix.

are significant predictors of the conflict outcome, but the coefficient for the statement score only becomes *more* significant after controlling for them, as shown in Table 3.3, which summarizes all robustness check results. Therefore, it does not appear that the coefficient for statements of resolve is picking up the effect of any of these other signals of resolve or MID characteristics that might influence the president's underlying level of resolve.

Furthermore, statements of resolve have a much bigger impact on the predicted probability of winning than either of the other signals of resolve that I control for. The average predicted probability of winning calculated based on this new regression goes from 6 percent when no resolved statements are made to 82 percent at the maximum amount of statements. In contrast, the decision of the United States to use force (a hostility level of 4) raises the predicted probability of winning by only 10 percentage points compared to taking no militarized action (a hostility level of 1). Imposing sanctions actually appears to reduce the predicted probability of winning, but only by 8 percentage points. It is true that the measures of force and sanctions, which were obtained from existing data, are less nuanced than the statement score that I created myself, and this may partially account for their weaker predictive power. Still, the fact that statements have more predictive power than these variables, which might seem like much costlier signals at first glance, is impressive.

It might be argued, however, that the observable MID characteristics controlled for in the previous regression do an inadequate job of capturing the president's true underlying level of resolve. These variables might affect resolve, but they are not the same as resolve itself. Resolve cannot be measured directly, but one way in which it might be possible to obtain a more nuanced approximation of the president's resolve is to control for the level of press reporting. I created a new variable, which codes the average number of *New York Times* articles per day mentioning the dyadic MID adversary during the time frame of each dyadic MID. This variable might approximate the president's resolve for two reasons. First, the *NYT* staff are well-informed individuals who, by virtue of being based in the United States, are likely to have some interest in US national security. Therefore, there might be natural overlap between the *NYT*'s view and the president's view of which conflicts are most important for the United States to win. Second, greater press reporting about a conflict will increase the conflict's salience with the public, and knowing that the eyes of the public are watching may actually increase the president's resolve. When I inserted the *New York Times* reporting variable into my original regression, as a proxy for resolve and salience, I found that the coefficient for statements of resolve still remains significant (see Table 3.3), even though the new variable is also significant. Furthermore, even with *NYT* reporting included in the regression, increasing the statement score from the minimum to the maximum still raises the predicted probability of a winning outcome by 42 percentage points. These findings offer further support for the position that statements are not merely acting as a proxy for the underlying level of resolve.

Another technique that can be used to address both the possibility of a confounding effect of resolve and the possibility of reverse causation is matching. These two alternate explanations for the results are each based on the premise that presidents do not make statements of resolve randomly, but rather base their level of statements on either their true level of resolve or the perceived likelihood of winning. Matching techniques seek to reduce the impact of nonrandom assignment of treatment (in this case, the level of statements) by creating a sample of observations that are balanced on observable variables, similar to the type of sample we would presumably have if treatment were assigned randomly. By attempting to approximate random assignment of statements to MIDs, matching aims to reduce the confounding effects that could occur if presidents do indeed make more statements when they are more resolved or more confident of winning (Simmons and Hopkins 2005).

To create a matched sample, I first converted the continuous statement score variable to an indicator for whether the level of statements was over the median. This became the treatment variable. I then matched on variables that I expected to be related to the conflict outcome and the decision to make statements, including relative military capabilities, the political party in control of Congress, the percentage of the MID that took place during an election year, whether the MID adversary had an ongoing rivalry with the United States, and the identity of the president. The technique used was Coarsened Exact Matching, which creates a completely balanced sample based on coarsened versions of the variables used in matching (Iacus, King, and Porro 2012).[7] After matching, I re-estimated the model in the matched sample, using both the original continuous measure of statements and the binary one used for matching. As shown in Table 3.3, the statement score remained significant at the 99 percent confidence level.

Matching is not a panacea for the problem of reverse causality or confounding factors because it cannot account for unobserved factors that might be related to resolve or the probability of winning. Therefore, based on statistical analysis alone, it is impossible to prove beyond doubt that statements of resolve truly have a causal effect on conflict outcomes.[8] However, the logical argumentation and the three robustness checks presented in this section make the case for a causal effect of statements stronger by attempting to rule out alternate explanations for the results. The case for a causal effect of statements will be further strengthened in subsequent chapters. Chapter 4 presents statistical results that would be even more difficult to explain based on reverse causality. Chapters 6–8 present historical evidence that the reason presidents made statements of resolve during the Cuban Missile Crisis, the Vietnam War, and US-Soviet tensions in the 1980s was not that they were confident of victory. These chapters also establish that presidential statements had a direct effect on adversary beliefs, which was distinct from the effect of other signals of resolve.

---

[7] More details regarding the matching procedure are available in the Online Appendix.
[8] For readers who are unconvinced of the causal effect of statements, my measure of statements might still be viewed as a useful approximation of the underlying level of resolve or of a broader set of expressions of resolve.

OTHER CONCERNS WITH THE STATEMENT SCORE

I also performed other robustness checks. The next set of checks deals with the statement score and whether it is adequately measuring statements of resolve. One concern might be that the statement score is picking up the effect of the frequency and length of presidential statements rather than the actual resolved words contained within them. It is true that the score for resolved words is correlated with the length and frequency of statements because a large portion of statements made about MID adversaries are resolved. However, if the words that the president says are meaningful, then resolved words should have a bigger impact on the conflict outcome than neutral words.

To test this, I created a count of the word "that" and a count of the word "the" in the statements I collected. After normalizing these counts by the duration of statement collection, I inserted each of them separately into the main model. The score for resolved words has a positive correlation of around 0.90 with each of the scores for neutral words, which weakens the significance of both the original resolved statement score and the new neutral word scores. However, there is still evidence that resolved words, and not neutral words, are driving the effect of statements. The coefficient for resolved statements remained positive and significant at close to the 85 percent confidence level after each of the neutral word scores was inserted. In contrast, the neutral word scores are never significant with more than 15 percent confidence. The "the" score actually has a negative coefficient, which could be taken to imply that after controlling for resolved statements, additional non-resolved "babble" is actually counterproductive. However, with such low significance, we should not make too much of this negative coefficient. The stronger and more important result is that resolved words have a more significant effect than neutral words.

Another concern about the statement score might be whether it is simply picking up how important or how tense a MID is, since presidents are likely to speak more about more important MIDs and in times of higher tension. If more serious MIDs are more likely to have definite outcomes, then this could be another alternate explanation for the relationship between higher levels of resolved statements and winning outcomes. This line of thinking would imply that a higher level of statements would also be associated with a greater probability of a *losing* outcome compared to a neutral outcome. The functional form used in the main regression model, an ordered probit, is based on the assumption that resolved statements have the same effect at each threshold of the dependent variable. In order to relax this assumption and test for the possibility that statements might increase the probability of both winning and losing, I switched to a multinomial logit model, with a neutral outcome as the base category. With this model, I found that a higher level of statements is associated with a lower probability of a losing outcome and a higher probability of a winning outcome. This indicates that statements do help to achieve more favorable conflict outcomes, rather than just predicting more definite outcomes. However, the coefficient for predicting losing outcomes is not significant, suggesting that most of the significance of the statement score coefficient in the main model is driven by the effect on the threshold between winning and neutral outcomes.

An additional concern about the result for the statement score might be whether it is driven by a few outliers. There are several ways to examine this possibility. I initially tested to see how many observations with the highest values of Cook's distance, a commonly used measure of influence, I could drop. I found that the coefficient for resolved statements remained significant when I dropped the top 13 most influential observations from the sample, as well as when I dropped a lesser number of influential observations.[9] I also examined the influence of outliers by transforming the measure of resolved statements in various ways. I found that the natural logarithm of the statement score and an indicator variable coding whether the statement score was greater than its 75th percentile value were also significant predictors of the conflict outcome.

Another important test of robustness is determining whether the results are robust to different methods of coding statements of resolve. I experimented with varying the time period for collecting statements and using different dictionaries and weighting schemes for measuring resolve. First, I varied the number of days before the dyadic MID when I started collecting statements between 10 and 60 days. Second, I developed two alternate weighting schemes for my dictionary. In one, each word is weighted equally. In the other, words are weighted between one and ten. I found that none of these things made much difference in the significance of the result, indicating that my finding is not driven by any specific decision regarding the statement collection period or the weighting scheme.

I also investigated whether one particular type of statement might be driving the result more than the others by breaking down the original statement score into three separate scores for each type of statement – threats, demands and refusals, and negative characterizations. We might expect threats, which make the clearest commitment, to have the biggest effect on the results and negative characterizations, which only create a vague impression of commitment, to have the smallest effect. When I initially inserted each of the three statement type scores individually into the original regression using the full sample, I did not find evidence of this. Instead, the results suggested that all three types of statements had almost identical effects. However, this finding was driven by the fact that all three types of statements are highly correlated, particularly in the observations that are most influential to the regression results. When I dropped the 13 most influential observations based on the calculation of Cook's D,[10]

---

[9] The only exception is that the result does lose significance when exactly the top eight most influential observations are dropped.

[10] In a previous robustness check, I found that this was the largest number of highly influential observations that I could drop without losing the significance of the original statement score.

I began to see more divergence in the effectiveness of the statement types. As shown in Table 3.3, I found that threats were significant with the highest confidence level (98 percent), followed by negative characterizations (97 percent), and demands and refusals (93 percent). The high effectiveness of threats fits my expectations, but the fact that negative characterizations seem to have greater effectiveness than demands and refusals is more surprising. This may be because negative characterizations convey more hostility. However, because all of the coefficients are significant, it tentatively appears that all types of statements are contributing to the main result that resolved statements are effective at influencing conflict outcomes.[11]

ADDITIONAL ROBUSTNESS CHECKS

I also performed other robustness checks unrelated to the statement score. Although I have previously addressed concerns about the influence of outliers, there might also be more general concerns about which observations are included in the sample. One concern might be whether the results are driven by conflicts in which resolved statements did not truly play a role. One reason this might happen is if a conflict was won entirely by force, rather than by convincing the other side to back down. To address this concern, I dropped the eight dyadic MIDs won by force from the analysis.[12] Another reason statements might not play a role is if some MIDs are accidents rather than true conflict bargaining situations. To eliminate possible accidents, I dropped MIDs which lasted only one day and MIDs in which neither side was coded as revisionist. In addition, I dropped MIDs with unclear or missing outcomes to avoid any concerns that my treatment of these outcomes as neutral distorts the results. A final potential concern with the observations in the sample is that some observations might not be independent from each other. To address whether nonindependence of dyadic MIDs that are part of the same overall MID biases the result, I re-estimated the regression in a subsample that contained only the dyad with the highest statement score in each MID. To address another source of nonindependence, I tried dropping all of the overlapping MIDs with the same adversary. In each case, statements of resolve retained significance.

I also performed a variety of other robustness checks. I used different ways of controlling for time, particularly a linear time trend and indicator variables for the president's identity. I corrected violations of the proportional odds assumption (Williams 2006). Finally, I dropped relative military capabilities

---

[11] The continued high correlation among the types of statements, which is above 0.80 even after dropping the most influential observations, makes the conclusions in this paragraph tentative. It would be ideal to include all three types of statements as separate variables in the same regression, but the multicollinearity is too high to produce a meaningful result.

[12] Again, these are the invasion of Grenada (accounts for two dyadic MIDs with Grenada and Cuba), pressure on Libya over terrorism in 1986, the invasion of Panama, the Gulf War (accounts for two dyadic MIDs with Iraq and Jordan), the Iraq War, and the Afghanistan War.

from the model, which enabled observations after 2007 to be included in the regression. In all cases, resolved statements remained significant. In sum, we can conclude that the statistical significance of resolved statements is highly robust.

SUMMING UP

This chapter has demonstrated a positive relationship between statements of resolve and the probability of achieving a more favorable MID outcome. This result is robustly statistically significant and substantively significant as well. As is common in statistical analysis, the possibility of reverse causality or other confounding factors cannot be eliminated entirely, but my theoretical argumentation and testing suggest that such issues are not very likely to be driving the results. Therefore, the findings support the notion that when US presidents make statements of resolve, it effectively conveys US resolve to adversaries and makes adversaries more likely to back down in disputes.

Even though the effectiveness of statements in international conflict has been widely theorized (Fearon 1994a; Sartori 2005; Trager 2010), this is the first research to find evidence of statements' effectiveness in a direct statistical test. It improves upon previous indirect statistical tests (Eyerman and Hart 1996; Gelpi and Griesdorf 2001; Partell and Palmer 1999; Schultz 1999; Weeks 2008) by including a measure of statements of resolve in the regression directly, instead of using regime type as a proxy for audience costs. It also improves on the times series analysis work of Wood (2012) by examining the effect of statements on ultimate conflict outcomes, instead of immediate adversary reactions. Finally, it offers a contrasting perspective to the case study research of Snyder and Borghard (2011) and Trachtenberg (2012) by performing a more systematic analysis over a larger number of cases.

Therefore, both the methodology employed in this chapter and the statistical result providing evidence of the effectiveness of resolved statements are unique. This makes the findings in this chapter interesting in their own right, but establishing that resolved statements are effective is also an important precursor to investigating the conditions of effectiveness. In the next chapter, I will build on the statistical analysis in this chapter in order to test the conditions under which statements of resolve are most effective.

4

Evidence Regarding the Conditions for Statements' Effectiveness

The previous chapter offered strong evidence that statements of resolve are generally effective at influencing international conflict outcomes. However, statements are unlikely to be equally effective in every situation. It is easy enough to think of cases in which statements have not been effective, such as the Vietnam War or the dispute over North Korea's nuclear weapons program. Additional analysis is therefore required to understand the primary question of interest for this book: Which conditions make statements of resolve most effective? This chapter will build on the statistical models in the previous chapter to explore the conditions that increase or decrease the effectiveness of resolved statements.

The main theoretical argument of this book is that an important condition impacting the effectiveness of statements of resolve is the ability to follow through on them. In Chapter 1, I explained that if adversaries perceive the physical or political impediments to following through on resolved statements as too great, they are likely to disregard the statements. I also proposed three conditions that can give leaders the ability to follow through on statements of resolve and make their statements more effective. These conditions will all be tested in this chapter.

The first of these conditions, which has already been recognized by other scholars (for example, Huth and Russett 1984; Mearsheimer 1983; Press 2005), is relative military strength. If the country issuing statements of resolve has greater military capabilities relative to its adversary, there are less likely to be physical obstacles to following through, and the risk of losing or incurring high casualties should also be lower. Therefore, statements of resolve issued by a country with relatively higher military capabilities will be taken more seriously by adversaries.

The second condition is the hawkishness of domestic veto players. While dovish veto players are likely to create political obstacles to following through on statements, hawkish veto players are unlikely to stand in the leader's way. Therefore, adversaries will know that leaders with more hawkish veto players will have an easier time following through on their resolved statements, which should make the adversaries more likely to back down. This condition is more unique to my theory. Other scholars have explored related topics, such as the role of domestic opposition parties (Ramsay 2004; Schultz's 1998) and the hawkish or dovish preferences of leaders (Clare 2014; Schultz 2005) on conflict bargaining, but I am the first to directly consider how the hawkishness of veto players affects threat credibility.

The third condition is security in office of the leader. Leaders who are secure in office are likely to have more bargaining leverage over veto players and face less risk in initiating or escalating military conflict because they are unlikely to lose office even if the conflict goes poorly. For both of these reasons, secure leaders should have a greater ability to follow through on their statements. Therefore, I argue that security in office will also be beneficial to the effectiveness of statements.

This chapter will also test the additional hypotheses derived in Chapter 1 based on domestic audience cost theory and international reputational cost theory. These theories both focus on the costs of backing down from statements as reasons for statements' effectiveness. Domestic audience cost theory would predict, in contrast to my theory, that security in office will be detrimental to the effectiveness of statements because it reduces the costs of backing down (Fearon 1994a; Schultz 1999; Weeks 2008). In principle, it is possible that my theory and audience cost theory are both correct because they rely on distinct mechanisms. However, because they predict effects that push in opposite directions, it is important to determine which one wins out.

Meanwhile, international reputational cost theory (Sartori 2005) would predict that statements of resolve will be less effective when the country issuing them has backed down from other resolved statements in the recent past. The theory of international reputational costs has no contradictions with my theory and even has the potential to complement my theory, but my dataset of resolved statements provides a unique opportunity to test it. In sum, this chapter tests all of the hypotheses about the conditions for effectiveness of statements developed in Chapter 1. For convenience, these hypotheses are summarized again in Table 4.1.

TABLE 4.1 *Hypotheses to Be Tested*

Hypotheses Associated with the Ability to Follow Through

H1: Statements of resolve will be more effective when the country issuing them has greater military strength relative to the target of the statements.

H2: Statements of resolve will be more effective when domestic veto players are more hawkish.

H3: Statements of resolve will be more effective when the leader issuing them is more secure in office.

Hypotheses Associated with the Costs of Backing Down

H4: Statements of resolve will be less effective when the leader issuing them is more secure in office.

H5: Statements of resolve will be less effective if the country issuing them recently backed down from a large number of previous statements of resolve.

RESEARCH DESIGN

Having reviewed the hypotheses, I will turn to describing how they are evaluated. I test the hypotheses using statistical models which build upon the main model used in Chapter 3. In Chapter 3, I examined the effect of statements of resolve on conflict outcomes. In this chapter, I also examine the effect of statements on conflict outcomes, but with a focus on how this effect is moderated by other conditions.

This chapter uses the same dataset used in Chapter 3, which consists of all 272 dyadic MIDs involving the United States between 1950 and 2010. As in Chapter 3, the dependent variable is the conflict outcome, which is measured ordinally, with higher values representing outcomes more favorable to the United States. The main independent variable is again the statement score, which is the measure of US presidential statements of resolve described in Chapter 2. As in the previous analysis, I mainly use the version of this variable that I created by using a three-tiered weighting scheme and starting collection of statements 30 days before the dyadic MID start date. I also use the same control variables as in the main model in Chapter 3.

The key difference from Chapter 3 is that the models in this chapter interact the score for statements of resolve with the conditions hypothesized to impact the effectiveness of statements. By interacting each of these conditions with statements of resolve, we can see how the effect of statements on conflict outcomes changes as the interacted variable moves from its minimum to its maximum value. This will tell us whether the interacted conditions indeed have the hypothesized impact on the effectiveness of resolved statements. In order to create these interactions, it is necessary to operationalize the abstract concepts in the hypotheses using specific variables. Some of the variables that I use to operationalize these concepts were briefly mentioned in Chapter 2, but here I will discuss the rationale for using them in more detail since this is where they play a critical role in testing my theory and other theories.

To test Hypothesis 1, I operationalized military strength using the same measure of relative military capabilities that I used as a control variable in Chapter 3. This variable captures the percentage of total capabilities among the dyadic MID participants which are held by the United States. Military capabilities are measured at the midpoint of the dyadic MID, using the widely utilized CINC score (Singer, Bremer, and Stuckey 1972).

To test Hypothesis 2, I operationalized the hawkishness of veto players using the percentage of total seats in Congress held by Republicans (US House 2014; US Senate 2014). This variable is also measured at the midpoint year of each dyadic MID. I focus on Congress as a veto player because it has the constitutional power to limit the president's ability to use force. Congress has rarely passed legislation restricting use of force, but the mere possibility of this can potentially restrain the president (Howell and Pevehouse 2007). I use the percentage of Republican seats to measure the hawkishness of Congress because

Republicans were generally more hawkish than Democrats throughout the period covered by my dataset. In the early 1950s, Senator McCarthy led the Republican Party toward a hawkish position against Communism. The difference between the parties was smaller in the 1960s, but the Republican Party was still more hawkish, as evidenced by the views of prominent Republicans such as Barry Goldwater (Dueck 2010). In the 1970s, a greater divergence between the parties reemerged due to the Vietnam War. This divide persisted after the end of the Cold War, with Republicans taking more hawkish positions toward countries such as Iraq and North Korea. This evidence that Republicans have tended to be more hawkish than Democrats is in keeping with the findings of cross-national research that right-wing parties are generally more hawkish and increase a country's propensity for involvement in military conflict (Arena and Palmer 2009; Koch and Sullivan 2010; Palmer, London, and Regan 2004).

Testing Hypotheses 3 and 4 requires operationalizing the concept of security in office for the US president. As my primary measure of this concept, I use the president's net approval rating, which is the percentage of people approving of the president's job performance minus the percentage disapproving in the most recent Gallup poll at the midpoint of the dyadic MID (Peters and Woolley 2016). For presidents in their first term, net approval is a good indicator of how likely their reelection is. Even presidents who are not running for reelection are likely to care somewhat about maintaining high approval because it may help them achieve domestic priorities, reflects on their legacy, and affects the likelihood that a successor from the same party will be elected.

Testing Hypothesis 5 required me to operationalize the extent to which the United States recently backed down from resolved statements. The MID dataset does not capture backing down directly, but since most MIDs are not won by force, I assume that non-winning outcomes are highly correlated with backing down. I treated neutral outcomes in conflicts in which the United States was on the initiating side as non-winning, based on the assumption that the United States would have preferred to change the status quo in most of these MIDs. After identifying the non-winning MIDs, I created a variable capturing the level of recent non-winning statements. Non-winning statements are measured using the statement score from the most recent non-winning MID that ended before the current MID.[1]

MAIN RESULTS

The main results are given in Table 4.2. Regarding the control variables, we see similar results as in Chapter 3. Turning to the results of interest, we see that the interaction term is positive and significant when statements of resolve are

---

[1] I code this variable by MID, rather than by dyadic MID, because all of the dyads within a MID have the same outcome and usually the same end date.

TABLE 4.2 *Main Models with Statement Score Interactions*

Conditioning Variable (listed across):	Relative Capabilities	Republicans in Congress	Net Approval	Non-Winning Statements
Statement Score	−0.399**	−3.009***	0.139*	0.325***
	(0.164)	(0.790)	(0.071)	(0.108)
Conditioning Variable	1.076*	−3.590	0.539	0.055
	(0.607)	(2.254)	(0.393)	(0.072)
Statement Score # Conditioning Var.	0.917***	7.949***	0.697**	−0.045***
	(0.336)	(2.063)	(0.279)	(0.017)
Relative Capabilities		1.681***	2.027***	1.847***
		(0.645)	(0.608)	(0.633)
Adversary Democracy	−0.642	−0.588	−0.810	−0.708
	(0.483)	(0.502)	(0.526)	(0.517)
Year	0.032**	0.037**	0.041**	0.032**
	(0.016)	(0.017)	(0.016)	(0.016)
Year Squared	0.0004	0.001	0.001	0.001
	(0.0004)	(0.001)	(0.0004)	(0.0004)
Year Cubed	−0.0001**	−0.0001***	−0.0001***	−0.0001**
	(0.00003)	(0.0003)	(0.00003)	(0.00003)
Observations	262	262	262	261

Note: * P <.10, ** P <.05, *** P <.01. The functional form is an ordered probit model with the conflict outcome as the dependent variable. "Conditioning variable" refers to the variables interacted with statements of resolve, listed across the top. Huber-White standard errors are in parentheses.

interacted with each of the three variables associated with the ability to follow through, namely, relative military capabilities, the percentage of Republicans in Congress, and the president's net approval rating. The coefficient for the interaction between the statement score and previous non-winning statements is also significant, but negative. This suggests support for Hypotheses 1–3 and for Hypothesis 5, but it is more useful and appropriate to analyze the substantive impact of the interactions by considering marginal effects and changes in the predicted probability of winning.

Figures 4.1–4.4 show the average marginal effect of the statement score on the probability of a winning outcome at different levels of each of the interacted variables. Figure 4.1 shows how change in the level of relative military capabilities impacts the marginal effect of statements. The upward slope of the line confirms that the effect of resolved statements on the probability of

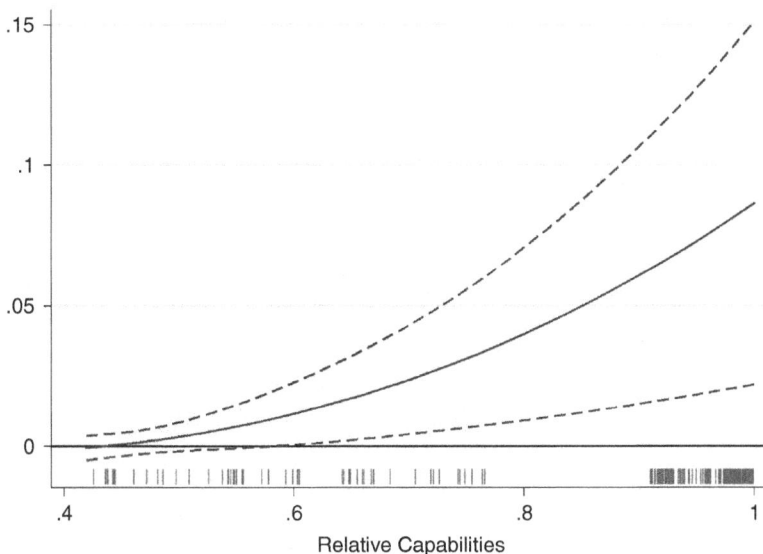

FIGURE 4.1 Impact of Relative Capabilities on the Marginal Effect of the Statement Score
Note: The solid line represents the average marginal effect of the statement score on the probability of winning. Marginal effects for each observation in the sample were calculated and averaged. The dotted lines are 95 percent confidence bounds. The rug plot shows the distribution of the variable interacted with statements.

winning becomes increasingly positive as the United States becomes more capable relative to its adversary. We see that the lower confidence bound is above zero at higher levels of relative capabilities, but is below zero when the United States has less than about 60 percent of the capabilities in the dyad. This means that resolved statements have a significant positive effect on the conflict outcome when the United States is notably stronger than its adversary, but not when both sides are about evenly matched.

Analyzing predicted probabilities also supports the same conclusion about the impact of capabilities on the effectiveness of statements. When the United States has only 50 percent of the capabilities in a dyad, the average predicted probability of winning remains less than 1 percent regardless of the statement score. In contrast, when the United States has 99 percent of the capabilities in a dyad, the average predicted probability of winning increases from 7 percent to 31 percent as the statement score increases from 0 to 2 (the range in which 95 percent of statement scores fall).

Among the influential observations in which the United States had much higher military capabilities than its adversary, made a high level of resolved statements, and achieved a winning outcome was the US pressure on leaders of a coup in Haiti to step down in 1993–1994. President Clinton made many

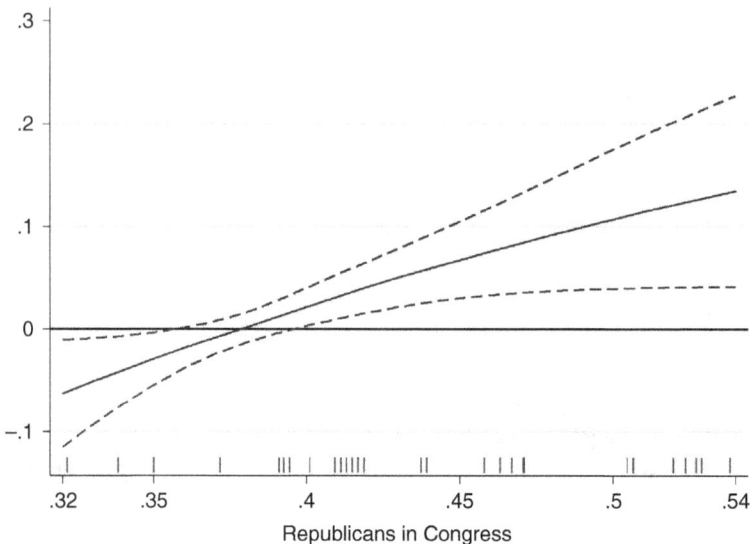

FIGURE 4.2 Impact of Republicans on the Marginal Effect of the Statement Score
Note: The interpretation is the same as for Figure 4.1.

resolved statements during this MID. After Clinton made a televised speech explicitly announcing an intention to invade Haiti (September 15, 1994, Peters and Woolley 2016), the Haitian leadership finally agreed to step down a few days later. The specific invasion preparations Clinton announced in his speech left little doubt about his resolve, and once it was clear that the United States was resolved to invade, the Haitian leadership knew that it could not win against superior US forces.[2] The cases in which the United States had the lowest relative capabilities and usually failed to achieve a winning outcome, despite often making high levels of resolved statements, were MIDs against the Soviet Union. Most MIDs against the Soviet Union end with neutral outcomes because the evenly matched capabilities of the United States and the USSR, combined with their large nuclear arsenals, made it difficult for either one to push the other too far.

Figure 4.2 shows how the average marginal effect of the statement score changes with the level of Republicans in Congress. The upward slope of the line shows that the marginal effect of statements on the probability of winning increases with the percentage of Republican seats in Congress. We see that the

---

[2] American aircraft had already taken off for an invasion of Haiti by the time an agreement was reached, but it is not clear that the Haitian leadership knew this because the White House asked US media not to report it (Carter 1994). Therefore, any sense of urgency to reach an agreement probably stemmed primarily from US public statements warning that an invasion was imminent and diplomatic efforts.

lower confidence bound is above zero at most levels of Republicans in Congress, but falls below zero when Republicans control less than about 40 percent of seats. When Republicans comprise less than about 36 percent of Congress, resolved statements actually have a negative and significant marginal effect, possibly because making statements without the ability to follow through on them draws attention to the president's impotence. The majority of MIDs with such a low level of Republicans in Congress occurred during the détente era, during which US presidents mostly refrained from making highly resolved statements.

The calculation of predicted probabilities also reveals how much the level of Republicans in Congress impacts the effectiveness of statements. When 39 percent of Congress members are Republicans, increasing the statement score from zero to 2 increases the average predicted probability of a winning outcome by only 2 percentage points. However, when 54 percent of Congress members are Republicans, the same increase in the statement score raises the average predicted probability of victory by 61 percentage points.

Several of the influential observations for the findings regarding Republicans in Congress were MIDs that took place under President Clinton, who had a majority of Republicans in Congress for most of his time in office and who also had a tendency to make fairly high levels of resolved statements. Clinton had a relatively high rate of successful MID outcomes. In addition to the Haiti case mentioned previously, he was able to compel Serbia to back down in the Bosnia and Kosovo conflicts and compel Iraq and Iran to halt some provocations. Another president with a fairly good record of MID outcomes was Eisenhower. For example, during the Suez Crisis, Eisenhower deterred Soviet intervention, while also eventually persuading US allies Britain and France to back down. During the crisis, Eisenhower made a relatively high level of resolved statements targeting the Soviet Union, and Republicans held 47 percent of seats in Congress, a high percentage in historical perspective. In contrast, the United States experienced no winning MID outcomes from the Johnson administration through the Carter administration, and this was also a time when the level of Republicans in Congress was at a low point.

Figure 4.3 illustrates the impact of the president's net approval rating on the average marginal effect of the statement score. The figure shows that the marginal effect of resolved statements gets larger as the president's popularity increases. At the lowest level of net approval, the marginal effect is insignificant, but it becomes positive and significant when net approval is slightly more than zero. It makes sense that the tipping point is close to zero because this is the point at which approval and disapproval for the president are equal. Therefore, the figure confirms that the president's security in office has a positive impact on the effectiveness of his statements, in keeping with Hypothesis 3 and contrary to Hypothesis 4.

We can also consider how net approval affects predicted probabilities. When the president has a net approval rating of zero, an increase in the statement score

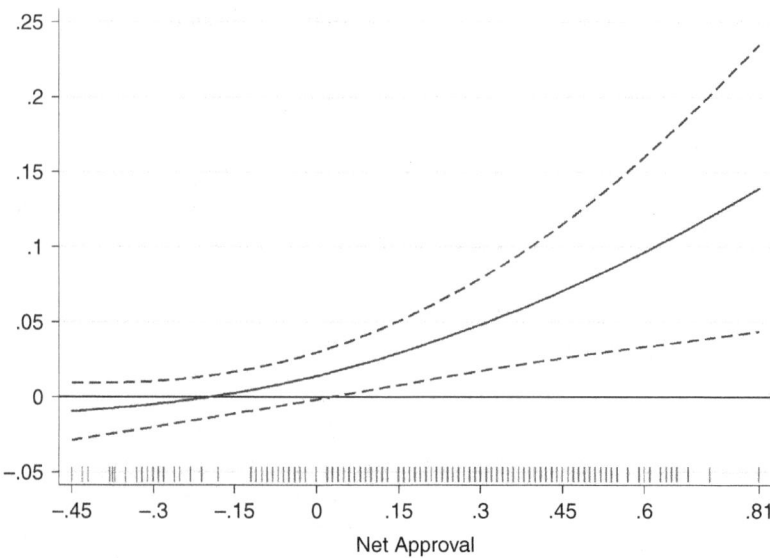

FIGURE 4.3 Impact of Approval on the Marginal Effect of the Statement Score
Note: The interpretation is the same as for Figure 4.1.

from zero to 2 raises the average predicted probability of winning by 3 percentage points. On the other hand, when the president has a net approval rating of 0.81, the same increase in the statement score causes the average predicted probability of victory to increase by 40 percentage points. One observation that exemplifies the effect of net approval is the Berlin Crisis of 1961, in which President Kennedy had a net approval rating of 0.64 and made a televised speech about the crisis. Kennedy succeeded in deterring the Soviet Union from attempting to forcibly drive the Western powers from Berlin. In contrast, President Carter, who became deeply unpopular due to the Iranian Hostage Crisis, was less able to influence the Soviet Union, particularly with regard to Soviet intervention in Afghanistan.

Now it remains to examine the interaction between the statement score and previous non-winning statements. Figure 4.4 shows how the level of statements made in the most recent non-winning MID impacts the average marginal effect of statements in the current dispute. The negative slope of the line confirms that backing down from more past statements decreases the positive effect of present statements. The statement score only has a positive and significant marginal effect on the probability of winning the current conflict when the statement score in the most recent non-winning MID was less than around five. The figure therefore indicates support for Hypothesis 5, although the skewed distribution seen in the rug plot makes it necessary to test whether this result is driven by outliers.

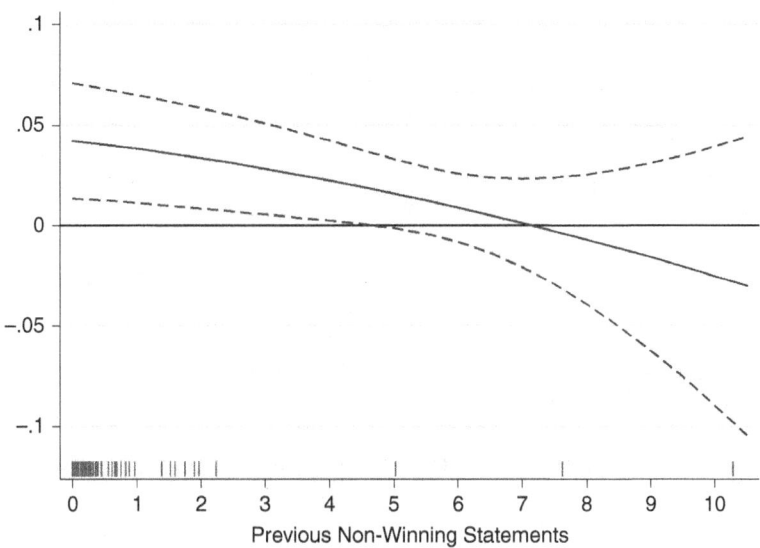

FIGURE 4.4 Impact of Previous Statements on the Marginal Effect of the Statement
Score
Note: The interpretation is the same as for Figure 4.1.

The conclusions regarding the impact of previous non-winning statements
based on the marginal effects graph can be reinforced by calculating predicted
probabilities. An increase in the statement score from zero to 2 raises the
average predicted probability of winning by 11 percentage points when the
level of previous non-winning statements is zero, but it only raises the average
predicted probability of winning by 3 percentage points when the level of
previous non-winning statements is 5. One prominent observation that has
among the highest levels of previous non-winning statements and influences
the results for this interaction is the Iranian Hostage Crisis MID. This MID is
recorded as having a high level of previous non-winning statements because of
the harsh statements that President Carter made about the Soviet invasion of
Afghanistan during a non-winning MID against the USSR that took place prior
to the end of the Iranian Hostage Crisis. The fact that President Carter made
such strong statements against the Soviet Union, without prompting
a discernable change in Soviet behavior or taking strong action against the
Soviet Union, may have made the Iranians take his statements of resolve less
seriously.

In sum, the effectiveness of statements increases as all of the variables
associated with the ability to follow through increase. The result for the
relative capabilities interaction indicates that US presidential statements are
more effective when the United States has relatively greater military power,
supporting my Hypothesis 1 and the similar expectations of previous scholars

(Huth and Russett 1984; Mearsheimer 1983; Press 2005). The result for the Republicans in Congress interaction indicates that presidents are able to make more effective resolved statements when their veto players are more hawkish. This result supports my Hypothesis 2. While Hypothesis 2 is unique to my theory, this finding also complements other work that has found that hawkish right-wing governments experience a greater frequency and duration of military conflicts (Arena and Palmer 2009; Koch and Sullivan 2010; Palmer, London, and Regan 2004). The result for the net approval interaction shows that US presidents are able to make more effective statements when they are more secure in office. This result supports my Hypothesis 3, and goes against Hypothesis 4, which was an alternative hypothesis derived from audience cost theory (Fearon 1994a; Schultz 1999; Weeks 2008).

Thus, the evidence shows clear support for my theory of the ability to follow through. When each of the variables associated with the ability to follow through is maximized, even a relatively small increase in the statements score (from zero to 2) can have a large effect on the predicted probability of winning – which helps to answer the question, raised in Chapter 3, of why presidents sometimes find it beneficial to make just a small number of statements. In addition to the support for my theory of the ability to follow through, there also appears to be at least tentative support for the theory of international reputational costs. The significance of the interaction between the statement score and previous non-winning statements suggests that previous non-winning statements damage the effectiveness of current statements, although this result requires more investigation because it may depend upon outliers.

IMPORTANCE OF STATEMENTS

The impact of the factors related to the ability to follow through on the effectiveness of statements is so strong that we might wonder whether these factors are more important than the statements themselves. However, this is not the case at all. The results indicate that statements of resolve do play a critical role. This could be seen in the previous section, in which it was observed that the marginal effect of statements on the conflict outcome keeps getting larger as each of the variables related to the ability to follow through increases. We saw that statements have a dramatic effect on the predicted probability of winning when each of the variables associated with the ability to follow through was maximized, indicating that a high ability to follow through does not crowd out the effect of statements.

It is possible to see even stronger evidence of the importance of statements by examining the interaction between resolved statements and the ability to follow through from the other direction. The second row of coefficients in Table 4.2 shows the effect of the variables interacted with the statement score when the statement score is equal to zero. We see that most of the interacted variables are not significant in this scenario, and even relative capabilities are only weakly significant for predicting the conflict outcome. This indicates that the factors related to the ability to follow through do not have much impact in international conflict by themselves, but they do have an impact in conjunction with statements of resolve.

This finding makes sense based on the logic of conflict bargaining and the relationship between statements of resolve and the ability to follow through posited by my theory. In conflict bargaining, an adversary is likely to back down only if it believes that the US president both has the ability to follow through *and* is resolved enough to follow through (and if the adversary is not equally resolved). There are likely to be some situations in which the president has the ability to follow through, but is not resolved. Because the United States is involved in so many international disputes, the president simply cannot care equally about them all. My theory assumes that adversaries can more or less accurately observe the president's ability to follow through, but they are likely to have greater difficulty observing the president's resolve because it is more of an internal characteristic. If an adversary knows that the president has the ability to follow through, how can it learn whether the president is also resolved? I argue that this learning takes place primarily through statements of resolve. As explained in Chapter 1, presidents who are genuinely more resolved are more likely to make statements of resolve, and therefore the statements can serve as informative signals. If a president does not make statements, then adversaries will assume (probably correctly) that the president is not resolved. In this situation, the ability to follow through becomes irrelevant because adversaries believe that the president is not resolved enough to take action anyway.

Given this logic, it makes sense that the coefficients for factors related to the ability to follow through are mostly insignificant when the level of resolved statements is zero. This finding therefore supports my theoretical expectations about the importance of resolved statements. It indicates that it is generally necessary to both make statements and have the ability to follow through on them in order to have successful conflict outcomes. A policy implication of this is that it is not enough for US presidents who have the ability to follow through to simply sit back and wait for other countries to take US interests into account. Instead, they must actively signal US interests and preferences.

STRATEGIC BEHAVIOR AND ALTERNATE EXPLANATIONS

In any situation in which statistical analysis is used to test predictions about a complicated strategic situation, it is necessary to consider whether strategic behavior by the actors involved might distort the results. One concern raised in Chapter 3 was whether leaders might make more statements when they anticipate that they will win, creating the potential for reverse causality.

In Chapter 3, I used a matching technique and logical argumentation to make the case that reverse causality is unlikely to be driving the result. The results in this chapter provide further evidence against the possibility of reverse causality. As previously stated, if statements did not truly affect the probability of victory, then the only reason to make them would be to draw attention to anticipated victories in order to gain glory domestically. However, for this explanation to fit with my results, one would have to believe that popular presidents seek more glory than unpopular presidents, that presidents with credible reputations seek more glory than those with damaged reputations, and that higher military capabilities and levels of Republicans in Congress also somehow make presidents seek more glory. Since these beliefs are mostly implausible, reverse causality is not a likely explanation for the results.

Another way that presidents might behave strategically is by making more statements not just when they expect to win militarily, but when they generally have a greater ability to follow through on their statements. Chapter 2 showed no evidence that a greater ability to follow through increases the propensity to make statements. The absence of a relationship is somewhat surprising under my theoretical framework, but as explained in Chapter 2, it does not undermine the predictions of my theory regarding the impact of the ability to follow through on the effectiveness of statements. With regard to the statistical regressions in this chapter, the fact that the level of resolved statements is not significantly affected by the factors interacted with the statement score is actually beneficial because it reduces concerns about multicollinearity and makes it easier to analyze the distinct effects of statements and the ability to follow through.

Another concern raised about the results in Chapter 3 was the possibility of a confounding effect of resolve itself. Since statements of resolve are expected to be positively correlated with the president's true underlying level of resolve, it is possible that the underlying level of resolve is influencing the conflict outcome in ways that are not controlled for in the regression and might be picked up by the statements coefficient. This would lead to the following alternate interpretation of the results presented in this chapter: That the president's underlying level of resolve only has a big impact on conflict outcomes when the ability to follow through is high, and that the ability to follow through only has a big impact on conflict outcomes when the president's underlying resolve is high. This interpretation is not entirely implausible, but it seems less likely because it would be difficult for adversaries to assess the president's level of resolve accurately without statements. Chapter 3 offered a more detailed argument regarding why this interpretation is less likely. This chapter does not offer any new theoretical arguments in this regard, but Table 4.4 at the end of the chapter does show that the results continue to be robust to using more control variables and matching in an attempt to rule out a confounding effect of resolve.

VALIDITY OF MEASURES INTERACTED WITH STATEMENTS

I performed a wide variety of robustness checks for each model. The first set of checks, summarized in Table 4.3, tests the validity of the measures which are interacted with statements of resolve. Compared to the other concepts discussed, military strength is relatively straightforward to measure. However, one concern might be whether the effect of relative military capabilities is driven by just a few countries. To address this concern, I dropped all dyadic MIDs against nuclear powers from the sample and then dropped only dyadic MIDs

TABLE 4.3 *Testing the Validity of Measures Interacted with Statements*

Validity Tests	Coef.	SE	P-Value
Military Strength			
Dropping nuclear adversaries	0.828	4.219	0.844
Dropping the Soviet Union	0.302	1.176	0.797
Hawkish Veto Players			
Average Republicans in Congress over MID	8.164	2.111	0.000
Republican control of at least one house	0.390	0.181	0.031
Nominate score, Senate Foreign Relations Chair	0.563	0.270	0.037
Nominate score, 67th senator	2.357	0.703	0.001
Republican CJCS	0.289	0.140	0.038
Original measure, Republican president	9.971	4.155	0.016
Original measure, Democratic president	7.010	2.809	0.013
Original measure, 1950–1991	6.067	2.966	0.041
Original measure, 1992–2007	9.554	5.159	0.064
Security in Office			
Average net approval over MID	0.643	0.285	0.024
Net approval at beginning of MID	0.428	0.234	0.067
Square of net approval	−0.218	1.035	0.833
Percentage of MID in election year with eligible president	−0.285	0.146	0.052
Percentage of MID with lame duck president	0.955	0.400	0.017
International Reputation			
Average statement score over last five non-wins	−0.139	0.055	0.012
Last non-winning statement score > 75th percentile	−0.288	0.142	0.042
Statement score in last win	0.188	0.120	0.117
Statement score in last non-win with same adversary	−0.040	0.020	0.044
Statement score in last non-win under same president	−0.042	0.018	0.021

Note: Only results for the interaction with the statement score are reported here. Full results are available in the Online Appendix.

against the Soviet Union. Both of these changes cause the interaction with relative capabilities to lose significance, and dropping just the Soviet Union is almost as bad as dropping all nuclear adversaries. Therefore, the Soviet observations appear to be driving the relationship between military strength and the effectiveness of resolved statements. This does not necessarily undermine Hypothesis 1, but we cannot be absolutely sure that it is military capabilities and not some other attribute of the USSR that is driving the result.

I next considered alternate measures of the hawkishness of veto players. I began by using different ways of measuring hawkishness in Congress. First, I averaged the percentage of Republicans in Congress over each dyadic MID, rather than using the midpoint value. Second, I used an indicator variable for whether Republicans controlled at least one house of Congress.[3] The interaction with resolved statements remained significant in both of these tests. Third, I used Nominate Scores (Carroll et al. 2011), which measure how liberal or conservative individual members of Congress are, based on their voting records. Using these scores allows me to measure the ideology of key Congress members who might be veto players by themselves, and the ideology of key members also provides additional insight into the ideology of Congress as an institution. Another important benefit of Nominate Scores is that they are not biased by shifts in party ideology, such as the exit of Southern conservatives from the Democratic Party. Focusing on the Senate because of its greater role in foreign policy, I interacted resolved statements with the Nominate Scores of the Senate Foreign Relations Committee Chair and of the senator who would be in position 67 if all senators' scores were lined up from low to high.[4] I found that the interactions of these scores with resolved statements were positive and significant, indicating that more conservative Congress members, who are presumably more hawkish, make statements more effective.

For my last alternate measure of the hawkishness of veto players, I looked outside of Congress to examine the effect of an executive branch veto player, namely, the Chairman of the Joint Chiefs of Staff (CJCS). Although the CJCS is subordinate to the president and has a formally apolitical role, Golby (2011) argues that the CJCS can shape policy outcomes due to private information on military matters and an ability to influence the public debate. There is also some evidence that the hawkishness of the CJCS and other top military officials is related to their party affiliations. For example, members of the Joint Chiefs of Staff appointed by Republican president Eisenhower opposed President Kennedy's idea of using limited military options in Laos and recommended stronger military action, even including the use of nuclear weapons (Golby 2011, 195–196). In contrast, after Democratic president Kennedy was able to appoint his own CJCS, the new CJCS was less hawkish than other Joint Staff members and willing to provide Kennedy with a range of limited military

---

[3] All alternate variables are measured at the dyadic MID midpoint, unless otherwise noted.
[4] I am grateful to Jon Pevehouse for sharing his manipulated version of the Nominate data.

options during the Cuban Missile Crisis (Golby 2011, 209–212). Therefore, I follow Golby and code the party affiliation of the CJCS based on which party controlled the presidency and Senate when he was appointed.[5] Interacting an indicator for a Republican CJCS with the statement score, I found that the interaction term was positive and significant. The fact that I found the same impact of hawkishness on the effectiveness of statements by looking at an entirely different veto player provides strong corroborating evidence that this condition is important.

In addition to using alternate measures of hawkish veto players, I tested the validity of the Republicans in Congress measure by splitting the sample. First, to address whether the impact of Republicans in Congress is dependent on the party of the president, I split the sample by the president's party. I found that the significance of the interaction changed little between the two samples, although the size of the coefficient is greater under a Republican president. I will further explore the impact of the president's own party on the effect of Republicans in Congress with a more sophisticated model in Chapter 5. Second, to see if the temporal correlation between the end of the Cold War and an increase in Republicans in Congress might be driving the result, I split the sample after 1991. I found that the interaction is significant at the 95 percent confidence level in the longer Cold War era and at the 93 percent confidence level in the shorter modern era, even though the coefficient is larger in the modern era.

Next, I considered alternate measures of presidential security in office. First, I used the president's average net approval over the course of the MID and then the president's net approval at the beginning of the MID, rather than using the midpoint value. Using the average produced little change in the result. Using the beginning value reduced the size of the interaction coefficient and lowered the significance of the interaction coefficient to the 93 percent confidence level. This is not surprising because the initial level of net approval is a worse measure of the president's continued ability to follow through over the course of longer MIDs. However, the fact that the interaction is still somewhat significant using this value suggests that the result is not driven by the public rallying around anticipated victories.

I also considered the possibility that the impact of the president's net approval on the effectiveness of statements might not be linear. This might be the case if the least popular presidents decide to "gamble for resurrection" by following through on their statements because military victory – even if it is a remote possibility – is the only thing that can revive their political fortunes (Downs and Rocke 1994). This would imply a U-shaped impact of security in office on the effectiveness of statements, with the most and least secure presidents being able to make the most credible statements. I tested for this by

---

[5] Golby argues and presents evidence that Republican presidents can almost always succeed in appointing Republican senior officers, while Democratic presidents can typically only succeed at appointing Democratic senior officers when Democrats also control the Senate.

interacting the square of the president's net approval rating with the statement score (while still retaining the original statement–net approval interaction in the regression as well to avoid bias). I found that the new interaction had a P-value of 0.833,[6] which allows a strong rejection of the possibility that the impact of security in office is U-shaped. Substantively, this suggests that presidents are rarely so unpopular that they feel they have nothing left to lose by following through on statements.

In addition, I considered other measures of security in office related to election eligibility and timing. Presidents who are eligible for reelection are generally less secure in office because they need to maintain public support in order to receive another term, and eligible presidents are likely to feel most insecure when an election is approaching. Therefore, I expect reelection eligibility and proximity to an election to jointly reduce the effectiveness of statements. To test this expectation, I interacted the statement score with a measure of the percentage of the dyadic MID that took place within one year before an election in which the president was eligible to run.[7] I found that the interaction had a negative and significant coefficient, indicating that the presidents who are most insecure because of the election calendar can make less effective statements of resolve than other presidents. This fits with my expectation about the impact of insecurity on the effectiveness of statements.

What about the presidents who are most secure? Ironically, the presidents who are most secure in office are probably those who are leaving office soon due to term limits. Recall that my definition of security in office in Chapter 1 was "that a leader is very unlikely to be removed from office in the near future, for any reason *except* constitutionally imposed term limits." Term limits are different from other reasons for removal from office because presidents can do nothing about them. Therefore, term limits provide a freedom from worrying about public opinion that is similar to the freedom enjoyed by highly popular presidents. I expect that presidents will not necessarily cease caring about public opinion as soon as they enter their second term because they might want to retain public support to pass their domestic agenda. However, as their second term draws to a close, presidents might feel increasingly free from public opinion concerns. President George H.W. Bush's decision to initiate a risky and unprecedented humanitarian mission in Somalia only about a month before leaving office might be an example of how such freedom can affect presidential decision-making. If presidents who will soon leave office due to term limits have a greater ability to follow through due to freedom from public opinion, then their statements of resolve should be more effective. To test this expectation, I interacted the statement score with the percentage of the MID

---

[6] The original statement–net approval interaction also loses significance in this regression due to multicollinearity, but it remains much closer to significant with a P-value of 0.149.

[7] I considered Truman's and Johnson's eligibility to end when they announced that they were not running for reelection.

that took place under a "lame duck" president, defined as a president in the last two years of his second term or a president who had announced he would not run for reelection (as Truman and Johnson did). I found that the interaction had a positive and significant coefficient, indicating that presidents who are highly secure in the sense that public opinion will not influence the duration of their remaining time in office can make more effective statements.

Finally, I considered alternate measures for testing the concept of international reputational costs. First, instead of focusing solely on the level of resolved statements made in the most recent non-winning MID, I averaged the statement scores in the last five non-winning MIDs. Next, to reduce the impact of the skewed distribution, I created an indicator variable for whether the level of previous non-winning statements was above the 75th percentile. Like the original measure, both of these variables had negative and significant interactions with the level of statements made in the current MID. This reduces concern that the result for international reputational costs is driven by outliers.

Another potential concern with the result for non-winning statements is the possibility that making a high level of statements in any previous conflict, not just non-winning conflicts, might make current statements less effective, perhaps due to decreased salience of statements when they are made frequently. To test this, I interacted the statement score for the present dyadic MID with the level of statements made in the previous *winning* MID. I found that the interaction was insignificant and even had a positive coefficient. This suggests that there is indeed a distinct reputational effect of statements made in *non*-winning MIDs.

It is also interesting to consider whether bluffs that were called in conflicts with the current adversary have a stronger impact, since some scholars have argued that reputations are context-specific (Huth 1997). To test this, I created an additional variable capturing the level of statements made in the last non-winning dyadic MID with the current adversary. The coefficient for the interaction of this variable with current resolved statements was less significant and slightly less negative than the interaction with the original non-winning statements variable. This could be attributed to the fact that 83 observations were dropped because there had been no previous non-winning MIDs with the adversary since data collection began. Still, it cannot be said that there is any evidence reputation is adversary-specific.

Another question that is sometimes debated is whether reputations are acquired by countries or leaders (Renshon, Dafoe, and Huth 2015). If reputations are acquired by leaders, this implies that a country can restore its reputation for credibility by removing a leader who backed down (Guisinger and Smith 2002). In contrast, if reputations adhere to a country as a whole, they will be more difficult to restore. To investigate this, I created a new version of the previous non-winning statements measure in which each new president who comes to office has missing values for the level of previous non-winning statements until he experiences a non-winning MID himself. I found that the significance of the interaction is lower using the new measure than using the original measure, and the interaction coefficient itself is slightly closer to zero. The lower significance might be attributed to 33 additional missing values, but a strong effect of leader-specific reputation probably would have been able to overcome this. Therefore, this test provides no evidence that a country's reputation is reset when its leader is replaced.

OTHER ROBUSTNESS CHECKS

I also performed a variety of other robustness checks intended to confirm that the results in this chapter are not driven by any peculiarity of the statement-coding process or the model specification. These tests are all similar to the robustness checks done in the previous chapter, so I will not discuss them in great detail. The results are summarized in Table 4.4. As shown in the table, dropping the 20 most influential observations and converting the statements score to an indicator variable causes the interaction between statements of resolve and relative military capabilities to lose significance. The interaction between current statements of resolve and previous non-winning statements also loses significance in the matched sample, when the statement score is converted to an indicator variable, and when one-day MIDs are dropped. On the whole, however, the significance of the results is impressively consistent. This further raises confidence about the validity of the results.

SUMMING UP

This chapter provides strong evidence that statements of resolve have a greater effect on conflict outcomes when a country has greater relative military strength, when a leader is more secure in office, and when veto players are more hawkish. These findings support my theory regarding the importance of the ability to follow through on resolved statements as a condition influencing statements' effectiveness. This indicates that considering the ability to follow through in a detailed way is important for understanding and predicting when resolved statements will influence adversary behavior.

The results also suggest support for the theory of international reputational costs. This too is an important finding because, although I have focused on the ability to follow through as an underexplored condition for understanding the effectiveness of statements, the costs of backing down also play a theoretically important role. Without any cost for backing down from or making statements, resolved statements would be made constantly and most likely dismissed as uninformative regardless of the ability to follow through. Therefore, considering both international reputational costs and the ability to follow through together provides a more complete understanding of when resolved statements are likely to be effective.

TABLE 4.4 *Summary of Additional Robustness Check Results*

Interacted Variable: (across)	Relative Capabilities	Republicans in Congress	Net Approval	Non-Win. Statements
Control for additional variables	***	***	**	***
Matched sample	**	***	*	–
Drop top 10 Cook's D values	**	***	***	**
Drop top 20 Cook's D values	–	***	**	*
Indicator for stat. score > 75th percentile	–	**	**	–
Natural log of statement score	***	***	**	**
10-day pre-MID collection period	*	**	*	**
60-day pre-MID collection period	**	**	*	**
1-weight dictionary	***	***	**	***
10-weight dictionary	***	***	**	***
Drop MIDs won by force	**	***	*	**
Drop one-day MIDs	**	***	**	–
Drop non-revisionist MIDs	***	***	**	**
Drop unclear/compromise outcomes	***	***	***	***
Drop overlapping MIDs	***	***	**	**
Retain only one dyad per MID	***	***	**	***
Linear time trend	***	***	***	***
President indicator variables	***	***	**	***
Correct proportional odds violations	**	***	**	***
Drop capabilities to include 2008–2010		***	***	***

Note: This table summarizes the significance of the interaction terms in the robustness checks.
* $P < .10$, ** $P < .05$, *** $P < .01$. A dash (–) indicates that the result is not significant ($P \geq .10$). All significant results are significant in the same direction as the main results. The first regression includes the same controls as the first regression in Table 3.3.

This chapter has not found any support for the popular theory of domestic audience costs. It is possible that the impact of audience costs exists but is difficult to identify empirically. One challenge is that although security in office has two potentially competing effects – making it less risky to follow through *and* less risky to back down – my research design is only capable of picking up whichever effect is strongest. Therefore, the results do not prove that domestic audience costs are nonexistent, but audience cost theory does not appear to have as much explanatory power as my theory of the ability to follow through or international reputational cost theory.

5

Relationship among the Conditions for Statements' Effectiveness

The previous chapter showed that various factors related to the ability to follow through, as well as international reputation, have a significant impact on the effectiveness of US presidential statements of resolve. Up until this point, I have considered each of the conditions that influence the effectiveness of statements separately in order to clearly understand the mechanisms and empirical evidence associated with each. In reality, however, all of these conditions can influence the effectiveness of statements simultaneously. From the results in Chapter 4, we can infer that it is helpful for the effectiveness of statements to have as many as possible of the factors related to the ability to follow through – hawkish veto players, strong security in office, and a strong military – and not to have backed down from a large number of statements in the recent past. Yet it is possible to go beyond this inference and consider whether the conditions for the effectiveness of statements interact together in more complicated ways.

This chapter will consider three main categories of relationships among the conditions that impact the effectiveness of statements. First, it will consider the relationship among the factors related to the ability to follow through – military strength, the hawkishness of veto players, and security of the leader in office – and discuss whether they enhance or undermine each other. Second, it will consider the relationship between the ability to follow through and the country's international reputation for following through on statements. Finally, it will consider the relationship between hawkish veto players and the domestic political opposition. Domestic opposition is not one of the factors about which I previously offered hypotheses, but some theories would suggest that it has the potential to complicate the impact of hawkish veto players on the effectiveness of statements.

RELATIONSHIP AMONG FACTORS ASSOCIATED WITH THE ABILITY TO FOLLOW THROUGH

I will begin by considering the relationship among military strength, hawkish veto players, and security in office – all factors associated with the ability to follow through on resolved statements. The previous chapter showed that all of these factors are individually associated with a greater positive impact of statements on conflict outcomes. However, it is possible to explore the relationship among these factors in more detail. Do these factors enhance each other, meaning that one has a greater effect when the others are present? Or do they crowd each other out, meaning that if one is present, the others provide little additional benefit?

I theorize that the answer to both of these questions is yes, but under different circumstances. I expect that when one of the factors related to the ability to follow through has a low value, an increase in that factor will enhance the impact of the other factors. In contrast, when one of the factors related to the ability to follow through already has a high value, a further increase in that factor will tend to crowd out the impact of the other factors. Thus, the relationship among the factors associated with the ability to follow through is predicted to be non-monotonic.

To see why this is the case, first consider the situation in which one or more of the factors associated with the ability to follow through has a very low value. In this situation, the low value of one factor has the potential to undermine the ability to follow through enough that the other factors become irrelevant. For example, if military strength is so low that a country has no reasonable chance of defeating its adversary in battle, then it will not have a credible ability to follow through on its statements regardless of domestic political conditions. Therefore, the level of hawkish veto players or security in office will be irrelevant when military strength is too low. Similarly, if veto players are so uniformly dovish that there is no chance military action will be approved, this alone will be enough to undermine the ability to follow through, and the level of military strength or security in office will not matter. Finally, if the leader is so insecure in office that he or she is unwilling to risk military action under any circumstances, then the level of military strength and hawkish veto players will not play a role. Thus, when one factor associated with the ability to follow through has a very low value, the other factors are likely to have little or no impact on the effectiveness of statements. In this situation, any increase in the factor with the low value will help to restore the ability to follow through and allow the other factors to become more influential. Therefore, at low values of the factors associated with the ability to follow through, I expect them to mutually enhance each other's influence on the effectiveness of resolved statements.

In contrast, when the factors related to the ability to follow through have very high values, they can begin to crowd out each other's impact. For example, if a country has much higher military strength than its adversary, the leader may be willing to risk military conflict even if he or she is somewhat insecure, and even somewhat dovish veto players might be willing to approve military action because the costs are expected to be low. Furthermore, if a country has extremely hawkish veto players, they may be willing to approve military

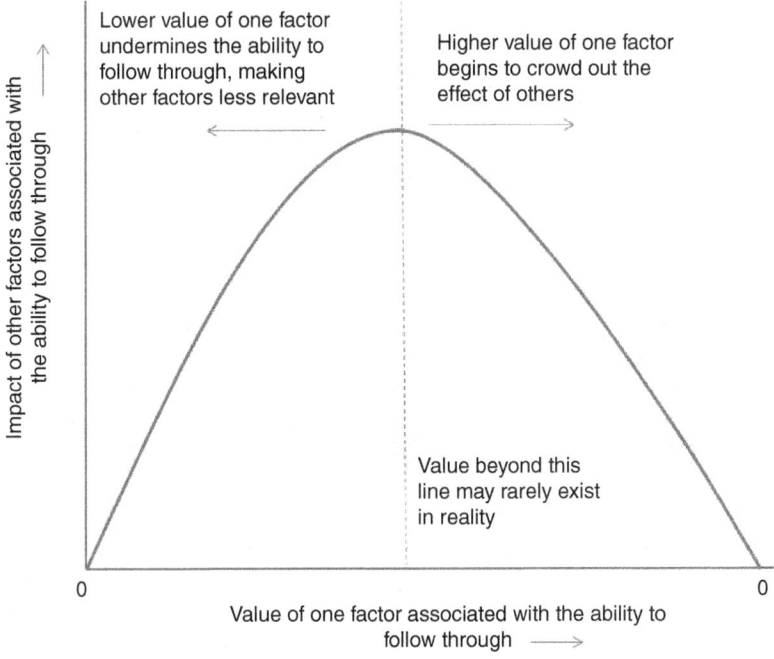

FIGURE 5.1 Expected Relationship among Factors

action even if the military balance is not extremely favorable and even if the leader is too insecure in office to have much leverage over them. Finally, if a leader is highly secure in office, he or she might be willing to risk military action even if the country's relative military strength is not very high and might be able to persuade veto players to go along with it even if they are not very hawkish. Therefore, a very high value of one factor related to the ability to follow through can potentially make the other factors less necessary.

The previous discussion suggests that each factor related to the ability to follow through should have the greatest impact on the effectiveness of statements when the other factors have middling values. This is because an overly low or overly high value of one factor can make the other factors less relevant. This expectation is depicted in Figure 5.1, which shows that the expected relationship among the factors related to the ability to follow through resembles an inverted U. One remaining question, however, is whether such low or high values occur in reality. Based on the results in Chapter 4, which showed that the average marginal effect of resolved statements cannot be distinguished from zero at the lowest values of relative military capabilities, Republicans in Congress, and net approval, it seems reasonable to believe that there are low enough values of these factors to make the other factors irrelevant. However, whether it is truly possible to have such high military strength that military conflict is virtually free of risk, to have veto players hawkish enough to approve almost any military action, or to have a leader so secure in office that he or she would take practically any military risk is more debatable. If such high values do not exist or only rarely exist in reality, then we may not actually observe much of the downward sloping portion of the curve depicted in Figure 5.1.

Empirical Testing

I will now turn to examining the relationship among the factors related to the ability to follow through empirically. I utilize the same dataset as in Chapters 3 and 4, which records the level of US presidential statements of resolve made in dyadic MIDs between 1950 and 2010. As in Chapter 4, I use the percentage of military capabilities in a dyad held by the United States to measure military strength, the percentage of Republicans in Congress to measure the hawkishness of veto players, and net approval to measure security in office. In Chapter 4, I interacted each of these variables with the statement score one by one in regressions predicting the conflict outcome. Here I use the same statistical model as a starting point, including the same dependent and control variables. Now, however, I interact the statement score with *two* variables related to the ability to follow through at once.[1] I estimate the following models:

Conflict Outcome = Statement Score + Relative Capabilities + Republicans in Congress +Statement Score*Relative Capabilities + Statement Score*Republicans in Congress +Relative Capabilities*Republicans in Congress + Statement Score*Relative Capabilities*Republicans in Congress + Controls

Conflict Outcome = Statement Score + Relative Capabilities + Net Approval + Statement Score*Relative Capabilities + Statement Score*Net Approval + Relative Capabilities*Net Approval + Statement Score*Relative Capabilities*Net Approval + Controls

Conflict Outcome = Statement Score + Republicans in Congress + Net Approval + Statement Score*Republicans in Congress + Statement Score*Net Approval + Republicans in Congress*Net Approval + Statement Score*Republicans in Congress*Net Approval + Controls

The full results of the models are available in the Online Appendix, but the large number of interactions makes them difficult to interpret by simply looking at the coefficients and standard errors. Therefore, I focus here on examining the marginal effects predicted by the models. I begin by graphing the average

---

[1] It is not feasible to interact more than two variables with statements of resolve at once because the need to include all of the related interaction terms (see Braumoeller 2004) would lead to too much collinearity, and the results would be too difficult to interpret.

marginal effect of statements of resolve on the probability of a winning outcome under various scenarios. The upper graph in Figure 5.2 illustrates how the marginal effect of the statement score is affected by the percentage of Republicans in Congress at the minimum and maximum levels of relative military capabilities. When the level of relative capabilities is at its minimum, 0.43, meaning that the United States is slightly less powerful than its MID adversary, the marginal effect of resolved statements is close to zero at all levels of Republicans in Congress. Thus, the level of hawkish veto players barely influences the marginal effect of statements in this scenario. In contrast, when the level of relative capabilities is at its maximum, 0.9999 (rounded to 1), the marginal effect of statements is not statistically distinct from zero at low levels of Republicans, but it increases and becomes positive and significant at higher levels of Republicans. Thus, the level of Republicans in Congress has a significant impact on the effectiveness of statements only when US military power is sufficiently high relative to the MID adversary. Insufficient military strength undermines both the effectiveness of statements themselves and the impact of hawkish veto players on the effectiveness of statements.

It is also possible to study the interaction between resolved statements, military strength, and hawkish veto players from the opposite direction. The bottom graph in Figure 5.2 shows how the level of relative military capabilities impacts the marginal effect of the statement score at the minimum and maximum levels of Republicans in Congress. At the lowest percentage of Republicans, the marginal effect of statements is never statistically distinct from zero, regardless of the level of military capabilities. In contrast, at the highest percentage of Republicans, the marginal effect of statements increases with capabilities and achieves statistical significance at high capability levels. Therefore, when comparing the effects at minimum and maximum values, military strength and hawkish veto players have been found to mutually enhance each other's impact on the effectiveness of statements. A lower level of one variable undermines the influence of the other, while a higher level of one variable increases the influence of the other.

Next, I analyze how relative military capabilities and net approval for the president interact with each other in influencing the effectiveness of resolved statements. The upper graph in Figure 5.3 shows that when the level of relative capabilities is minimized, net approval does not have a significant impact on the marginal effect of statements, which never gets far above zero. In contrast, when relative capabilities are maximized, an increase in the level of net approval causes a substantial increase in statements' marginal effect, and the marginal effect becomes positive and significant when net presidential approval is in the low positive range. Graphing the marginal effect of statements the opposite way, as shown in the lower graph in Figure 5.3, reveals a similar pattern. When net approval is minimized, the marginal effect of statements is not statistically distinct from zero at any level of capabilities, but when net approval is maximized, the marginal effect increases significantly as the United States

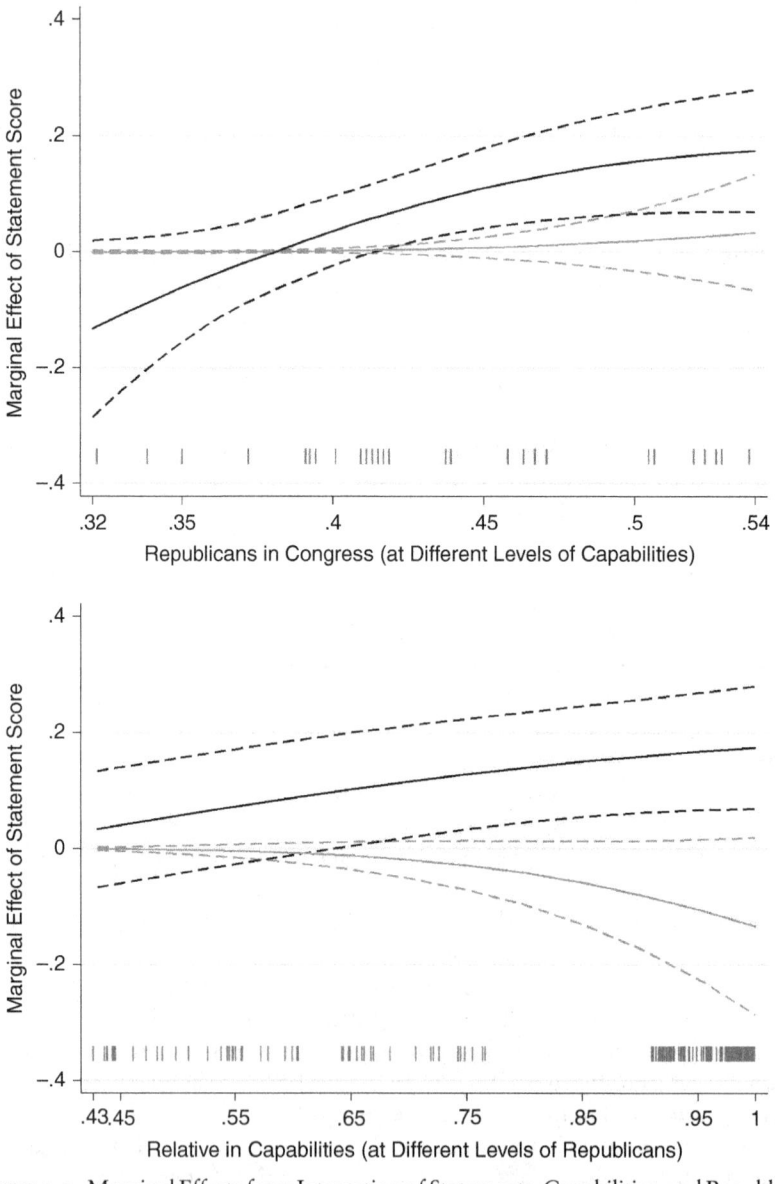

FIGURE 5.2 Marginal Effects from Interaction of Statements, Capabilities, and Republicans
Note: Each graph shows the impact of one variable on the average marginal effect of statements at different levels of a third variable (identified in parentheses). The black line represents the scenario in which the third variable is *maximized*, while the gray line represents the scenario in which it is *minimized*. The dotted lines are 95 percent confidence bounds, which are generally wider than in the previous chapter because the additional interactions increase the level of multicollinearity. The rug plots show the distribution of the variable on the x axis.

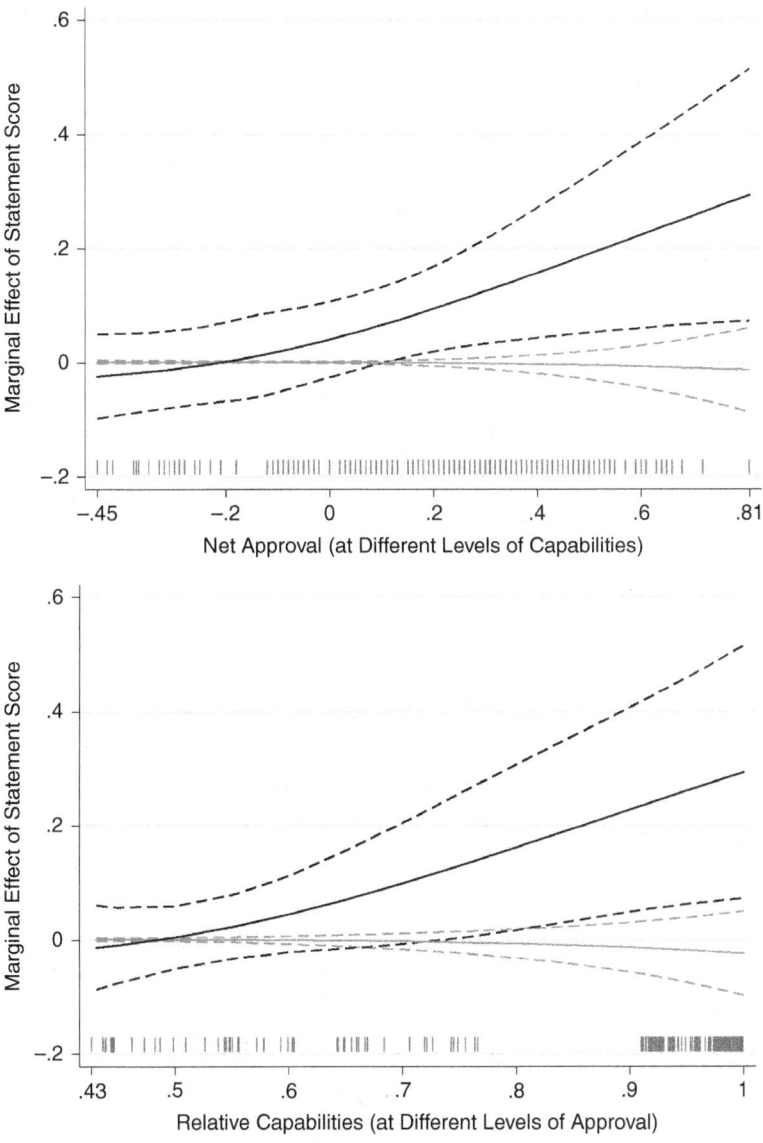

FIGURE 5.3 Marginal Effects from Interaction of Statements, Capabilities, and Approval
Note: The interpretation is the same as for Figure 5.2. Each graph shows the impact of one variable on the average marginal effect of statements at different levels of a third variable (identified in parentheses). The black line represents the scenario in which the third variable is *maximized*, while the gray line represents the scenario in which it is *minimized*.

becomes more powerful relative to its adversary. Therefore, Figure 5.3 indicates that security in office and military capabilities also enhance each other's impact on resolved statements' effectiveness.

Finally, I analyze the joint impact of hawkish veto players and security in office on the effectiveness of resolved statements. The top graph in Figure 5.4 shows how the marginal effect of statements changes with the percentage of Republicans in Congress at the minimum and maximum levels of net approval. In this case, the confidence bounds are wider, and the marginal effect is never statistically distinct from zero due to greater multicollinearity. However, the substantive increase in the marginal effect as the level of Republicans rises is clearly greater when the approval level is maximized than when it is minimized. Therefore, the evidence does indicate that a higher level of net approval enhances the impact of Republicans in Congress, although the evidence is weaker than in the previous cases. Similarly, the lower graph in Figure 5.4 shows weak evidence that a higher level of Republicans enhances the impact of net approval. When the percentage of Republicans is maximized, increasing approval produces a positive though insignificant change in the marginal effect of statements. In contrast, at the lowest percentage of Republicans, the impact of net approval on the marginal effect of statements is negative and insignificant. Therefore, it also appears that security in office and hawkish veto players augment each other's impact on the effectiveness of statements.

So far, the evidence has indicated that all of the factors related to the ability to follow through mutually enhance each other's impact on the effectiveness of statements. We have seen that an overly low value of one factor can undermine the influence of the other factors as well as the effectiveness of statements themselves. Thus, the evidence so far fits with the first part of the inverted-U relationship portrayed earlier in Figure 5.1. What about the second part of the relationship in which the effects of variables related to the ability to follow through are predicted to crowd each other out at very high levels? To see if there is truly a crowding-out effect and an inverted-U relationship, it is necessary to compare the impact of each factor at more than just the minimum and maximum values of the other factors. Because a graph with so many comparisons would be unreadable, I instead present Table 5.1.

Table 5.1 shows how each variable related to the ability to follow through influences the average marginal effect of statements at five different levels of the other variables. For example, the first line of the table shows that when the percentage of Republicans in Congress is at its minimum level, the change in the marginal effect of statements between the lowest and highest level of relative military capabilities is −0.133. This indicates that when the percentage of Republicans is minimized, statements have a smaller marginal effect at high levels of military strength than at low levels of military strength, which fits with Figure 5.2. The P-value indicates that this negative effect is only weakly significant. The subsequent rows show that as the percentage of Republicans in Congress increases, the impact of military strength on the marginal effect of

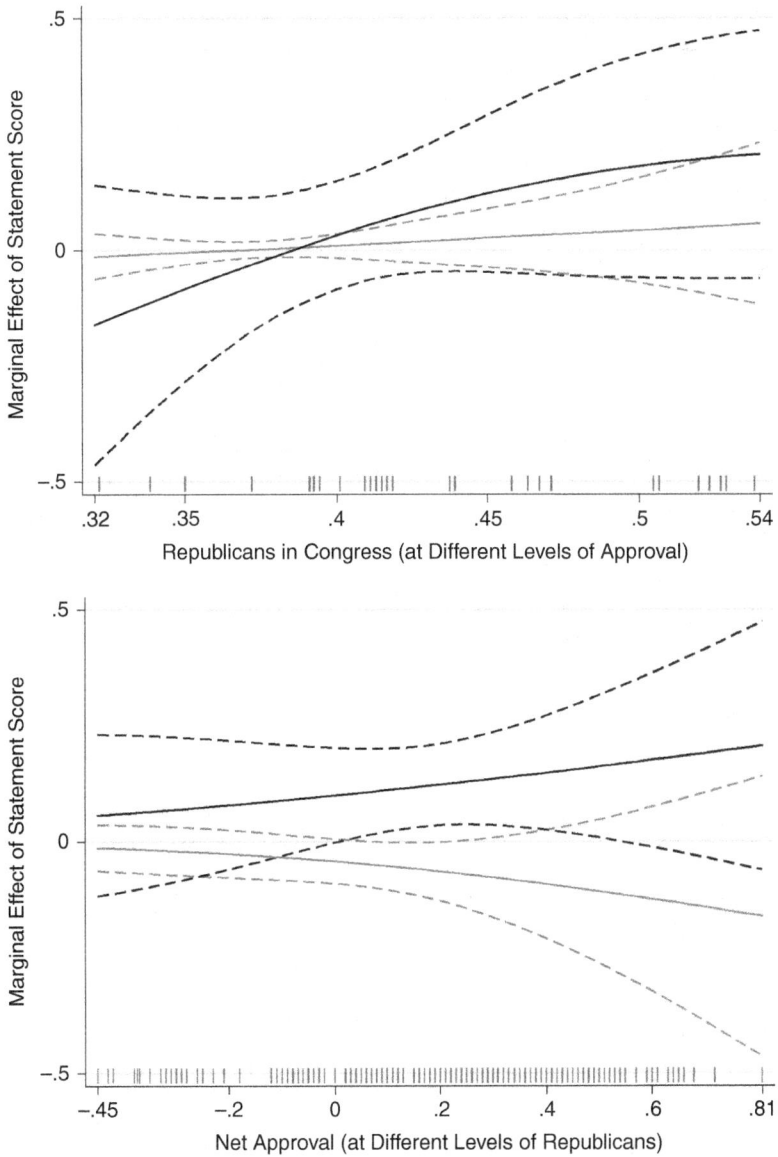

FIGURE 5.4 Marginal Effects from Interaction of Statements, Republicans, and Approval
Note: The interpretation is the same as for Figure 5.2. Each graph shows the impact of one variable on the average marginal effect of statements at different levels of a third variable (identified in parentheses). The black line represents the scenario in which the third variable is maximized, while the gray line represents the scenario in which it is minimized.

TABLE 5.1 *Changes in the Marginal Effect of the Statement Score*

Change when Relative Capabilities Goes from Min. to Max.		P-Value
At Republicans in Congress = 0.32 (min)	−0.133	0.088
At Republicans in Congress = 0.38	−0.003	0.937
At Republicans in Congress = 0.43	+0.079	0.014
At Republicans in Congress = 0.49	**+0.133**	**0.007**
At Republicans in Congress = 0.54 (max)	+0.141	0.056
At net approval = −0.45 (min)	−0.025	0.506
At net approval = −0.14	+0.010	0.775
At net approval = 0.18	+0.089	0.017
At net approval = 0.49	**+0.192**	**0.006**
At net approval = 0.81 (max)	+0.307	0.008
Change when Republicans Goes from Min. to Max		**P-Value**
At relative capabilities = 0.43 (min)	+0.034	0.511
At relative capabilities = 0.58	+0.087	0.071
At relative capabilities = 0.62	+0.143	0.002
At relative capabilities = 0.86	**+0.215**	**0.0003**
At relative capabilities = 1 (max)	+0.308	0.001
At net approval = −0.45 (min)	+0.070	0.491
At net approval = −0.14	+0.116	0.130
At net approval = 0.18	**+0.183**	**0.002**
At net approval = 0.49	+0.266	0.032
At net approval = 0.81 (max)	+0.368	0.123
Change when Net Approval Goes from Min. to Max.		**P-Value**
At relative capabilities = 0.43 (min)	−0.015	0.701
At relative capabilities = 0.58	+0.036	0.279
At relative capabilities = 0.62	+0.055	0.165
At relative capabilities = 0.86	+0.212	0.026
At relative capabilities = 1 (max)	**+0.318**	**0.017**
At Republicans in Congress = 0.32 (min)	−0.149	0.393
At Republicans in Congress = 0.38	−0.016	0.830
At Republicans in Congress = 0.43	+0.070	0.436
At Republicans in Congress = 0.49	**+0.132**	**0.410**
At Republicans in Congress = 0.54 (max)	+0.149	0.479

Note: The middle column gives the change in the average marginal effect of the statement score on the probability of winning. The right column gives the P-value for whether the change is statistically different from 0, based on Wald tests.

statements becomes positive and more significant. However, the change in the marginal effect of statements caused by a change in military strength is most significant when the level of Republicans is slightly *below* its maximum. Therefore, the first five rows of Table 5.1 do provide some evidence of an inverted-U relationship in which the factors related to the ability to follow through enhance each other's impact at low levels but begin to crowd out each other's effect at the highest levels.

The rest of Table 5.1 shows a similar pattern. In almost every case, the change in the marginal effect of statements caused by an increase in one factor is most significant when the other interacted factor is at less than its maximum value. Therefore, there is evidence of both an undermining effect and a crowding-out effect, which is in keeping with the inverted-U relationship depicted in Figure 5.1. However, we usually do not observe the full "U" because in most cases, the impact of one variable does not actually become insignificant again as the other variables reach their maximum. This fits with the expectation that a low value of one factor undermining the impact of the other factors is a more common problem than a high value of one factor crowding the impact of the other factors out.

THE ABILITY TO FOLLOW THROUGH AND INTERNATIONAL REPUTATION

I will next consider the relationship between the conditions related to the ability to follow through on statements and international reputation. We found in the previous chapter that a damaged international reputation can undermine the effectiveness of resolved statements. It seems likely that reputational damage will also undermine the influence of the factors related to the ability to follow through on the effectiveness of statements. If the leader already has a damaged reputation for credibility, this implies that the leader does not have much to lose by backing down again (Sartori 2005) or perhaps is a generally dishonest or unreliable individual. This is likely to make the adversary doubt that the leader's statements are truly a costly signal of resolve. If the adversary believes that the leader's statements are empty words, then the adversary is less likely to care about whether the leader has the ability to follow through on the statements. Therefore, I expect the factors related to the ability to follow through – namely, military strength, hawkish veto players, and security in office – to have a greater impact on the effectiveness of statements made by leaders with good international reputations for credibility than by leaders with damaged reputations.

I investigate this expectation using the same basic strategy used previously. Again, I utilize the same dataset and control variables as in Chapter 4. I operationalize the concept of international reputation using the measure of non-winning statements introduced in Chapter 4. Recall that this variable

TABLE 5.2 *Changes in the Marginal Effect of the Statement Score in More Scenarios*

Change when Relative Capabilities Goes from Min. to Max.		P-Value
At previous non-winning statements = 0 (min)	+0.090	0.011
At previous non-winning statements = 2.5	+0.069	0.097
At previous non-winning statements = 5	+0.031	0.704
At previous non-winning statements = 7.5	−0.028	0.850
At previous non-winning statements = 10.3 (max)	−0.111	0.644
Change when Republicans in Congress Goes from Min. to Max.		P-Value
At previous non-winning statements = 0 (min)	+0.213	0.001
At previous non-winning statements = 2.5	+0.193	0.322
At previous non-winning statements = 5	−0.029	0.961
At previous non-winning statements = 7.5	−0.147	0.705
At previous non-winning statements = 10.3 (max)	−0.101	0.670
Change when Net Approval Goes from Min. to Max.		P-Value
At previous non-winning statements = 0 (min)	+0.152	0.015
At previous non-winning statements = 2.5	+0.073	0.609
At previous non-winning statements = 5	−0.104	0.759
At previous non-winning statements = 7.5	−0.252	0.498
At previous non-winning statements = 10.3 (max)	−0.279	0.385

Note: The middle column gives the change in the average marginal effect of the statement score on the probability of winning. The right column gives the P-value for whether the change is statistically different from zero, based on Wald tests.

captures the level of resolved statements that the US president made in the last non-winning US MID. I include this variable in three-way interactions with the statement score for the current MID and with each of the factors associated with the ability to follow through in turn. As before, I show the full results of these models in the Online Appendix, but here I present a summary of the substantive effects.

Table 5.2 shows how the average marginal effect of statements changes as each factor associated with the ability to follow through goes from its minimum to its maximum value at various levels of previous non-winning statements. Looking at the differences in marginal effects, we can see that relative military capabilities, Republicans in Congress, and net approval for the president each causes a positive and significant change in the marginal effect of resolved statements when the level of previous non-winning statements is at its minimum value, which is zero. This means that all three variables have the expected positive impact on the effectiveness of statements when the US international reputation has not been damaged by backing down from resolved statements in the most recent previous MID. However, as the level of previous non-winning statements increases, the significance of these factors' impacts rapidly diminishes. At a level of previous non-winning statements of only 2.5, there is already very little evidence that factors related to the ability to follow through have any significant impact on the effectiveness of statements. Graphs of the marginal effects based on the same models (shown in the Online Appendix) also show that the marginal effect of statements themselves never achieves significance when the score for previous non-winning statements is 2.5 or above.

These regression results confirm that a damaged international reputation can undermine the impact of factors related to the ability to follow through on the effectiveness of statements. It appears that if the adversary believes a leader's statements lack credibility due to a substantial history of bluffing, then having military strength, hawkish veto players, or security in office will not do much to help the effectiveness of statements. Therefore, the ability to follow through matters more when the United States has a credible reputation and less when it has a reputation for bluffing.

IMPACT OF DOMESTIC OPPOSITION

Finally, I will consider the impact of domestic opposition parties on the effectiveness of resolved statements. Up until now, I have largely left aside the question of how domestic competition among political parties interacts with my theory of the ability to follow through on statements. However, the political incentives of the domestic opposition could have an influence on the ability to follow through. In many countries, the opposition has some veto power (Levy and Mabe 2004). This is certainly true in the United States because the political party in opposition to the president always has at least some representation in Congress, and it is not uncommon for the opposition party to have a majority in Congress.

It is therefore necessary to consider the incentives of the opposition party to support or oppose following through on statements of resolve. Schultz (1998) argues that it is in the interest of the opposition to support a leader's threats when the leader is highly resolved because a supportive opposition can share the political benefits of a successful conflict outcome. Ramsay (2004) makes a similar argument, starting with different assumptions. In contrast, Shea, Teo, and Levy (2014) make the case that the opposition may oppose military conflict even when the leader is highly resolved, in large part because the opposition will fear the increased power and popularity that war can confer upon a leader. Howell and Pevehouse (2007, 35–38) similarly argue that opposition members of the US Congress are less likely to support presidential use of force because they trust the president less, are less likely to share in the political gains from a successful outcome, and are less dependent on the president for political favors. Howell and Pevehouse also show that

US presidents are less likely to use force when their opposition in Congress is stronger.

Much of the research cited previously suggests that the domestic opposition may have the incentive to oppose following through on statements of resolve for domestic political reasons. If this is the case, then having a large number of opposition veto players might reduce the ability to follow through and undercut the effectiveness of resolved statements. However, as noted in Chapter 1, veto players are motivated not only by political incentives but also by ideology. Most politicians have genuinely held policy preferences and seek office with the goal of implementing those preferences. A complete betrayal of those preferences upon achieving veto player status would not only run counter to that goal but also alienate their electoral base. Therefore, we should not necessarily assume that political incentives related to party competition will overwhelm the underlying hawkish or dovish preferences of veto players.

It is not difficult to think of examples from modern history in which the hawkish or dovish ideologies of US political parties seem to have trumped their partisan loyalty or antagonism toward the president. The Republican Party was supportive of Kennedy's blockade during the Cuban Missile Crisis, Johnson's commitment not to back down during the Vietnam War, Carter's decision to arm Islamic fighters in response to the Soviet invasion of Afghanistan, and Clinton's show of force during the 1996 Taiwan Strait Crisis. Furthermore, when President Obama requested congressional authorization to use force in response to Syria's use of chemical weapons in 2013, he was supported by some prominent Republicans and opposed by many Democrats (Blake and Sullivan 2013; Gearan, O'Keefe, and Branigin 2013). Even more recently, in 2014 congressional debates over authorizing military action against the Islamic State, most Democrats supported restrictions on the use of ground troops, while many Republicans opposed placing this type of restriction on the commander in chief (Peters 2014).

Therefore, it remains an open question whether party politics or hawkish or dovish policy preferences will dominate the decision-making process of veto players when they are confronted with an opportunity to support or oppose following through on statements of resolve. A related, but distinct, question for predicting the effectiveness of resolved statements is whether *adversaries* view policy preferences or party politics as more important when analyzing a leader's ability to follow through. Ultimately, this is an empirical question. In Chapter 4, I addressed this question briefly by splitting the sample between Republican presidents and Democratic presidents and found that the level of Republicans in Congress had a similar effect regardless of whether the president was also a Republican. In this chapter, I address the question of the relationship between the effect of parties in Congress and the president's own party in a more sophisticated way, using a three-variable interaction between the statement score, the percentage of Republicans in Congress, and an indicator variable for a Republican president.

TABLE 5.3 *Average Marginal Effect of the Statement Score in Different Scenarios*

	Under Democratic President	Under Republican President	Difference
At Min. Republicans	−0.074	−0.090	−0.016
At Max. Republicans	0.095	0.187	0.092
Difference	0.169***	0.277***	

Note: The stars indicate whether the difference in marginal effects is statistically distinct from 0, based on Wald tests. * P < .10, ** P < .05, *** P < .01.

As before, I present the full results of the model in the Online Appendix and discuss only substantive effects here. Table 5.3 shows the average marginal effect of the statement score on the probability of a winning outcome at the minimum and maximum levels of Republicans in Congress under both Democratic presidents and Republican presidents. The table shows that under presidents from both parties, an increase in the number of Republicans in Congress increases the marginal effect of presidential statements. The size of the increase is larger under Republican presidents, but the significance of the increase is almost identical in both cases. The fact that an increase in congressional Republicans has a strong positive effect under presidents from both parties indicates that party politics play very little role in the effectiveness of resolved statements. This also suggests that both Democratic and Republican presidents should prefer to have more Republicans in Congress for purposes of making their statements effective on the international stage (although Democratic presidents would undoubtedly prefer more Democrats in Congress for other purposes).

It is possible to further examine the role of opposition by comparing the columns in Table 5.3 instead of the rows. We see that when the level of Republicans in Congress is minimized, and Democrats thus have their largest possible majority in Congress, statements are slightly more effective (or at least slightly less ineffective) under Democratic presidents. In contrast, when the majority of Republicans in Congress is as large as possible, statements are more effective under Republican presidents. This provides a hint that being part of the opposition party might make veto players slightly more likely to play an obstructionist role, but these effects are far from significant. Thus, there is no clear evidence that domestic opposition dynamics impact the effectiveness of resolved statements very much. At least from the perspective of how adversaries evaluate statements of resolve, the hawkish or dovish ideological beliefs of veto players appear to matter much more than whether they have the political incentive to undermine the president.

One final insight to take away from this analysis is that the president's own political party does not matter very much for the effectiveness of presidential statements. Regardless of the percentage of Republicans in Congress, the marginal effects of statements by Republican and Democratic presidents are statistically indistinguishable.[2] This might be because even though Democrats generally have more dovish reputations, making resolved statements reveals enough about their own preferences to compensate for this. Some research also suggests that presidents gain more domestic approval by acting contrary to their type, giving Democrats the incentive to be more hawkish and Republicans the incentive to be more dovish after assuming the presidency (Trager and Vavreck 2011). This could wash out the differences between the parties, making adversaries expect similar behavior from presidents of both parties.

SUMMING UP

This chapter has explored the relationship among various conditions that might influence the effectiveness of statements of resolve. It has found that all of the factors related to the ability to follow through enhance each other's impact on statements' effectiveness for the most part, although they can begin to crowd out each other's impact at the highest levels. It has also found that having an international reputation for credibility enhances the impact of factors related to the ability to follow through. In general, the findings indicate that the effectiveness of resolved statements is somewhat fragile because the absence or near-absence of even one of the conditions that contribute to effectiveness – either a credible reputation or one of the factors related to the ability to follow through – can render statements ineffective. Keep in mind, however, that Chapter 3 found statements are, for the most part, effective. Therefore, cases in which the absence of a single condition undermines the effectiveness of statements are the exception, not the rule. This is not a contradiction because middling values for the factors related to the ability to follow through are more common than very low values, and the United States begins most disputes without a reputation for backing down from many previous statements.

In addition, this chapter has found that the effectiveness of resolved statements is influenced much more by the hawkishness or dovishness of veto players than by party politics. Adversaries seem to view resolved statements as more credible when there are more Republicans in Congress, regardless of whether the Republican Party is the president's party or the opposition party. It also appears that Democratic and Republican presidents can make about equally effective statements of resolve. These findings provide some evidence in favor of the traditional idea that politics stops at the "water's edge," or at least that the adversaries who respond to US statements of resolve perceive that it does.

---

[2] I confirmed that this is the case at intermediate levels of Republicans in Congress as well as at the minimum and maximum levels.

This chapter has presented the most nuanced description yet of how the effectiveness of resolved statements is influenced by various conditions simultaneously. However, statistical analysis naturally has limits in its ability to distinguish between multiple possible causes of an effect or to definitely prove the existence of a causal relationship at all. The next chapters will use case studies to explore the causal impact of conditions related to the ability to follow through in more detail.

PART III

CASE STUDIES

6

Cuban Missile Crisis

The statistical tests in the preceding chapters indicate support for my theory regarding the importance of the ability to follow through on statements of resolve. The results show that higher levels of resolved statements are more likely to be associated with favorable conflict outcomes when military strength is higher relative to the adversary, when domestic veto players are more hawkish, and when the leader issuing the statements is more secure in office. The previous chapter presented evidence that these conditions enhance each other's impact, at least up to a point. Although the statistical results in Chapters 3–5 are strong and robust, an inherent limitation of statistical analysis is that while it can tell us that a statistical association exists, it cannot tell us *why* it exists. Therefore, although my theory is the most compelling explanation for the statistical relationships that we observed, the statistical analysis alone cannot fully confirm the causal mechanisms posited by the theory.

In order to gain greater insight into the validity of the causal mechanisms proposed by my theory, I will also discuss three historical cases: the Cuban Missile Crisis, US-Soviet tensions under President Reagan, and the Vietnam War. This chapter begins with a fuller discussion of the purpose of the case studies and how they were selected. It then provides an analysis of the Cuban Missile Crisis case, describing President Kennedy's statements of resolve and how Soviet leaders evaluated them. The other two cases are discussed in the following chapters.

PURPOSE OF CASE STUDIES AND CASE SELECTION

The main argument of this book is that statements of resolve will be more effective when the leader issuing them has a greater ability to follow through on them. When a leader lacks the ability to follow through, adversaries are likely to feel free to ignore his or her statements. In contrast, when a leader has the ability to follow through, adversaries must pay close attention to the leader's statements in order to determine his or her resolve to follow through. The statistical evidence presented so far fits with this theoretical argument, but it cannot provide direct insight into the actual decision-making process of government officials who hear statements of resolve. In order to verify that government officials actually recognize that certain conditions increase the ability to follow through on statements of resolve and that this influences how the officials interpret and react to the statements, it is necessary to do more in-depth qualitative analysis of certain historical cases.

My examination of historical cases focuses on how officials in one country perceived and reacted to statements of resolve by the leader of another country. My research analyzes the memoirs of officials and historical records of their private deliberations from both primary and secondary sources in order to understand their influences and motives. If my theory of the ability to follow through is correct, we would expect to see several pieces of evidence in the case studies. First, we would expect to see evidence that officials evaluate factors related to their adversaries' ability to follow through on statements of resolve, including military strength, the hawkishness of veto players, and security in office. Second, we would expect to see that particularly when their adversaries' ability to follow through is high, officials pay close attention to statements of resolve and make inferences about their adversary's resolve based on them. Third, we would expect to see that when officials become convinced that an adversary has both the resolve and the ability to follow through, they back down or at least give more consideration to backing down.

In selecting the cases to test these expectations, I took into account several considerations. First, I wanted the qualitative analysis to maintain continuity with the statistical chapters and be able to shed additional light on some of the observations that were part of the quantitative analysis. I therefore opted to select cases from the universe of US military conflicts and crises in the post–World War II era and analyze how US adversaries perceived and reacted to US statements of resolve in these cases. Second, it was important to select cases for which information on the US adversary's analysis of US statements and ability to follow through is available. I therefore decided to focus on significant conflicts and crises during the Cold War because these are well documented from both sides, and more historical information has become available since the Cold War ended. Focusing on Cold War conflicts and tensions also allowed me to select cases that are somewhat comparable to each other in terms of the nature of the adversary and the values at stake. This similarity makes the effects resulting from differences in the ability to follow through easier to observe.

The case study analysis focuses primarily on the impact of the hawkishness of veto players and the president's security in office on the effectiveness of US statements of resolve. The impact of military strength, the other main condition associated with the ability to follow through, is uncontroversial enough to require less in-depth analysis, although I do discuss it briefly in each case study. I therefore selected my cases in order to have variation in the

TABLE 6.1 *Summary of Case Selection Criteria*

		Veto players	
		More dovish	More hawkish
Security in office	Lower	Vietnam War	Cuban Missile Crisis
	Higher	Reagan-era tensions	

hawkishness of veto players and the president's security in office. Specifically, from the universe of major Cold War conflicts and crisis, I selected one case in which the president had particularly hawkish veto players, but not great security in office; a second case in which the president did have high security in office, but not extremely hawkish veto players; and a third case in which the US president had neither hawkish veto players nor security in office. The case in which the president had very hawkish veto players is the Cuban Missile Crisis, while the case in which the president had strong security in office is the increase in US-Soviet tensions under President Reagan. The case in which the president lacked both hawkish veto players and security in office is the Vietnam War, particularly the later years of the war. This combination of cases allows me to compare the impact of each condition individually to the situation in which both conditions are lacking. Table 6.1 summarizes which conditions are present and absent in each case.

THE CUBAN MISSILE CRISIS

Having explained the purpose of the case studies and the case selection, I now turn to analyzing the Cuban Missile Crisis. The Cuban Missile Crisis began on October 16, 1962, when President Kennedy learned of Soviet nuclear missiles in Cuba from spy plane photos. The Kennedy administration kept the news private for several days, but Kennedy made a public speech on October 22 announcing the presence of the missiles, demanding their removal, and declaring a blockade around Cuba. The Soviet Union's initial public response was unyielding, and for several days, neither the United States nor the Soviet side budged. Then, on October 26, Soviet premier Khrushchev sent a message to Kennedy suggesting that he could withdraw the missiles from Cuba in exchange for a US pledge not to invade Cuba. On October 27, Khrushchev sent a second message adding the demand that US missiles be removed from Turkey. The Kennedy administration opted to publicly agree only to the conditions of Khrushchev's first offer, but it privately promised to withdraw its missiles from Turkey as well (Dobrynin 1995, 89–91). Khrushchev accepted this, and on October 28 the Soviet Union issued a message announcing the withdrawal of the missiles from Cuba and ending the crisis.

The Cuban Missile Crisis is therefore a case in which the United States achieved its desired outcome without resorting to the use of force. Although both sides made some concessions, the Soviet concession was bigger, and the crisis is generally considered a success for the United States. Because President Kennedy made high-profile statements of resolve both during and before the crisis, this is an excellent case for evaluating what makes these statements effective. My research shows that Khrushchev and other Soviet leaders paid close attention to Kennedy's statements. Their eventual decision to comply with Kennedy's public demand to remove the missiles was influenced by a variety of factors, including an increase in the US nuclear alert level and rising tension due to the shoot-down of a US spy plane (Taubman 2003, 566–573). Another crucial factor, which came up frequently in Soviet discussions but has not yet received much scholarly attention, is the hawkishness of US domestic veto players. Awareness that US veto players were hawkish made Soviet leaders take Kennedy's statements seriously from the beginning, and new intelligence indicating that veto players were pushing Kennedy more toward war played a key role in ultimately convincing them to comply with the demand in Kennedy's statements of resolve.

KENNEDY'S STATEMENTS

Chapter 2 showed that presidents in the first few decades after World War II made considerably fewer statements of resolve than modern presidents, and President Kennedy was no exception. As shown in Figure 6.1, Kennedy issued few resolved statements directed at the Soviet Union throughout most of the six months prior to the Cuban Missile Crisis. The figure shows a few spikes in the level of statements in the spring and summer, but they are small and not focused on Cuba. The statements represented by the most notable spikes in May through July were about West Berlin and Southeast Asia. Kennedy did not make any resolved statements about the Soviet relationship with Cuba until August 29, and even during his remarks on that date, most of his resolved words were about the Limited Test Ban Treaty negotiations rather than Soviet activities in Cuba.

In my previous quantitative analysis, I assumed that all resolved statements targeted at a particular country help to increase perceptions of resolve, even if they do not mention a specific issue in dispute. This case study helps to validate that decision because I show below that Khrushchev perceived Kennedy as generally unresolved across a range of issues, suggesting that he formed a holistic rather than issue-specific impression of resolve. However, considering all statements targeting the Soviet Union or only statements about the Soviet relationship with Cuba leads to a similar conclusion in this case – that the level of resolve conveyed in April

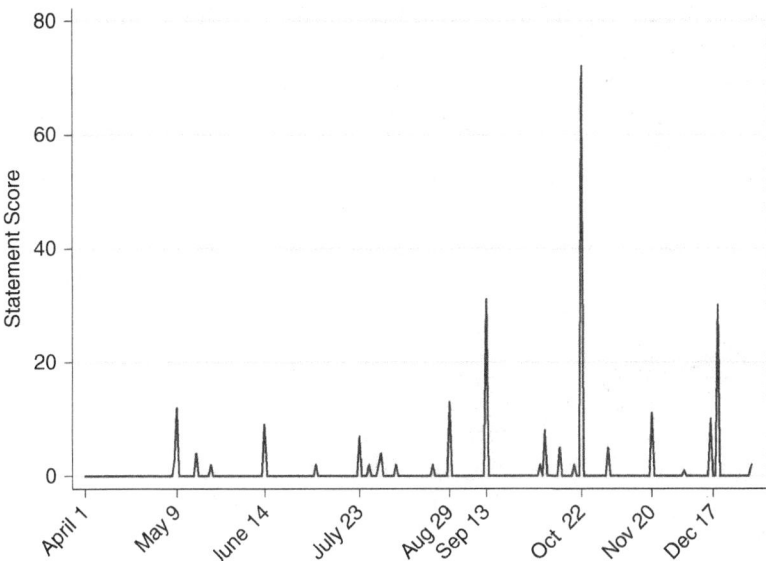

FIGURE 6.1 Kennedy's Resolved Statements Directed at the USSR in April–December 1962
Note: This figure measures statements of resolve using the main dictionary used in previous chapters.

through August, as Soviet leaders were considering and implementing their missile plan, was low.[1]

As concern about a Soviet military buildup in Cuba began to grow in the late summer and early fall, Kennedy's resolved rhetoric began to increase. The first statement specifically about Soviet missiles in Cuba was not actually spoken by Kennedy, but read by the White House press secretary on September 4, 1962. The statement said, "There is no evidence ... of the presence of offensive ground-to-ground missiles [in Cuba]; or of other significant offensive capability either in Cuban hands or under Soviet direction and guidance. Were it to be otherwise, the gravest issues would arise" (Department of State 1962). Kennedy reiterated this sentiment personally in a press conference on September 13, saying, "[I]f Cuba should ever ... become an offensive military base of significant capacity for the Soviet Union, then this country will do whatever must be done to protect its own security and that of its allies" (Peters and Woolley 2016). Figure 6.1 shows that Kennedy used more resolved language during this press conference than he had on any one day in

---

[1] Khrushchev apparently began considering the idea of nuclear missiles in Cuba in April, and the Soviet Presidium formally approved his plan on June 10 (Fursenko and Naftali 1997, 171, 187–189).

several months. Thus, for the first time Kennedy clearly convened his resolve to prevent a Soviet military buildup in Cuba. As demonstrated later in the chapter, this caused Khrushchev to raise his estimate of Kennedy's resolve.

After learning of the missiles in Cuba from U-2 spy plane photos on October 16, the Kennedy administration kept the news to itself for several days in order to take the time to examine its options. On October 22, Kennedy announced the presence of the missiles to the domestic public and the world in a highly resolved public speech. He denounced the Soviet Union for placing missiles in Cuba and demanded their withdrawal, saying, "[T]his secret, swift, and extraordinary buildup of Communist missiles ... in violation of Soviet assurances, and in defiance of American and hemispheric policy ... is a deliberately provocative and unjustified change in the status quo which cannot be accepted by this country." He went on to announce a US "quarantine" – effectively, a blockade – around Cuba to prevent the entry of additional weapons (Peters and Woolley 2016). This speech employed a large number of resolved words and represents by far the largest spike on Figure 6.1.

After this speech, Kennedy did not personally make any other public statements until the crisis was resolved, although the White House released several other written statements with similar sentiments (Peters and Woolley 2016). Some of the most significant communications between the US and Soviet governments, including Khrushchev's offer to exchange the Soviet missiles in Cuba for US missiles in Turkey, Kennedy's official response to the offer, and Khrushchev's formal acceptance of Kennedy's terms, were also issued as written public statements, which were disseminated by the press. This was done in large part because it was faster than waiting for communications to pass through official channels (Khrushchev 2000, 596, 615).

After the crisis was over, Figure 6.1 shows that Kennedy continued to make some resolved statements, although at a considerably lower level than during the height of the crisis. In November, he made statements urging the Soviets to continue carrying out the withdrawal of equipment from Cuba. In December, he used a fairly large number of resolved words in two question-and-answer sessions looking back on the crisis.

THE SELECTION QUESTION: WHY KENNEDY MADE RESOLVED STATEMENTS

Although the primary purpose of this chapter is to evaluate how and why Kennedy's statements of resolve affected Soviet beliefs and decision-making, at this point I will briefly discuss why Kennedy made such highly resolved statements. One concern raised earlier in the statistical chapters was the possibility that statements of resolve might only appear to be effective because presidents are more likely to make them when they already expect victory in international conflict. I attempted to rule out this concern using both statistical methods and logical argumentation. However, to further refute this concern, it is useful to analyze the specific reasons why the US president made a high level of resolved statements in the cases I have chosen to study in depth.

In the Cuban Missile Crisis case, there is some evidence that domestic politics influenced Kennedy's decision to make statements, but it does not appear that Kennedy made statements because he was confident of victory and wished to capitalize on that victory domestically. Kennedy's first statements about missiles in Cuba were made in part to avoid public criticism. His warning before the crisis erupted that the consequences of deploying "offensive ground-to-ground missiles" would be "grave" (Department of State 1962) was intended to ward off criticism from congressional Republicans, who had expressed concern about a Soviet arms buildup in Cuba (Taubman 2003, 554). In a sense, Kennedy was confident of success when he made this statement, but only in the sense that he did not expect a high-profile confrontation over this issue to occur at all. National Security Advisor McGeorge Bundy later said that the statement was made for domestic purposes, "not because we seriously believed that the Soviets would do anything as crazy from our standpoint as placement of Soviet nuclear weapons in Cuba" (Taubman 2003, 554). Kennedy's advisor and speechwriter Ted Sorensen also stated that "the President drew the line precisely where he thought the Soviets were not and would not be.... If we had known that the Soviets were putting forty missiles in Cuba, we might under this hypothesis have drawn the line at one hundred" (Beschloss 1991, 420).

This is not to say that Kennedy's warning was not a genuine statement of resolve. Indeed, Kennedy was quite resolved on the issue of missiles in Cuba and on standing firm against the Soviet threat in general, as became clear after the discovery of the missiles. Kennedy viewed the placement of Soviet missiles in Cuba as unacceptable for a variety of reasons that went beyond domestic politics. For example, Kennedy and his advisors worried about how the missiles changed the military balance of power (Fursenko and Naftali 1997, 226) and were even more concerned about the blow to US prestige and reputation that would result if the missiles were allowed to remain (Stern 2005, 48). At one point during the crisis, Kennedy did privately express regret that he had issued the public warning about missiles. This, along with Sorensen's retrospective comment in the previous paragraph, might suggest that Kennedy otherwise would have been willing to tolerate the missiles (Stern 2005, 48). However, based on how strongly Kennedy reacted to discovering the missiles, it is unlikely that Kennedy's statement about this was truly the only reason he cared.

After Kennedy learned that there were indeed Soviet nuclear missiles in Cuba, his calculations in the decision to make a resolved public speech were different. At this point, Kennedy and his advisors were far from confident of victory. On October 20, when Kennedy authorized the blockade of Cuba, he also ordered preparations for a military attack on Cuba to continue, revealing his doubt about whether the speech would persuade the Soviets to back down. In fact, Kennedy stated, "We are very, very close to war" (Stern 2005, 73–74). On October 22, hours before making his speech, Kennedy worried, "Khrushchev will not take this without a response, maybe in Berlin or maybe here" (Stern 2005, 80). If Kennedy was not confident of publicly basking in the glow of victory, why then did he make such a tough speech?

It seems that Kennedy never seriously considered not making a speech. Although his White House advisors debated some of the details of the speech (Stern 2005, 76–77), there is no evidence of a discussion over whether or not to make a public speech at all. In fact, even before Kennedy made the decision to employ a blockade, an alternative speech announcing an air assault on Cuba had been drafted (Dobbs 2008, 31). Therefore, to some extent the Kennedy administration may have been following the usual norm of addressing the public about major crises without questioning it. Furthermore, it is clear from White House deliberations that Kennedy and his advisors believed that it was important for the Soviets to know that Kennedy's position had support, from both Congress and US allies (Stern 2005, 85–91, 98). It would have been difficult to obtain this type of support without making the crisis public in a speech. Finally, it is beyond doubt that Kennedy was truly resolved on this issue. He considered it necessary for the missiles to be removed even if he had to go to war to achieve this (Stern 2005, 73–74, 80). Thus, Kennedy's speech was a genuine expression of his resolve, despite his uncertainty about the outcome.

Although Kennedy's motives for making a resolved public speech remain somewhat ambiguous because they were never explicitly debated, there is strong evidence that Kennedy did not make the speech because he was confident of victory. Kennedy's first statements on Cuba were made in part because Kennedy was confident that they would go unchallenged, but also partly to alleviate domestic criticism. Therefore, this case does not offer much support for the perspective that presidents are more likely to make statements of resolve when they already expect to win. This helps to alleviate concerns about treatment selection effects in my earlier statistical analysis.

SOVIET REACTION TO KENNEDY'S STATEMENTS

Premier Khrushchev and other Soviet officials paid close attention to Kennedy's statements. In the first part of 1962, during which Kennedy made few resolved statements directed at the Soviet Union, Khrushchev had a low opinion of Kennedy's resolve. Soviet defector Arkady Shevchenko stated that Khrushchev ignored warnings by some Soviet officials about a strong US reaction to Soviet missiles in Cuba because of his low opinion of Kennedy (Weisbrot 2001, 100). According to Khrushchev's son-in-law,

Khrushchev had "near certainty that Kennedy would not choose war" over the missiles (Taubman 2003, 552). In addition, Khrushchev made the case that because Kennedy was too weak to take the initiative on a Berlin settlement, he needed to be pushed. He said, "Kennedy is waiting to be pushed to the brink – agreement or war? Of course, he will not want war; he will concede. No rational being could not but agree with us" (Fursenko and Naftali 2006, 458).

As Kennedy began to increase his level of resolved statements about Soviet activities in Cuba, Khrushchev heeded them and raised his estimate of Kennedy's resolve. Though Khrushchev had initially hoped that the United States would reluctantly accept the Soviet missiles in Cuba (Dobbs 2008, 113), he became worried after hearing Kennedy's September statement warning against placing offensive missiles in Cuba. He took Kennedy's words largely at face value, interpreting them as evidence that Kennedy was less likely to accept the missiles. However, despite raising his estimate of Kennedy's resolve and the likelihood of conflict, Khrushchev himself was too resolved to abandon his plan so quickly. Therefore, rather than backing down, he sped up the delivery of the missiles and sent additional tactical nuclear weapons to Cuba (Fursenko and Naftali 1997, 206–207; Taubman 2003, 554).

The Soviets also paid a great deal of attention to Kennedy's televised speech on October 22. Upon learning that Kennedy planned to make a speech, Khrushchev assumed it would be about Cuba and called a late-night meeting of the Soviet Presidium even before the speech started. At 1:00 A.M. Moscow time, the entire Presidium listened to the text of the speech (Taubman 2003, 562). Although Khrushchev expressed considerable relief that Kennedy had not announced an invasion (Dobbs 2008, 42), his flurry of activity after the speech shows that it further dashed his hopes that Kennedy would acquiesce easily to the presence of the missiles. He ordered an increase in the military alert level to be prepared for war and slept that night in his office, "ready for alarming news to come at any moment" (Fursenko and Naftali 1997, 247–248). Furthermore, while Khrushchev did not instantly acquiesce to Kennedy's public demand to remove the missiles, he did immediately take Kennedy's threat to stop ships approaching Cuba at face value. He quickly ordered Soviet ships with military cargo that were not already close to Cuba to halt before the blockade line or turn back (Dobbs 2008, 43–44, 88–89; Fursenko and Naftali 2006, 477; Politburo 1962). Therefore, the evidence suggests that Kennedy's national speech was at least partially effective right away in further increasing Soviet perceptions of his resolve and causing Khrushchev to make at least some immediate modifications to his plans.

In addition, Soviet expectations of a second major public address by Kennedy slightly hastened the Soviet decision to back down and agree to remove the missiles. While meeting on October 28, Soviet leaders received a report that Kennedy would address the nation again later that day. They assumed that the address would be an announcement of an invasion, although it turned out to be merely a rebroadcast of Kennedy's October 22 speech (Frankel 2004, 159–160). According to his son's account, upon hearing this report, Khrushchev emphasized the need to respond quickly to Kennedy's proposal to the other Soviet officials present (Khrushchev 2000, 624–625). He said, "We don't have the right to take risks. Once the president announces there will be an invasion, he won't be able to reverse himself" (Khrushchev 2000, 630). This comment shows Khrushchev's belief in the committing function of public statements. Therefore, although Soviet leaders were already discussing the decision to back down, the prospect of a second public speech by Kennedy appears to have accelerated the decision at least somewhat. Indeed, the Soviets were in such a hurry to concede that they rushed Khrushchev's reply to Kennedy to Moscow's Radio Center and demanded that the announcer read it on the air immediately, without even practicing first (Dobbs 2008, 332–333).

Therefore, it appears that Kennedy's public statements did play an important role in the Cuban Missile Crisis. In Chapter 3, the question was raised of whether statements of resolve are often accompanied by other signals of resolve and whether these other signals might actually be more influential than the statements themselves. Kennedy's September statements were not accompanied by any other signals, so the updating of Soviet beliefs in September can be attributed to statements alone. Kennedy's October 22 speech was accompanied by a naval blockade, a strong additional signal of resolve. While the blockade undoubtedly helped to confirm Soviet beliefs about Kennedy's resolve, the evidence above showed that an initial flurry of Soviet activity and updating of beliefs about resolve occurred in response to the speech itself. After Kennedy announced the blockade and demanded the removal of the missiles, Khrushchev and other Soviet leaders did not wait for intelligence on the actual extent of the blockade to react or draw conclusions. Therefore, it is possible to observe a distinct effect of Kennedy's resolved words on October 22. It is also worth noting that the speech was necessary to provide context for the blockade and clarify US goals.

Therefore, statements of resolve played an important role during the Cuban Missile Crisis. Yet they did not do so alone. If statements alone had been perfectly persuasive, Khrushchev would have actually withdrawn the missiles immediately upon hearing Kennedy's October 22 speech or perhaps even upon hearing Kennedy's September warning about missiles in Cuba. In fact, Khrushchev did not make the initial proposal to withdraw the missiles from Cuba until October 26 (Fursenko and Naftali 1997, 263; Taubman 2003, 569) and did not make the final decision to acquiesce to the terms of Kennedy's offer until October 28. Therefore, it is necessary to consider what other factors caused Khrushchev's response to Kennedy's public demand to change between October 22 and October 28. The blockade, of course, also cannot provide a compelling explanation for this by itself because it also preceded Khrushchev's reversal by several days.

INTERNATIONAL REPUTATIONAL COSTS

One possible explanation for why the Soviets were eventually persuaded by US statements of resolve was that the statements had created international reputational costs that would make it difficult for the United States to back down. Kennedy and his advisors certainly believed that the international reputation of the United States was in danger. Kennedy said in his public speech, "The 1930's taught us a clear lesson: aggressive conduct, if allowed to go unchecked and unchallenged, ultimately leads to war" (Peters and Woolley 2016). Private discussions within the Kennedy administration also indicated reputational concerns. For example, President Kennedy worried that allowing the missiles to remain in Cuba would make Cuba appear "coequal" with the United States, and Assistant Secretary of State Edwin Martin stated that not appearing to "let 'em do it to us" was "more important than the *direct* threat" (Stern 2005, 48). Secretary of State Dean Rusk also opined that responding weakly would "undermine our alliances all over the world very promptly" and cause the Soviet Union to "feel like they've got it made as far as intimidating the United States is concerned" (Weisbrot 2001, 109).

It is not entirely clear from the statements quoted in the preceding paragraph that US officials believed the reputational consequences of backing down were directly linked to having made a statement. However, there is one private statement by President Kennedy that makes this link. On October 16, Kennedy said, "Last month, I said we weren't going to [accept offensive missiles in Cuba] and last month I should have said we don't care. But when we said we're *not* going to, and then they go ahead and do it, and then we do nothing, then I would think that our risks increase." Making it clear that he was talking about risks resulting from a damaged international reputation, Kennedy went on to add, "They've got enough to blow us up now anyway. After all, this is a political struggle as much as military" (Stern 2005, 48). Therefore, it is clear that US policymakers believed the US reputation was at stake, and there is some evidence that Kennedy believed his statement had raised the international reputational costs associated with backing down.

A more important question for the explanatory power of international reputational costs, however, is whether the Soviet side took these costs into account in its decision-making. Aside from the brief comment that Kennedy would be "unable to reverse himself" if he announced an invasion (Khrushchev 2000, 630), there is no evidence that this was the case. The idea that Kennedy might have been unwilling to back down from his public statements because it would damage the US reputation and thus make it more difficult for the United States to credibly signal resolve in the future does not appear to have been part of the Soviet discussions. Perhaps this was because Soviet leaders viewed themselves as reasonable and nonaggressive and may not have been able to understand the US fear of further conflict with the Soviet Union in the future. Therefore, evidence is lacking that an understanding of the international reputational costs faced by the United States influenced the Soviet decision to back down.

DOMESTIC AUDIENCE COSTS

Another possible explanation for why the Soviets became convinced of US resolve and ultimately backed down is domestic audience costs generated by Kennedy's statements of resolve. There is also ample evidence that members of the Kennedy administration believed there would be domestic consequences for backing down. Both President Kennedy and his brother, Attorney General Robert F. Kennedy, expressed the belief that the president would have been impeached for allowing the missiles to remain in Cuba (Stern 2005, 106). Treasury Secretary Douglas Dillon opined that allowing the missiles to become operational would lead to a Republican majority in Congress (Weisbrot 2001, 108). In the most direct link between domestic political consequences and statements of resolve, Defense Secretary Robert McNamara referred to the situation as "a domestic *political* problem," making the argument that Kennedy's previous commitment not to allow offensive missiles in Cuba did not lock the administration into invading because Kennedy had only said that "we'd *act*," which could have different interpretations (Stern 2005, 52). Thus, there is evidence that the US administration believed it would face domestic audience costs for backing down and some evidence that it believed these costs were increased by making statements.

There is also some evidence that the Soviets understood it would be domestically difficult for the Kennedy administration to accept the missiles in Cuba. Upon first hearing the proposal to send the missiles, Soviet foreign minister Andrei Gromyko warned that it could cause a "political explosion" in the United States (Taubman 2003, 544). Two days after Kennedy announced the presence of the missiles to the world, Anatoly Dobrynin, the Soviet ambassador to the United States, sent a cable to Moscow warning that "the president himself, like a gambler, actually was staking his reputation as a statesman, and his chances for reelection in 1964, on the outcome of this crisis" (Dobrynin 1995, 87).

Khrushchev himself also showed some awareness that the revelation of the missiles before the 1962 congressional elections would be particularly awkward for Kennedy. He sent Kennedy a message falsely assuring him, "Nothing will be undertaken before the American congressional elections that could complicate the international situation or aggravate tension in the relations between our two countries" (Fursenko and Naftali 1997, 197). He also privately expressed that the congressional elections increased the necessity of keeping the missiles secret (Taubman 2003, 543). On the other hand, Khrushchev also sometimes completely disregarded Kennedy's domestic audience costs, particularly during the tensions over the status of Berlin, which preceded the Cuban Missile Crisis. In a substantial misreading of American politics, he said,

"If only Kennedy understood that in solving the Berlin problem [by the US backing down] and thus consolidating peace, 90% of Americans (and not just Americans) would carry him in their arms" (Fursenko and Naftali 2006, 458).

However, even if Khrushchev and other Soviet officials did have some awareness that accepting the missiles in Cuba would damage Kennedy's domestic political standing and the electoral chances of the Democratic Party, there is no evidence that this actually influenced Khrushchev's decision-making once the crisis began. Although Khrushchev's comment that Kennedy would be "unable to reverse himself" after announcing an invasion (Khrushchev 2000, 630) could be taken as evidence in favor of either domestic audience cost theory or international reputational cost theory, there is no evidence that the Soviet leadership ever directly considered Kennedy's domestic audience costs during the crisis. The idea that Kennedy might be unable to back down from his resolved statements because of the threat of domestic political punishment seems to have been absent from their discussions. Therefore, as Snyder and Borghard (2011) and Trachtenberg (2012) have previously concluded, US domestic audience costs were not a major factor impacting Soviet decision-making.

HAWKISHNESS OF VETO PLAYERS

Most of the comments which Soviet policymakers made about US domestic politics during the Cuban Missile Crisis were not related to audience or reputational costs, but rather focused on the hawkishness of veto players. Even prior to the onset of the crisis, Soviet leaders believed that Kennedy's veto players were hawkish. As the crisis developed, they gained even more information about the hawkishness of veto players and became correspondingly more worried that the United States would attack Cuba in order to enforce Kennedy's public demand that the missiles be removed.

The evidence presented in this chapter shows that beyond having the understanding that domestic veto players would not block Kennedy from following through on his public threats, the Soviets were worried that some of these domestic actors would actively encourage him to follow through by attacking Cuba. This fear was separate from the idea that Kennedy would face domestic criticism for backing down because the Soviets' primary concern was about the hawkish influence of individuals within the White House and the military, who would find it difficult to criticize Kennedy publicly. In keeping with the theory developed in Chapter 1, the Soviets were aware that these informal veto players had a great deal of influence on Kennedy's decision-making. However, while my argument in Chapter 1 focused on how the advice of dovish informal veto players could make a leader hesitate to use force, in this case the Soviets believed that the advice of hawkish informal veto players would actually encourage Kennedy to use force. This belief helped persuade Soviet leaders to concede to Kennedy's public statement demanding removal of the missiles. Therefore, the influence of hawkish veto players on the effectiveness of Kennedy's statements of resolve in this case was actually even greater than anticipated by my theory.

Soviet Views on Veto Players Prior to the Crisis

From the beginning of his interactions with Kennedy, Khrushchev had believed that Kennedy was highly influenced by veto players. Even before Kennedy was elected, Khrushchev worried about his youth and inexperience (Beschloss 1991, 34). After discussing the status of Berlin with Kennedy at a June 1961 summit in Vienna, Khrushchev concluded that hawkish veto players in the US government were preventing Kennedy from making concessions (Fursenko and Naftali 2006, 413). He said of Kennedy, "The man himself has very little authority among those that decide and direct the policy of the United States" (Haslam 2011, 188). There is also evidence that Khrushchev understood the specific ability of Congress to constrain Kennedy and the fact that Congress was more hawkish than Kennedy himself. He told an American visitor on September 6, 1962, "[T]he President is boxed in – he can't move ... as it now stands, if the two of us made an agreement [on Berlin], Congress would veto it" (Memorandum 1962). Khrushchev also expressed fears that the influence of other hawkish actors on Kennedy could make the United States more aggressive. Speaking to Warsaw Pact leaders in 1961, Khrushchev said of Kennedy, "He is too much of a lightweight for both Republicans and Democrats, whereas the state is so big and powerful that it poses certain dangers." Therefore, Khrushchev believed that "anything is possible, including war; they could unleash it" (Taubman 2003, 502).

Aside from his general perception that veto players in the United States were hawkish, Khrushchev had ample evidence that many members of Congress had hawkish views specifically with regard to Cuba. In the months preceding the crisis, many Congress members from both parties criticized Kennedy for not doing enough about Soviet forces in Cuba. For example, Senator John Tower called Kennedy's policy "massive appeasement" (Weisbrot 2001, 83), and Representative William Miller, Chair of the National Republican Committee, called Cuba "a symbol of the tragic irresolution of the Administration" (Paterson and Brophy 1986, 99). Some Congress members advocated for military action in Cuba even before the missiles were discovered. Republican Senator Homer Capehart said on August 28, 1962, that America had the right "to land troops, take possession of Havana, and occupy the country" if Soviet forces remained there (Weisbrot 2001, 80). In late September 1962, Congress passed a resolution authorizing the president "to prevent by whatever means may be necessary, including the use of arms ... the creation or use of an externally supported military capability [in Cuba] endangering the security of the United States" (Weisbrot 2001, 91). Therefore, Kennedy had congressional authorization to use force in the Cuban Missile Crisis even before the crisis began.

Despite all of the evidence that most US veto players were hawkish, Khrushchev initially believed that Kennedy would accept the missiles in Cuba. The difficulty in reconciling this belief with his expressed views about the influence of hawkish interests over Kennedy stems in large part from a contradiction in Khrushchev's own thinking (Taubman 2003, 552). Khrushchev seems to have based his hope that Kennedy would acquiesce primarily on his view of Kennedy as weak and indecisive (discussed in the preceding text) and partly under the influence of more dovish veto players. Khrushchev viewed Kennedy's refusal to use greater force to prevent the failure of the 1961 Bay of Pigs invasion as a sign that Kennedy had insufficient determination (Beschloss 1991, 150; Khrushchev 2000, 436) and ascribed this decision at least partially to the impact of dovish veto players. Soviet officials had learned through the US media and their own intelligence of UN ambassador Adlai Stevenson's role in influencing Kennedy to cancel a second round of airstrikes against Cuba during the Bay of Pigs invasion, and attributed importance to this information. Some speculated that Kennedy's inexperience and deference to his liberal advisors might prevent him from acting decisively (Beschloss 1991, 149).

Soviet Perceptions of Veto Players during the Crisis

The discussion in the preceding section indicates that before the onset of the Cuban Missile Crisis, Khrushchev and other Soviet leaders viewed Kennedy as indecisive and able to be influenced by both hawkish and dovish veto players. Therefore, even though hawkish veto players were dominant, they maintained the hope that he could be pushed in a more dovish direction or would be constrained by his own fear of war. After Kennedy's initial public speech demanding the removal of the missiles, however, it became apparent to Soviet leaders that he was taking a resolved position.

After hearing the statements of resolve in his public speech, Soviet leaders never doubted for an instant that Kennedy had the ability to follow through on his demand that the missiles be removed with military action. This point is so obvious that it is rarely mentioned, but it is important and shows a great contrast to the situation during the Vietnam War, which will be discussed in Chapter 8. If President Kennedy had faced a Congress as dovish as the Congresses of the early 1970s, we probably would have observed the Soviets debating or even scoffing at Kennedy's domestic ability to follow through on his public statements and enforce his demand. However, given all of the evidence that had accumulated prior to the crisis that most of Kennedy's veto players were hawkish, the Soviets never expressed any opinion that there might be domestic constraints on Kennedy's ability to follow through. Therefore, Soviet leaders seemed to take Kennedy's statements of resolve at face value, and, as noted previously, they immediately ordered many of their ships to turn around.

As the crisis evolved, more evidence emerged that many members of Congress and the public had equally, if not more, hawkish views on this issue as the president. A Gallup poll showed that 84 percent of the public supported the blockade around Cuba, while only 4 percent opposed it (Weisbrot 2001, 136). Kennedy's approach also received widespread support from political commentators and members of Congress. Senator Kenneth Keating, who had previously been one of the most prominent critics of Kennedy's policies toward Cuba, said on the day after Kennedy's speech that "the firm stand of the President will have the 100% backing of every American regardless of party. It is what the American people have been waiting for" (Weisbrot 2001, 146). However, some Congress members still expressed concern that Kennedy's approach was insufficiently aggressive. For example, Senator Hugh Scott noted that the president's speech did not actually do anything to remove the large amount of Soviet military hardware in Cuba, and Representative William Miller worried that Kennedy would display "the same timidity and indecision which doomed the Bay of Pigs" (Beschloss 1991, 486–487).

Soviet officials were clearly aware of the sentiments in the US press and Congress. The Soviet embassy reported on the tense atmosphere in Washington, DC (Dobrynin 1995, 84). In his memoirs, Khrushchev recalled the intense reaction in the United States, saying, "[A]n unbelievable uproar broke out in the U.S. press. The pro-Republican press was the first to raise the hue and cry, and Republican Party leaders began speaking out, and then the Democrats joined in" (Khrushchev 2007, 334).

Soviet officials were also receiving information that veto players within the Kennedy administration were very hawkish. The pressure from these hawks on Kennedy was a theme in reports from the Soviet embassy in Washington to Moscow. An October 23 cable to Moscow warned of intelligence indicating that some of Kennedy's advisors saw the crisis as an opportunity to reverse the trend of growing Soviet power by fighting the Soviet Union in Cuba, which was a more favorable location for a fight than Berlin (Dobrynin 1995, 83). The embassy later repeated to Moscow reports that certain top advisors and the military were urging the president to be firm in the goal of eliminating the missiles and advocated invading Cuba if necessary. The embassy concluded that it "could not rule out – especially given the more aggressive members of his [the president's] entourage – the possibility of a reckless reaction such as a bombing raid on the Cuban missile bases or even an invasion" (Dobrynin 1995, 87). The embassy's most influential report to Moscow was based on information from US journalist Warren Rogers, who was overheard talking about Pentagon plans for having reporters cover the invasion of Cuba and apparently indicated in a later conversation with a Soviet agent that the decision to invade had already been made in principle. Although Rogers had no inside knowledge in reality, this information was urgently reported to Moscow (Dobbs 2008, 117–118; Frankel 2004, 128; Khrushchev 2000, 583, 591).

In what seems to have been a successful strategy, the Kennedy administration encouraged the perception that the president was surrounded by hawkish advisors. Kennedy made a specific effort to rein in the ability of UN ambassador Adlai Stevenson, one of the most dovish administration members, to interact with the Soviets by sending another advisor to "chaperone" him (Frankel 2004, 110). Even more importantly, Robert F. Kennedy, who met with Soviet ambassador Dobrynin regularly during the crisis, used a classic "good cop, bad cop" strategy. He portrayed President Kennedy as a reasonable man who wanted peace, but emphasized that many people around the president were advocating for war. As Dobrynin recalled, Robert F. Kennedy "kept dropping hints about the highly charged atmosphere among members of the presidential crisis team. Occasionally he seemed to overdramatize somewhat the pressure from the military.... But in general he rather correctly reflected the tense mood inside the White House. I reported this to Moscow, and it helped Khrushchev understand the seriousness of the situation" (Dobrynin 1995, 79).

According to Dobrynin's telegram recounting their decisive final meeting during the crisis on October 27, Robert F. Kennedy warned Dobrynin that the US military wanted to retaliate for the downing of a US U-2 plane over Cuba and that there were "hotheads among the generals, and in other places as well, who were spoiling for a fight" (Taubman 2003, 573–574). Khrushchev's memoirs state that Attorney General Kennedy further warned, "You should take into account the particular features of our governmental system. It's hard for the president. Even if he doesn't want a war and doesn't wish for war, against his will something irreversible might happen" (Khrushchev 2007, 339).

Khrushchev's Decision to Back Down

Khrushchev himself appears to have believed that Kennedy was under the influence of hawkish advisers during the crisis. In a letter to Kennedy on October 24, Khrushchev denounced Kennedy's "ultimatum" and demanded to know, "Who asked you to do this?" suggesting that Kennedy was not taking the initiative in his own foreign policy (Taubman 2003, 566). On October 25, he told his son that Kennedy was under pressure "from all directions: the military, the press, Congress. All were demanding military action. Kennedy might not be able to resist such pressure" (Khrushchev 2000, 582).

Khrushchev also took very seriously the erroneous information that Soviet agents had learned from journalist Warren Rogers, which he received early on October 26. Together with other intelligence information, this report convinced Khrushchev that Kennedy had given in to the hawks in his administration and that the United States was ready to invade (Fursenko and Naftali 1997, 262; Taubman 2003, 568). According to his son's account, Khrushchev told the Soviet Presidium, "We have been warned that war could start today. Of course, it's possible that the information has been planted, but the risk is too great. America is gripped by a real frenzy and the military are thirsting for action" (Khrushchev 2000, 584). In a crucial turning point, Khrushchev then began dictating a letter making the initial offer to withdraw the missiles.

Another turning point arrived on October 28, when Khrushchev had to decide whether to accept Kennedy's response to his initial offer. According to Khrushchev's interpreter Oleg Troyanovksy, the "entire tenor" of Robert F. Kennedy's October 27 conversation with Soviet ambassador Dobrynin, warning that the military was pushing for action, showed that "the time of reckoning had arrived" (Taubman 2003, 575). According to Khrushchev's son, "The tone of the conversation was evidence of the fact that to delay could be fatal" (Khrushchev 2000, 622). His son further states that Khrushchev believed Kennedy "was reaching the limit of his strength" to resist hawkish influences (Khrushchev 2000, 623).

Therefore, there is strong evidence that Khrushchev was highly influenced by new information coming in related to the pressure of hawkish veto players on Kennedy. This, along with the belief that Kennedy was about to make another public speech, encouraged the Soviet leadership to quickly agree to the demand laid out previously in Kennedy's statements of resolve.

This case reveals several aspects of the role of hawkish veto players that were not discussed very much in the previous chapters. First, as noted earlier, the Soviets not only realized that Kennedy's hawkish veto players would not block him from following through but also feared that they would encourage him to follow through. Thus, hawkish veto players played an even more decisive role in the crisis outcome than might be expected. Second, Soviet officials, and particularly Khrushchev himself, believed that US veto players were even more hawkish than they probably actually were. This shows that adversaries' perceptions may not always be fully accurate, but they are likely to have a strong basis in reality, as they did in this case. Third, the hawkish veto players in this case were both Democrats and Republicans. Although it could be argued that the Republicans were slightly more hawkish, even Democrats were hawkish enough to approve and even encourage military action. This shows that the percentage of Republicans in Congress is only a rough measure of the hawkishness of veto players, which is not necessarily surprising. Therefore, if there were a more precise way of coding the hawkishness of veto players for each individual crisis, this would quite possibly strengthen the statistical results. On the other hand, in smaller crises with fewer public statements revealing veto player preferences, political party affiliations might be the best way to approximate hawkishness.

OTHER FACTORS RELATED TO THE ABILITY TO FOLLOW THROUGH

Having demonstrated that hawkish veto players had an important role in convincing Soviet leaders to back down in response to Kennedy's demand, I will also briefly consider whether this case supports the importance of military strength and security in office as other factors influencing the effectiveness of resolved statements. Press (2005, 121–123) discusses the military balance during the Cuban Missile Crisis extensively, arguing that it was primarily the strategic nuclear balance that mattered. The United States had a definite advantage over the Soviet Union in strategic nuclear warheads and delivery vehicles, but it could not be confident of destroying the Soviet Union's entire arsenal in a first strike. Therefore, nuclear war would probably have been devastating for both sides and undoubtedly would have been devastating for the Soviet Union. Khrushchev was aware that the strategic situation did not favor the Soviet Union, and in fact his deployment of the missiles to Cuba was intended as a way to amend this (Taubman 2003, 536–537). However, many of the intermediate-range missiles that had been sent to Cuba were not yet operational or had not yet even arrived during the crisis (Fursenko and Naftali 2006, 468–469).

Khrushchev and his colleagues understood that nuclear war would be devastating for the Soviet Union and for the world (Fursenko and Naftali 2006, 469, 484). Clearly, US nuclear capabilities and the Soviet fear of nuclear war influenced the Soviet decision to give in to Kennedy's demand because at crucial moments, Khrushchev used phrases such as "the risk is too great" (Khrushchev 2000, 584) and "In order to save the world we must retreat" (Taubman 2003, 574). However, the nuclear balance did not change over the course of the crisis, and thus, US military strength alone cannot explain why the Soviet Union backed down. Therefore, while US military strength was high enough not to undermine the ability to follow through, it was not enough in itself to convince the Soviets that the United States was likely to follow through. It was only as more information about hawkish veto players came to light that Soviet leaders began to believe the risk of a devastating nuclear war was too great to bear.

The final condition that I have argued can give a leader the ability to follow through on statements of resolve is security in office. It does not appear that security in office played a very important role in the crisis because Kennedy was not in an extremely secure position. He had been elected by a relatively narrow margin and was concerned about the performance of the Democratic Party in upcoming congressional elections, which would be a bellwether for his own anticipated reelection campaign in 1964 (Paterson and Brophy 1986). Typically, my theory would predict that this type of vulnerability would make statements of resolve less effective. In this case, however, high security in office was not really necessary to have the ability to follow through because veto players in Congress and within the executive branch were hawkish enough that Kennedy did not need to use any political leverage to obtain their support to follow through. Furthermore, since public opinion was very hawkish, it is not clear that Kennedy would have been blamed for following through even if it went poorly. In this sense, the extreme hawkishness of veto players and the US public "crowded out" the importance of security in office. Since Kennedy had the ability to follow through regardless of security in office, it is not surprising that Kennedy's electoral vulnerability did not factor prominently in Soviet discussions.

SUMMING UP

In conclusion, the hawkishness of veto players appears to have been a more important factor impacting the effectiveness of Kennedy's statements in the Cuban Missile Crisis than international reputational costs, domestic audience costs, or other factors related to the ability to follow through. There is strong evidence that Soviet beliefs about hawkish veto players played a crucial role in convincing Khrushchev to heed Kennedy's public statements of resolve and remove the missiles.

Kennedy's address to the nation clearly served as a turning point in Soviet beliefs about his resolve. Whereas Khrushchev had previously hoped that Kennedy would accept the missiles, he became much more fearful that the United States would attack after Kennedy's speech. Because they always understood that Kennedy's veto players were hawkish, Soviet leaders never had any doubt about Kennedy's ability to follow through on his statements with force if he decided to do so. Therefore, they immediately ordered their ships not to challenge the blockade that Kennedy announced. While he did not doubt Kennedy's ability to follow through and his estimate of Kennedy's resolve increased after the speech, Khrushchev retained some doubt about whether Kennedy had enough "courage" to actually go through with an attack (Fursenko and Naftali 1997, 274). However, after learning more information about exactly how hawkish the veto players surrounding Kennedy were on this issue, Khrushchev came to believe there was a great danger that these actors would convince Kennedy to follow through. Therefore, as his perception of how hawkish US veto players were increased, Khrushchev took the demand and implicit threats in Kennedy's previous statements of resolve increasingly seriously. This, along with the prospect of a new resolved speech by Kennedy and other situational factors, ultimately encouraged Khrushchev to back down.

In sum, this case supports my theoretical argument about the importance of hawkish veto players in making statements of resolve effective. The role of hawkish veto players in this case even goes beyond my theory because Soviet leaders thought that the veto players would not only fail to restrain the president from attacking but also actively encourage him to attack. This was a case in which hawkish veto players gave the president the ability to follow through even though his security in office was not terribly strong. The next case to be explored involves a president with stronger security in office, but less hawkish veto players.

7

Refreezing of the Cold War

In this chapter, I will evaluate the reasons for effectiveness of resolved statements in another case: the upsurge in US-Soviet tensions in the 1980s, which is sometimes referred to as the refreezing of the Cold War. After a period of détente in the 1970s, US-Soviet relations drastically deteriorated in the early 1980s, following the Soviet invasion of Afghanistan and the election of Ronald Reagan as president of the United States. Tensions between the United States and the Soviet Union escalated over many issues, including Soviet policy toward the Warsaw Pact countries, interventions in developing countries, and human rights within the Soviet Union. However, the biggest areas of concern from the Soviet perspective were arms buildups and disagreements in arms control negotiations. While touching on other aspects of US-Soviet tensions, this case study will focus primarily on arms control disagreements, not only because this was a major Soviet concern but also because this is the first area in which Soviet foreign policy began to shift.

This case study will analyze how President Reagan's statements of resolve affected the Soviet position on arms control as well as Soviet foreign policy toward the United States in general. President Reagan issued many public statements declaring his resolve to take a tougher position in arms control negotiations and challenge Soviet interests around the world. At first, Reagan's resolved statements and policies led to greater tensions. Arms control efforts stalled, and Soviet ambassador Dobrynin (1995, 541) characterized relations in 1983 as having "reached a new low." Yet, by 1987, Reagan and Soviet secretary general Mikhail Gorbachev had signed the historic Intermediate-Range Nuclear Forces (INF) Treaty, which eliminated an entire class of nuclear weapons and required deeper cuts on the Soviet side than the US side. From that point onward, arms reductions continued at a rapid pace, as US-Soviet relations warmed.

This chapter will analyze the conditions that made Reagan's statements effective at persuading Soviet leaders of Reagan's resolve and eventually convincing them to modify their approach to arms control negotiations and relations with the United States. The analysis will particularly focus on the impact of security in office. I will demonstrate that while a variety of factors contributed to the successful negotiation of the INF Treaty and the end of the Cold War, Reagan's public statements of resolve, combined with his security in office, played an important role in convincing the Soviet Union to make concessions. While the Soviet leadership initially reacted hostilely to Reagan's resolved statements, they became more accommodating after they realized that Reagan had significant public support and security in office.

BACKGROUND

US-Soviet relations had improved in the 1970s due to the policy of détente with the Soviet Union initiated under President Nixon. Relations began to sour under President Carter, particularly after the Soviet Union invaded Afghanistan in late 1979. President Reagan came to office in 1981 with the belief that the Soviet Union had exploited détente by continuing to build arms and intervening in the Third World, while the United States held back. Therefore, Reagan's administration was determined to challenge the Soviet Union more directly and demonstrate US strength (Matlock 2004, 5). This determination was seen most clearly in the realm of arms control. Whereas Presidents Nixon, Ford, and Carter had all pursued arms control negotiations with the Soviet Union, Reagan believed that the United States should focus on building up its military. In his view, arms control could not be seriously considered until the United States had built up enough arms to negotiate from a position of strength (Matlock 2004, 11).

Reagan put his beliefs about the importance of military strength into action. Within his first two weeks in office, he requested a $32.6 billion defense budget increase (Garthoff 1994, 33). Over the next few years, Reagan expanded and modernized the US strategic nuclear forces, including bombers, long-range missiles, and submarines. In 1983, the United States began deploying new intermediate-range nuclear missiles in Europe (Kimball 2004). In the same year, Reagan announced that the United States would begin research on a space-based missile defense system, which Reagan called the Strategic Defense Initiative (SDI) and critics dubbed "Star Wars" (Graebner, Burns, and Siracusa 2008, 54–56).

Meanwhile, arms control negotiations with the Soviet Union went nowhere. In 1981, due to pressure from NATO allies, the United States resumed negotiations with the USSR over intermediate-range nuclear forces in Europe (Garthoff 1994, 71). The United States proposed the "zero option," under which the United States would forgo deploying new intermediate-range missiles in Europe in exchange for the Soviet Union removing existing ones. However, Moscow rejected this proposal as one-sided, and INF negotiations eventually broke off (Matlock 2004, 38–45; Wilson 2014, 25, 54). In 1982, the United States and the Soviet Union began separate talks on strategic nuclear forces. The US proposal focused on cuts to land-based nuclear forces, which comprised a larger portion of the Soviet arsenal than the US arsenal, and this proposal was also rejected by the Soviets (Matlock 2004, 45). In late 1983, the Soviet Union suspended arms control negotiations with the United States (Kimball 2004).

However, in June 1984, the Soviet Union made the first move toward resuming negotiations by proposing talks on "prevention of the militarization of space." The United States proposed broadening the negotiations to include other disarmament issues and changing the name of the talks so as not to imply that the militarization of space was to be prevented. After some delay, the Soviet Union agreed to this in late November 1984, and negotiations resumed in 1985 (Dobrynin 1995, 565–566; Matlock 2004, 99). Still, little progress was made because the United States continued to insist that pursuing SDI was crucial, while the Soviet Union continued to insist that SDI was unacceptable. At a summit between Reagan and Gorbachev, which took place in Reykjavik in 1986, both leaders were willing to agree to deep cuts in nuclear forces, but no deal was reached due to the disagreement over SDI (Graebner, Burns, and Siracusa 2008, 93–94; Matlock 1995, 93–97).

In 1987, Gorbachev changed his position and agreed to stop linking an agreement on SDI to the reduction of nuclear arms. He also reversed previous Soviet policy by agreeing to a deal similar to the "zero option," which the United States had proposed in 1981 (Kimball 2004). These Soviet concessions allowed the INF Treaty to be signed in 1987. This treaty proved to be a turning point, after which arms control proceeded rapidly. It is often considered a critical event in establishing trust between the United States and the Soviet Union and ending the Cold War. The following sections will analyze how this rapid reversal of the Soviet position occurred, beginning with an analysis of Reagan's statements of resolve.

REAGAN'S STATEMENTS

President Reagan was known for making very resolved and highly critical statements directed at the Soviet Union. As shown in Figure 7.1, Reagan's average level of resolved statements during militarized disputes with the Soviet Union was higher than the level of any other US president, with the exception of Carter, whose level of statements varied widely.[1] Therefore, there is quantitative support for the common portrayal of Reagan as a president who used particularly harsh rhetoric against the Soviet Union. Most US-Soviet MIDs under Reagan were minor shows of force and did not challenge key US interests, so the high level of resolved statements reflects a general decision by Reagan to speak harshly about the Soviet Union.

---

[1] Carter made few statements of resolve directed at the Soviet Union before the invasion of Afghanistan, but many afterward.

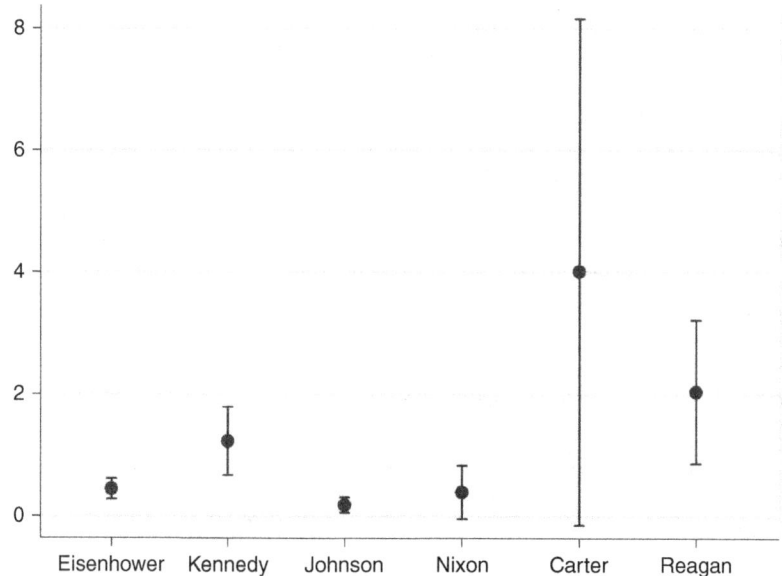

FIGURE 7.1 Average Statement Scores in US-Soviet MIDs by President
Note: The points give the mean level of statements, while the lines denote 95 percent
confidence bounds. The statement score is calculated using the main dictionary from the
previous chapters and normalized by MID duration. There were no US-Soviet MIDs
under President Ford, and President Truman is omitted because he is president in so few
observations in the sample.

Regarding the content of his statements, Reagan made both specific
commitments regarding US policy toward the Soviet Union and more general
criticisms of the Soviet Union. Reagan declared, on October 2, 1981, that the
United States would "strengthen and modernize" its nuclear forces in order to
"signal our resolve to maintain the strategic balance," which he called "the
keystone to any genuine arms reduction agreement with the Soviets." On
November 18, 1981, he said that the US position in arms control negotiations
would be based on the principles of "substantial, militarily significant reduction in
forces, equal ceilings for similar types of forces, and adequate provisions for
verification." Reagan said on January 8, 1983, "If there are to be better mutual
[US-Soviet] relations, they must result from moderation in Soviet conduct." He
added that the Soviet Union could improve relations "by ending the bloodshed in
Afghanistan, by showing restraint in the Middle East, by permitting reform and
thus promoting stability in Poland, by ending their unequaled military buildup."
Reagan also pledged to directly challenge Soviet efforts to spread communism in
the Third World. In particular, he argued, on April 27, 1983, that the United States
had "a vital interest, a moral duty, and a solemn responsibility" to defeat
communism in Central America (Peters and Woolley 2016).

In addition to the commitments discussed in the preceding paragraph, Reagan's statements of resolve also contained many harsh criticisms and negative characterizations of the Soviet Union. At his first press conference on January 29, 1981, he stated that Soviet leaders "reserve unto themselves the right to commit any crime, to lie, to cheat" for the "promotion of world revolution" (Peters and Woolley 2016). In a June 8, 1982, speech to the British Parliament, Reagan famously said that "the march of freedom and democracy … will leave Marxism-Leninism on the ashheap of history" (Peters and Woolley 2016). In what is probably Reagan's most well-known statement about the Soviet Union, on March 8, 1983, he called the Soviet Union an "evil empire" and the "focus of evil in the modern world," phrases which he repeated and defended in subsequent statements. He also strongly condemned the Soviet Union for shooting down a civilian airliner, flight KAL007, which strayed over its territory. In a televised speech on September 5, 1983, he called the event "an act of barbarism, born of a society which wantonly disregards individual rights and the value of human life and seeks constantly to expand and dominate other nations" (Peters and Woolley 2016).

As discussed in Chapter 2, while negative characterizations do not commit a country to any specific policy position, they can still raise expectations that the country will take some sort of action to remedy the situation or behavior about which it is complaining. Thus, as discussed in the next section, Reagan's negative characterizations of the Soviet Union not only raised expectations that he would follow through on his commitments to stand firm against the Soviet Union but also raised the fear that he sought to destroy the Soviet Union, possibly with a military attack. Indeed, this chapter provides strong evidence of the importance of negative characterizations as a type of resolved statement that can influence adversary beliefs.

Despite all his resolved statements, Reagan did not directly threaten to attack the Soviet Union.[2] Therefore, when I refer to Reagan "following through" on his statements, I primarily mean continuing to hold the tough line he committed to in disputes with the Soviet Union, particularly with regard to arms building and the Third World. "Following through" in this case does not necessarily involve use of force. Nonetheless, bargaining between the United States and the Soviet Union took place in a context of such heightened tensions that holding a tough line could have inadvertently led to force.[3] Therefore, the United States

---

[2] In one instance, he did joke about launching a nuclear attack against the Soviet Union, saying, "My fellow Americans, I'm pleased to tell you today that I've signed legislation that will outlaw Russia forever. We begin bombing in five minutes." This joke was made privately before a radio address, but it was recorded and leaked to the press (De Groot 2011). Although the Soviets viewed this joke as threatening (Dobrynin 1995, 556; Garthoff 1994, 160), it was not an intentional threat.

[3] In one instance that could have inadvertently led to war, Soviet nuclear forces went on alert in response to the NATO exercise Able Archer in 1983 (Holloway 2015).

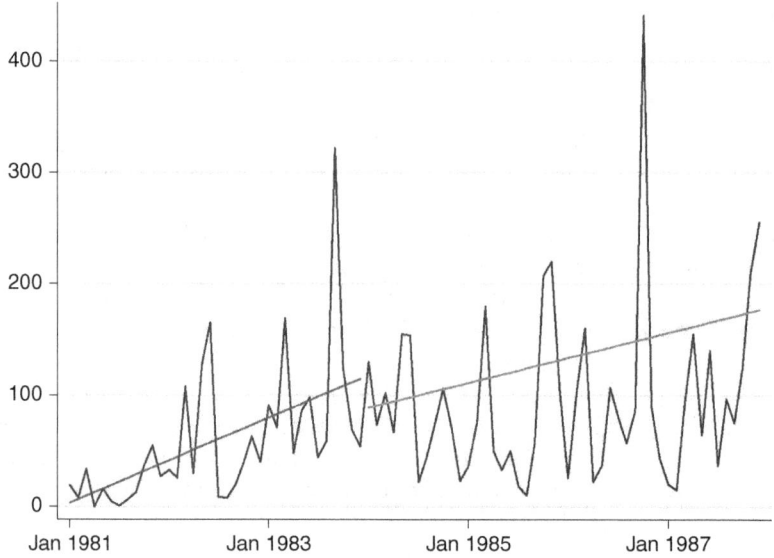

FIGURE 7.2 Reagan's Statements of Resolve over Time
Note: The fluctuating line is the measure of Reagan's resolved statements directed at the
Soviet Union, using the main dictionary from the previous chapters. The straight lines are
separate regression lines for 1981–1983 and 1984–1987.

and the USSR could be considered to be in a situation of international conflict,
broadly construed.

Some scholars have asserted that Reagan began to moderate his statements of
resolve in 1984. It is true that Reagan's most famous anti-soviet statements, such as
the "evil empire" and "ashheap of history" comments, were made before this year
(Peters and Woolley 2016). Fischer (1997, 32–39) and Wilson (2014, 81) see
Reagan's January 1984 speech, in which he spoke about how fictional Soviet
citizens Ivan and Anya could find things in common with fictional US citizens
Jim and Sally, as an important shift in tone. However, whereas Fischer (1997) sees
this speech as an irrevocable turning point in US-Soviet relations, Wilson (2014,
108) gives examples of resolved and provocative rhetoric by Reagan as late as
1986. Evidence from Soviet records, discussed in this chapter, shows that Soviet
anger at Reagan's public statements continued through at least 1987.

With my new data on US presidential statements of resolve, it is possible to
analyze more systematically whether Reagan's public statements truly became
less resolved over time. Figure 7.2 shows the level of resolved statements made
in each month between Reagan's inauguration in January 1981 and the signing
of the INF agreement in December 1987. It is true that Reagan made fewer
resolved statements in 1984 than in 1983, but there is no evidence that
a permanent reduction in Reagan's resolved rhetoric occurred in this year.

Although there is a great deal of variation between months, the general trend in resolved statements is upward between the beginning of 1984 and end of 1987, as shown by the regression line plotted across the monthly level of statements. Furthermore, the average number of resolved statements per month is actually higher in 1984–1987 than in 1981–1983. This is not to say that there were no changes in Reagan's policies between 1983 and 1987, since he did begin to engage more with the Soviet Union and discuss arms control seriously, as described later in this chapter. However, his rhetorical strategy of issuing highly resolved statements continued even as his administration's policy shifted.

THE SELECTION QUESTION: WHY REAGAN MADE RESOLVED STATEMENTS

As in the previous chapter, I will briefly divert from the main topic of how Soviet officials responded to statements of resolve in order to discuss why Reagan made the statements. This discussion is intended to address the concern that presidents make more statements of resolve when they already expect to win, creating the spurious appearance that statements are effective even if they actually are not. In this case, there is no evidence that Reagan made statements because he was confident of winning and wished to get credit for it. It should be noted that Reagan did generally express faith in democracy and capitalism and seemed to have confidence that the US system would triumph over communism in the long run. Indeed, while running for president, he told a campaign advisor that his goal was to "end the Cold War" (Wilson 2014, 9). Therefore, it is clear that Reagan was genuinely resolved to challenge Soviet power. However, there is no indication that he expected victory against communism to happen imminently.

In the near term, Reagan believed that the Soviet Union was a major threat to the United States. In his public statements, Reagan often emphasized the Soviet military threat. For example, on April 17, 1982, he accused the Soviet Union of undertaking an "unprecedented buildup of both its conventional and nuclear forces" and worried that the United States could "progressively lose the ability to deter the Soviet Union from employing force or threats of force against us" (Peters and Woolley 2016). Other public comments, such as at a press conference on October 1, 1981, indicate that Reagan believed Soviet leaders considered a nuclear war to be winnable by the Soviet Union (Peters and Woolley 2016), a view that would have increased his fear of a Soviet nuclear first strike. This view was also promoted by one of his top advisors on Soviet affairs, Richard Pipes (Pipes 1977).

It appears that Reagan's belief that the Soviet Union was a danger to the United States was long-standing and deeply entrenched. Reagan was affiliated with the Committee on the Present Danger, an organization with the primary goal of promoting awareness of what its members viewed as a massive Soviet military threat. Reagan brought 32 members of the committee into his administration when he assumed office (Sanders 1983, 8). Even though Reagan was aware of evidence that the Soviet Union was declining economically, he and his advisors thought this would make the Soviet Union more reliant on military force and therefore potentially even more dangerous (Matlock 2004, 7). His first secretary of state, Alexander Haig (1981), stated in his confirmation hearing that the "years immediately ahead will be unusually dangerous" for the United States.

If Reagan was not confident of winning the Cold War in the near future, why then did he make so many resolved statements? It appears that Reagan was motivated by several factors. First, Reagan may have felt it was his duty as a Christian to speak out against communism. Wilson (2014, 13–14) presents evidence that Christian and anti-communist ideas had deep roots in Reagan's past. This again suggests that Reagan's resolve to stand up against communism was genuine. Second, Jack Matlock (2004, 6), one of Reagan's advisors, states that Reagan believed previous presidents had not been candid enough with the American people about the true nature of the Soviet Union and that this had led to inflated public expectations about the prospects for US-Soviet cooperation. Therefore, Reagan was determined to be more forthright in speaking what he believed to be the truth about the USSR.

Third, Reagan was getting at least some advice that resolved statements had the ability to effectively convey his resolve to Soviet leaders. A National Security Council memo titled "The Truth and The Strength of America's Deterrent," argued that a key element in the Soviet assessment of overall US strength was the strength of the US "moral-political conviction" and that this strength was bolstered by speaking "plainly about the nature and goals of communism." The memo asserted, "So long as our leaders deliver this message, the Soviets will know that we are not spiritually weak" (Wilson 2014, 67–68). Therefore, there is evidence that Reagan made statements of resolve not because he was already confident of winning the Cold War but because he hoped that the statements would help him win it. The belief that resolved statements were helpful in winning the Cold War probably also helps explain why Reagan continued to make them even as relations with the Soviet Union began to improve under Gorbachev. He may have reasoned that his previous resolved statements had helped bring the Soviet Union to the bargaining table and believed that continuing to make such statements would ensure a continued improvement in Soviet behavior.

SOVIET REACTION TO REAGAN'S STATEMENTS

Soviet leaders paid close attention to Reagan's statements of resolve. Their primary initial reaction to the statements was anger. Soviet ambassador Anatoly Dobrynin reported that the Soviet Politburo "roundly and unanimously denounced" Reagan's first press conference and observed, "During my long career as ambassador the collective mood of the Soviet leadership had never been so suddenly and deeply set against an American president. It was a catastrophe in personal relations at the highest level" (Dobrynin 1995, 492–493). At a Communist Party Congress in February 1981, Soviet secretary general Leonid Brezhnev said, "Unfortunately, since the change of leadership in the White House, openly belligerent statements and cries are still being heard from Washington seemingly deliberately calculated to poison the atmosphere of relations between our countries" (Garthoff 1994, 57). The Soviet leadership viewed Reagan's 1983 "evil empire" speech, given at a time when the United States and USSR were privately engaging in a dialogue intended to improve relations, as a sign of "duplicity and hostility" (Dobrynin 1995, 533). In a Politburo meeting a few months after the speech, the new Soviet secretary general, Yuri Andropov, referred to Reagan as "a bearer and creator of all anti-soviet [sic] ideas, creator of all the untrue insinuations regarding our country" (Politburo 1983, 1).

The Soviets were also incensed at Reagan's "hysterical" reaction to the downing of flight KAL007, which they believed was on a US reconnaissance mission (Dobrynin 1995, 544). Soviet foreign minister Andrei Gromyko (1989, 297) accused the United States of "brazenly exploiting" the KAL incident for "propaganda purposes." A few weeks after the incident, Secretary General Andropov released a statement criticizing the "unseemly spectacle" of US leaders issuing "abuse mingled with hypocritical sermons on morality" (Garthoff 1994, 130). Andropov condemned Reagan's communication methods as "inadmissible in state-to-state relations" and added that "if anybody ever had any illusions about the possibility of an evolution to the better in the policy of the present American administration, these illusions are completely dispelled now" (Zubok 2007, 274). Similarly, Andropov also told Ambassador Dobrynin in private that Reagan's public statements made it impossible to achieve "even a small measure of reconciliation with Washington" (Dobrynin 1995, 556).

Soviet leaders seemed to take Reagan's statements as genuine indications of his resolve to stand firm against the Soviet Union. Indeed, many members of the Soviet leadership felt threatened by Reagan. Foreign Minister Gromyko reportedly told his son that based on Reagan's statements, he believed, "The US is trying to challenge the status of the Soviet Union as a great power." He told another confidant, "Reagan and his team ... are trying to destroy us" (Grachev 2008, 21). Shortly after the KAL incident, Sergei Vishnevsky, a Soviet journalist with reputed ties to the KGB, told a US official: "the leadership is convinced that the Reagan Administration is out to bring their system down and will give no quarter" (Wilson 2014, 77–78).

The Soviets even feared that Reagan's resolve, which they believed "bordered on fanaticism" (Dobrynin 1995, 541), might be great enough to make him launch a first strike on the Soviet Union with nuclear weapons. In early 1981, the Soviet Union launched a global intelligence operation designed to detect indications of a first strike with nuclear weapons by the United States.

The operation, referred to by the Russian acronym VRYaN or sometimes simply RYaN, intensified in 1983 (Mastny 2009, 112–116). A Soviet defector reported that in both May 1981 and November 1983, the KGB station in London was told to be on alert for signs of an imminent US attack (Garthoff 1994, 60, 139).

Even Mikhail Gorbachev, the Soviet secretary general who presided over the end of the Cold War, viewed Reagan's rhetoric as hostile. In his memoirs, he accused Reagan of leading "anti-communist hysteria" with his rhetoric in 1985 and complained that the United States was "accusing the Soviet Union of all the deadly sins" in 1987 (Gorbachev [1995] 1997, 532, 566). There is also evidence that the Soviet leadership under Gorbachev analyzed the meaning of Reagan's statements closely. When former president Nixon visited Moscow in 1986, former ambassador Dobrynin, who was by then the head of the Communist Party Central Committee International Department, asked Nixon to analyze the meaning of a single word, "coy," in Reagan's description of Soviet behavior (Nixon 1986, 10).

As in the Cuban Missile Crisis case, we might ask whether it was really Reagan's statements of resolve or other signals of resolve made at the same time that caused Soviet leaders to view Reagan as highly resolved or even hostile. The evidence in the preceding paragraphs reveals several instances in which Soviet leaders reacted to specific statements of Reagan, including the "lying and cheating" statements at Reagan's first press conference, the "evil empire" speech, and the national address about the KAL incident. In each instance, a Soviet official is directly quoted as saying that the statement caused the Soviet leadership to view Reagan as more hostile than before. Between this and the other more general Soviet reactions to Reagan's resolved statements, it is clear that Reagan's statements influenced Soviet beliefs.

Of course, it was not only Reagan's public statements that made Soviet leaders believe he was resolved and even hostile. Reagan also took tough actions against the Soviet Union, such as building up arms, taking a hard line in arms control negotiations, and supporting anti-communist fighters abroad. Georgy Arbatov, a Soviet academic who often represented Soviet views to Western audiences, noted, "The bully-boy rhetoric [of Reagan] was supplemented by corresponding policies – primarily, by whipping up the arms race" (Wilson 2014, 54). Thus, in this relatively prolonged confrontation between Reagan and the Soviet leadership, Reagan's statements and other policies signaling resolve bolstered each other's impact. If Reagan had made resolved statements without any resolved policies, eventually the Soviets would have viewed the statements as empty words. On the other hand, if Reagan had pursued resolved policies without resolved statements, it is not clear that the Soviets would have viewed the policies as so threatening. As evidence of the weight that Soviet officials placed on public statements in gauging US intentions, Soviet ambassador Dobrynin (1995, 532–533) tells how the "evil empire" speech caused Soviet leaders to view the United States as more hostile despite the fact that the United States had been making private overtures which the Soviets perceived as more cooperative. Therefore, it is clear that statements of resolve played a role in the confrontation between the Reagan administration and the Soviet leadership that was distinct from, and quite possibly more important than, any other resolved behavior.

Soviet leaders had a strong reaction to Reagan's statements not only because they believed them to be true indicators of Reagan's intentions, but also because they were concerned about the impact of Reagan's statements on US public opinion. For example, Soviet defense minister Dimitri Ustinov stated that Reagan's claims about Soviet military superiority over the United States were "calculated at deceiving the public" with "the purpose of justifying the unprecedented U.S. military programs and aggressive doctrines" (Garthoff 1994, 91). In addition, Gorbachev complained to the Politburo in 1986 that Reagan was "undertaking fraudulent maneuvers in order to distort the facts and to confuse the public" (Wilson 2014, 122). Soviet leaders were concerned about the link between Reagan's statements of resolve and public opinion because they viewed Reagan's need to maintain security in office by retaining public support as one factor that could prevent him from following through with his confrontational policies indefinitely. The next section will discuss Soviet beliefs about Reagan's security in office, and the following sections will show how changes in Soviet beliefs about this affected arms control negotiations.

SECURITY IN OFFICE AS A LIMITATION ON THE ABILITY TO FOLLOW THROUGH

In evaluating Reagan's statements of resolve, Soviet leaders took into account his security in office. The Soviets appeared to view public opinion and Reagan's need to win reelection as factors restraining Reagan's continued ability to follow through on his pledges to take a tough line against the Soviet Union. In late 1982, Soviet academic Georgy Arbatov cited Republican losses in the midterm elections as a sign that "common sense, which is a national trait of the Americans, is beginning to manifest itself in the United States" and expressed hope that the coming year "would see a return to normal international relations based on the true perception of one's own interests" (Garthoff 1994, 89). Dobrynin (1995, 535) assessed in 1983 that tensions between the United States and the Soviet Union would harm Reagan's reelection campaign.

The Soviets were so certain that public opinion was a restraining force on Reagan, that rather than considering his statements of resolve to be pandering to the public, they viewed his more conciliatory statements and gestures as pandering. They suspected that Reagan's initial attempts at conciliation were not genuine, but were rather intended to deceive the American public about his true hostility toward the Soviet Union. Soviet academic Georgy Arbatov referred to Reagan's minor efforts to improve relations in 1983 as "ruses ... needed in view of the upcoming election campaign in 1984" (Garthoff 1994, 125). Soviet foreign minister Gromyko (1984, 1) described indications that Reagan wished to improve relations before the 1984 presidential election as a "façade" designed to "facilitate the lessening of the concerns of the American public about their future." Initially, Soviet leaders deliberately sought to avoid playing along with this perceived deception by declining opportunities to meet with administration officials (Garthoff 1994, 156, 174). Gromyko (1984, 2) asked, "Why should we hold him [Reagan] up by his elbows when he is climbing the stairway to the White House in connection with the presidential elections?"

The belief that the need to maintain public approval limited Reagan's ability to follow through with anti-soviet policies persisted even under Gorbachev. In his memoirs written after the end of the Cold War, Gorbachev described Reagan's willingness to negotiate as being driven not by his own internal motivations but by public opinion, saying, "[T]he steps we took to carry out our new policy [of more conciliatory foreign relations] were met by a wall of prejudice and refusal in the political centres of the West. But in the end Western politicians yielded to pressure from the general public, who understood that the world was on the brink of catastrophe" (Gorbachev [1995] 1997, 518).

The Soviet view that the need to maintain public support was a restraining factor for Reagan had some basis in US political realities. US media outlets were devoting substantial coverage to the nuclear arms race, and many commentaries blamed the Reagan administration, rather than the Soviet Union, for the situation (Wilson 2014, 70). Concerns about nuclear war grew among the American public. In fall 1983, about half the US population watched the first airing of the ABC made-for-television movie *The Day After*, which depicted the gruesome effects of nuclear war on average people in Kansas (Zaitchik 2013). In 1982–1983, a "nuclear freeze" movement began to gain popularity in the United States. Referenda calling for a freeze on the level of nuclear weapons were passed in many localities, nearly one million people protested in favor of a nuclear freeze in New York, and the movement was endorsed by many major religious denominations. As of 1983, public opinion polls showed an average of 72 percent public support for a nuclear freeze (Wittner 2010).

Although the Soviet perception that Reagan's ability to follow through on his resolved statements toward the Soviet Union was constrained by public opinion had some basis in reality, it also reflected some wishful thinking. Even though many Americans disapproved of the arms race, they did not necessarily disapprove of Reagan's policies overall. Gallup polls showed that approval for Reagan's general foreign policy and his policy toward the Soviet Union increased during 1983, despite very poor US-Soviet relations. Some 1984 polls found that a majority of Americans agreed with Reagan that the Soviet Union was "an evil empire trying to take over the world" and that "the Soviets are constantly testing us" (Fischer 1997, 62–63). In general, Reagan was able to maintain fairly strong public support throughout his presidency. According to Gallup polls, Reagan had positive net approval ratings for most of his first term.[4] His net approval rating did dip into negative territory in late 1982 and early 1983, but the dip was not very prolonged or deep. In his second term, Reagan's average net approval rating was even higher and only became negative briefly in response to the Iran-Contra scandal (Peters and Woolley 2016).

Because the Soviets viewed public disapproval and reelection concerns as constraints on Reagan, they became more convinced of Reagan's continued ability to follow through on his statements of resolve as they increasingly recognized the extent of his security in office. Dobrynin (1995, 501) notes the fact that "American public opinion was on the whole willing to give Reagan the benefit of the doubt and even support him" as a factor that caused concern in Moscow. I will show below that because they believed security in office gave Reagan a greater continued ability to follow through on his resolved statements, the Soviets became more accommodating toward the United States when Reagan was more secure in office. The Soviets also tried to influence Reagan's security in office by appealing to US public opinion.

ARMS NEGOTIATIONS, 1981–1984

The preceding discussion shows that the Soviets believed Reagan was genuinely resolved to confront the Soviet Union and that greater security in office would enhance his ability to follow through with this hard-line policy. I will now examine how these beliefs affected negotiations. The initial impact of Reagan's resolved statements was to push Soviet leaders to take a harder line in order to demonstrate their own resolve as well. The Soviet Union denounced Reagan's statements and increased its own military spending (Singer, Bremer, and Stuckey 1972). It also refused to budge in arms control negotiations, as it considered the US proposals to be too one-sided to take seriously (Dobrynin 1995, 539). A few months later, the Soviet side decided to halt arms control negotiations completely. In making this decision, Soviet leaders hoped to increase public pressure on Reagan by conveying to the domestic publics in the United States and Europe that the United States had raised the risk of war through its inflexibility (Garthoff 1994, 132–133). Therefore, as seen in Chapter 2, the initial effect of statements of resolve is sometimes not to immediately cause the other side to back down, but rather to create a competition to demonstrate the most resolve.

However, eventually the Soviets developed a greater willingness to negotiate with Reagan. Importantly, this began to happen even before Gorbachev came to power in 1985. The first turning point was when the Soviet Union expressed interest in negotiating on space weapons in June 1984 and then agreed to more wide-ranging negotiations in late November 1984. The reasons that the Soviet

---

[4] Recall that a positive net approval rating means that more people approve of the president than disapprove. I found in Chapter 4 that statements of resolve are predicted to have a positive and significant marginal effect only when the president's net approval rating is positive.

attitude began to change have been subject to some debate. As discussed later in the section about alternate explanations, some have argued that Reagan's own attitude began to change, making it easier for the Soviets to engage with him (Dobrynin 1995; Fischer 1997).[5] However, even Soviet ambassador Dobrynin's (1995) account attributes the Soviet move to return to negotiations at least in part to Soviet fear of SDI and Soviet awareness of Reagan's increased security in office.

The request to negotiate about weapons in space was directly linked to Soviet fears of SDI. The Soviet leadership took the threat of SDI seriously. They believed that SDI could destabilize the strategic balance by depriving Moscow of its capability to retaliate against a US nuclear strike and would certainly launch a new arms race, which the Soviet Union could ill afford (Dobrynin 1995, 534; Wilson 2014, 124). The Soviet reaction to SDI must be considered in the context of Soviet beliefs about the Reagan administration's resolve and public support. Because they viewed Reagan as determined to undermine them, based in large part on his resolved statements, the Soviets interpreted SDI as a hostile initiative. They also had reason to believe that Reagan had sufficient domestic support to go through with building SDI. Soviet ambassador Dobrynin (1995, 534) assessed that most Americans "welcomed" the SDI proposal.[6] Therefore, it appears that Reagan's statements of resolve, combined with public support for him, influenced Soviet threat perceptions.

In addition to enhancing the perception that SDI was a threat, Soviet acknowledgment of Reagan's security in office also contributed more directly to the decision to resume negotiations. As of December 1983, when the Soviets withdrew from negotiations, it was not entirely clear that Reagan would win reelection. Although Reagan always had a lead on his rival, Walter Mondale, in the polls, sometimes the lead was much narrower than at other times. Reagan and Mondale were within 6 percentage points of each other in terms of support in December 1983, May 1984, and July 1984, but the gap widened after that (Harris Survey 1983–1984). Therefore, at least until July, the Soviets had reason to hope that Reagan would be replaced by Mondale, whom Moscow greatly preferred. Dobrynin (1995, 565) admits that after the Reagan administration asked to broaden the scope and change the name of the space weapons negotiations proposed by the Soviet Union, the Soviets decided to delay agreeing until after the election.

Ultimately, however, Reagan won reelection by a large margin. He won 58.8 percent of the popular vote, and he won more electoral votes than any

---

[5] As an example of the conflicting perspectives, both US and Soviet participants viewed Soviet foreign minister Gromyko's visit to the White House in September 1984 as a symbolically important turning point, but each side asserts that the initiative for the meeting came from the other side (Anderson and Anderson 2009, 160; Dobrynin 1995, 560; Gromyko 1989, 306; Matlock 2004, 100).

[6] Opinion polls indicate that the actual level of support depended a great deal on question wording. See, for example, Harris Survey (1983) and Roper Report (1984).

other candidate in history (Peters and Woolley 2016). This resulted in a "flood" of warm letters from Soviet officials. Eleven days after the election, Moscow agreed to resume negotiations (Anderson and Anderson 2009, 177–180). According to Dobrynin (1995, 565), "The decision [to resume negotiations] was prompted in no small measure by Reagan's landslide reelection, which awarded a complete mandate to his foreign and domestic policies." Therefore, the knowledge that not only would they have to deal with Reagan for four more years but also that Reagan was free to continue his policies with few constraints imposed by public opinion helped to persuade the Soviets to return to the negotiating table. Still, the positions of the United States and Soviet sides remained far apart.

ARMS CONTROL NEGOTIATIONS UNDER GORBACHEV

After Gorbachev came to power, the Soviet position on arms control began to shift more dramatically. A major reason for this change was undoubtedly that Gorbachev himself had an inherently different way of thinking about US-Soviet relations from his predecessors. He believed in the benefits of collective security and was generally more open-minded (Brown 1996; English 2000; Risse-Kappen 1991). In addition, Soviet economic difficulties were getting worse, making the need to limit military spending more urgent (Brooks and Wohlforth 2000/2001). For these reasons, Gorbachev was more eager to reach an arms control agreement with deep cuts than the previous Soviet leadership. However, like the previous leadership, he was strongly opposed to SDI, which created an obstacle to reaching an agreement. As Gorbachev attempted to negotiate an agreement with Reagan, Soviet beliefs about public support for Reagan's tough line influenced his strategy.

Because he believed that public support was an important factor influencing Reagan's ability to maintain his tough line, Gorbachev's strategy aimed to reduce public support for Reagan's policies. Many of Gorbachev's arms control initiatives were presented in public in order to gain the initiative in influencing public opinion. For example, in January 1986, Gorbachev disclosed a phased plan to completely eliminate nuclear weapons to the press mere hours after sharing it with the Reagan administration (Dobrynin 1995, 603). Since Reagan's statements of resolve were made in the public sphere, Gorbachev sought to discredit them by showing Soviet peacefulness in the public sphere.

As of late 1985, Gorbachev judged that his strategy of public pressure had been effective because it had persuaded Reagan to meet with him in Geneva. Gorbachev viewed Reagan as "a product of the military-industrial complex, of its most right-wing, reactionary wing." Therefore, Gorbachev attributed Reagan's willingness to meet as being due to Soviet pressure and public opinion. He noted that Reagan was particularly vulnerable to this type of pressure as the 1986 congressional elections approached (Haslam 2011, 354). The Geneva Summit itself was not a great success, as the United States and the

Soviet Union remained at an impasse over the issue of SDI. Gorbachev left Geneva frustrated with Reagan. During a discussion with his own colleagues about the summit, Gorbachev referred to Reagan as "not simply a conservative, but a political 'dinosaur'" (Gorbachev [1995] 1997, 524). He also complained of Reagan's "crude primitivism, caveman views and intellectual impotence" (Wilson 2014, 100). Still determined to reach an arms control agreement, Gorbachev continued trying to undermine public support for Reagan's position by issuing new proposals. In January 1986, Gorbachev publicly proposed eliminating all nuclear weapons within 15 years in exchange for banning SDI. The proposal generated a great deal of interest across the US political spectrum and took the Reagan administration by surprise (Dobrynin 1995, 603–604).

In response to Gorbachev's strategy of pressuring Reagan through public opinion, US officials sought to convey to the Soviets that Reagan was sufficiently secure in office that this strategy would not work. Prior to the Geneva Summit, US national security advisor Robert McFarlane warned the Soviet ambassador not to think that Reagan was overly influenced by public opinion (Dobrynin 1995, 585). Former president Nixon also warned Gorbachev in a meeting in July 1986 that Reagan was sufficiently secure in office to be unconcerned about public opinion. According to his own account, Nixon (1986, 15) "emphasized strongly that President Reagan politically did not *need* [emphasis original] an agreement, that his popularity was at an all time high and would remain so for the balance of his term regardless of whether he reached an agreement with Gorbachev or not." Nixon also told Gorbachev that even after Reagan left office, "he would be enormously popular and would have great influence on public issues due to his incomparable communication skills." Therefore, Nixon said, it was in Gorbachev's interest not to alienate Reagan (Nixon 1986, 15). According to the accounts of both Nixon and Gorbachev's aid Anatoly Chernyaev, Gorbachev acknowledged Reagan's popularity and strong political position (Chernyaev [1993] 2000, 77; Nixon 1986, 15). Contrary to the speculation of some commentators that it would be better for the Soviets to wait out Reagan and make an arms control agreement with his successor, Gorbachev expressed a desire to reach an agreement with Reagan (Nixon 1986, 14–15).

Being determined to reach an agreement, Gorbachev proposed another summit meeting in Reykjavik. As before, Gorbachev attributed Reagan's acceptance of his summit proposal to public opinion pressure rather than a genuine desire for peace (Gorbachev [1995] 1997, 535–536). Although the Reykjavik Summit, held in October 1986, is now considered a turning point in the Cold War because of the radical disarmament proposals that were exchanged, no actual agreement was reached at the summit. As at the Geneva Summit, Reagan insisted that the United States be allowed to continue work on SDI, and Gorbachev insisted that this was unacceptable. Therefore, the summit ended without an agreement, and both leaders left frustrated. After the summit,

Gorbachev made optimistic public comments, but privately referred to Reagan's administration as "political scum" and expressed doubt over whether an agreement could ever be achieved (Wilson 2014, 122).

Shortly after the Reykjavik Summit, US-Soviet relations took another downturn due to the summit's failure and a spate of tit-for-tat diplomatic expulsions (Matlock 2004, 242). Because of these events and the 1986 congressional election campaign, Reagan's statements of resolve targeted at the Soviet Union reached an all-time high in October 1986, as measured by my dictionary and shown previously in Figure 7.2. Reagan put blame on Gorbachev for the failure of the summit and said that the United States would never back down on SDI. Soviet leaders appear to have paid attention to this rhetoric as well as the diplomatic expulsions. In an October 1986 Politburo meeting, Gorbachev complained that members of the Reagan administration were "doing everything to inflame the atmosphere" and "acting like bandits" (Politburo 1986a, 1). During this time, Gorbachev still placed hope in the ability of US public opinion to restrain Reagan. He expressed optimism that the failure of the Reykjavik Summit would be a political blow to the Republican Party in the United States (Politburo 1986b, 3). He said, "We need to continue to put pressure on the American administration, explaining our positions to the population and showing that the American side is responsible for the breakdown in the agreement" (Politburo 1986a, 1).

However, evidence continued to mount that Reagan was unlikely to be constrained by the need to maintain public support. Reagan had automatically gained some security in office after his reelection because he no longer had to face another election campaign. Reagan also had security in office in the form of public support. As Nixon had noted, Reagan's popularity was at a high point between the Geneva and Reykjavik Summits. During that time period, Reagan maintained a net approval rating ranging from 31 to 52 percentage points, meaning that substantially more Americans approved, than disapproved, of his job performance (Peters and Woolley 2016). Public opinion continued to support Reagan after the failure of the Reykjavik Summit. The public seemed persuaded by Reagan's statements resolving to stand firm on SDI and blaming Gorbachev for the summit's failure. A *New York Times*/CBS News poll found that 44 percent of Americans blamed Gorbachev for the failure, while only 17 percent blamed Reagan (Matlock 2004, 239).

Reagan's approval rating did decline when the Iran–Contra scandal broke, less than one month after the Reykjavik Summit. However, even in 1987, as new information about the scandal was slowly being revealed, Reagan maintained an average net approval rating around 8.5 percent (Peters and Woolley 2016). The fact that Reagan managed to maintain more approval than disapproval in such circumstances is testament to his great skill at getting the American people to like him, which earned him the reputation of being a "Teflon president" that no scandal could stick to. Reagan's political troubles did not make him any more accommodating toward the Soviet Union. He continued to stand firm on the same positions and make statements of resolve. In his January 1987 State of the Union Address, Reagan listed numerous ways in which he viewed Soviet conduct as unacceptable and accused the Soviet leaders of "single-minded determination to expand their power" (Peters and Woolley 2016).

In February 1987, Gorbachev changed his position and decided to delink SDI from arms reductions (Anderson and Anderson 2009, 335; Charles 2015, 66). This decision allowed the United States and the Soviet Union to negotiate and sign the INF Treaty, which essentially codified the "zero option" proposal for intermediate-range forces in Europe that the United States had made in 1981. A variety of factors contributed to the change in Soviet strategy, including economic pressure, Gorbachev's ideas about collective security, and an increasing Soviet belief that SDI was unworkable.[7] However, Soviet desire to influence public opinion also played a role in the decision to delink SDI.

In early 1987, Gorbachev told his Politburo colleagues that he thought Reagan was only pretending to want arms reductions to mollify the American public. He therefore suggested that the Soviet Union could call Reagan's bluff by suggesting large mutual arms reductions with no linkage to an SDI agreement (Matlock 2004, 251). Gorbachev's advisor Aleksandr Yakovlev wrote a memo analyzing the merits of delinking SDI, in which he argued that it would improve public opinion of the Soviet Union because "it would look objectively as one more expression of our goodwill and common sense." Politburo member Yegor Ligachev likewise thought that by delinking SDI, the USSR "would win a lot in public opinion" (Charles 2015, 78–79). In his memoirs, Gorbachev himself portrayed the decision as an opportunity to regain the initiative in the public sphere, even though he was not yet sure if further cooperation with the Reagan administration was possible ([1995] 1997, 566–567).

Therefore, the Soviet decision to delink SDI from other arms control issues and accept the INF zero option is crucially linked to Soviet beliefs about Reagan's security in office and his ability to continue to follow through on his statements of resolve. Initially, Soviet leaders had hoped that public opinion and concerns about security in office would force Reagan to back down from his resolved statements and modify his negotiating position. When Soviet leaders realized that Reagan would be in office for four more years and that the resolved positions that he took had substantial US public support, they began to modify their own position in hopes of gaining an advantage in public opinion which would increase pressure on Reagan. Even though Gorbachev's February 1987 decision to delink SDI was not made at the height of Reagan's popularity, it followed two years of frustration among Gorbachev and his advisors that Reagan had managed to maintain high public support while making highly resolved statements and taking what they perceived as an inflexible position in negotiations.

---

[7] For example, Andrei Sakharov, the famous Soviet scientist and dissident, argued that SDI could be easily overwhelmed (Charles 2015, 75).

ALTERNATE EXPLANATIONS

Many explanations have been offered for the successful negotiation of the INF Treaty and the end of the Cold War. To be clear, I make no claim that Reagan's statements of resolve and security in office are the sole causes of these events. I only claim that these factors played a significant role. Other factors, including the economic situation in the Soviet Union, the Soviet inability to keep up with the United States in the arms race, the role of ideas, Gorbachev's own background and personality, and the influence of other individual actors, also clearly played important roles. Most of the other factors contributing to the end of the Cold War have already been well analyzed by other research, and they complement, rather than contradict, my own account. Therefore, I will not attempt to compare every alternate explanation for the end of the Cold War in this section. Rather, this section will focus on alternate explanations that are specifically related to the effectiveness of statements of resolve, including domestic audience cost theory, international reputational cost theory, and other factors related to the ability to follow through. I will also discuss the explanation that Reagan showed increased flexibility before the Soviets did, since this explanation is somewhat in contradiction to my own.

Costs of Backing Down

In keeping with the theory of domestic audience costs, there is some evidence that Reagan believed he would face domestic political costs for backing down. A State Department official told Soviet ambassador Dobrynin (1995, 493) that Reagan believed he owed his public support to the tough line he took with the Soviet Union and that backing away from that policy would have negative political repercussions. Furthermore, at his meeting with Gorbachev in Reykjavik, Reagan said that he could not back down on SDI because of domestic public opinion (Anderson and Anderson 2009, 307–314). However, Reagan's beliefs about US public opinion were not shared by the Soviets. As shown in detail in the preceding sections, the Soviets believed that domestic public opinion was a factor that could *persuade* Reagan to back down, rather than punish him for backing down. Therefore, it does not seem that the Soviets gave any serious consideration to the idea that Reagan would face domestic audience costs for backing down from his statements, and audience cost theory therefore cannot explain their decision-making.

Another possible explanation for the effectiveness of Reagan's statements is international reputational costs. Reagan himself and his advisors seemed to believe in the existence of such costs. At the outset of his term, Reagan believed that America's international reputation had been damaged by weak policies and that it was necessary for him to restore it. According to US defense secretary Caspar Weinberger, the Soviet Union had "tested"

Carter and had taken advantage of the situation when it found him to be weak. He also believed that the Soviet Union was now testing Reagan in the same way (Dobrynin 1995, 495). It follows from this belief that backing down would have negative consequences for the United States. However, this type of logic does not necessarily link international reputation to statements of resolve. More importantly, there is no evidence that the Soviets thought Reagan would face international reputational costs for backing down. As during the Cuban Missile Crisis, Soviet leaders seemed to consider themselves to be reasonable people who would not represent a real danger to the United States in the future. Therefore, the costs of backing down do not seem to have figured prominently into the Soviet response to Reagan's statements of resolve.

Other Factors Related to the Ability to Follow Through

We can also consider the impact of other factors related to the ability to follow through. In addition to security in office, the other factors that contribute to the ability to follow through are military strength and hawkish veto players. Military strength undoubtedly played a role in the effectiveness of statements in this case as well. Even though Reagan never made an explicit threat to attack the Soviet Union, the evidence earlier in this chapter showed that some Soviet leaders feared this was a real possibility. These fears were due both to the extreme hostility that Soviet officials inferred from Reagan's statements and the physical reality of a large US nuclear arsenal. Under Gorbachev, there was less fear that a US nuclear strike was imminent. However, Gorbachev and his advisors understood that the balance of power favored the United States in the long term. Gorbachev's advisor Alexander Yakovlev told him "not to lose real opportunities in terms of improving relations with the USA, because in the next quarter of a century the USA will remain the strongest power in the world" (Wilson 2014, 92–93). Therefore, the fact that the United States had the military capability to stand firm against and even overtake the Soviet Union undoubtedly also influenced Soviet officials to take Reagan's statements of resolve seriously and eventually modify their position. However, military capabilities by themselves would not have been as influential to the Soviets if they had continued to believe that the need to maintain public support would hinder Reagan's ability to follow through on his statements.

The final factor related to the ability to follow through is the hawkishness of veto players. It appears that hawkish veto players did also have some impact on Soviet beliefs. In his account of relations with the Reagan administration, Soviet ambassador Dobrynin often notes the hawkishness of officials in the administration. For example, he notes that "the top echelon charged with American disarmament policy consisted mostly of those essentially opposed to what they were supposed to be doing," that is, opposed to arms control (1995, 486). The Soviets also blamed Reagan's advisors for some of his intransigence. After the failure to reach an agreement at the Reykjavik Summit, Gorbachev complained that Reagan was "unable to handle his gang" (Zubok 2007, 293). Therefore, as during the Cuban Missile Crisis, Soviet officials in the 1980s understood that no one within the Reagan administration would prevent Reagan from following through on his statements of resolve and that some administration officials might even push him to be tougher.

On the other hand, Reagan had additional veto players who were more dovish. In particular, Congress as a whole was notably more dovish than Reagan. Democrats controlled the House of Representatives throughout Reagan's time in office and controlled both houses of Congress during his last two years in office. Democratic members of Congress criticized Reagan's policy toward the Soviet Union, and Congress even blocked funding for aid to rebels in Nicaragua (Howell and Pevehouse 2007). Congress initially authorized large defense budget increases requested by Reagan, but his military spending requests faced increased resistance. Over Reagan's two terms in office, Congress cut $61 billion from his proposed defense spending budgets (Campagna 1994, 65).

On the whole, there is no evidence that Soviet leaders considered Congress or other actors in the US government to be great obstacles to his ability to follow through. Therefore, Reagan's veto players were hawkish enough not to undermine his statements. On the other hand, Reagan did not enjoy the freedom of having completely hawkish veto players, and the hawkishness of veto players does not appear to have played as big a role in this case as security in office. One reason for this conclusion is that based on Soviet records, the Soviets did not pay a great deal of attention to changes in the hawkishness of Reagan's veto players over time. Another reason is that veto players in Congress and to some extent within Reagan's own administration were actually less hawkish when the Soviets began to modify their negotiating position than they had been earlier when the Soviets stood firm.

Reagan's Own Policy Changes

A final alternate explanation for the signing of the INF Treaty and the end of the Cold War is that Reagan's own policy changed before Soviet policy, and thus changes in the Soviet position represent reciprocation of Reagan's conciliation rather than backing down in the face of Reagan's resolve. Fischer (1997, 40–45) argues that Reagan's 1984 "Ivan and Anya" speech (discussed earlier) was a true turning point after which the Reagan administration began to focus more on common interests with the USSR. Dobrynin (1995, 485) also argues that Reagan's own position toward the Soviet Union eventually softened, making it easier to have a dialogue with him. There is indeed evidence that Reagan became more interested in engaging with the Soviet Union over time and reducing the number of nuclear weapons in the world (Fischer 1997). The summit meetings between Reagan and Gorbachev also enabled greater rapport between the leaders.

However, regardless of Reagan's personal desire for engagement, it cannot be said that his administration's policy positions substantially softened over his years in office. In negotiations, the United States continued to insist on greater Soviet arms reductions, the right to build SDI, and improvement in the Soviet human rights record. Therefore, the breakthrough in arms control negotiations and subsequent improvement in US-Soviet relations resulted more from a shift in the Soviet position than from a shift in the US position. The INF Treaty that was signed in 1987 closely resembled the position that the United States had been insisting on since 1981. Furthermore, Gorbachev's angry and even rude private comments about Reagan, quoted earlier, show that the Soviet leadership did not view Reagan's policies as conciliatory even as late as 1986 or 1987. Thus, while greater engagement by Reagan in his second term may have contributed to the eventual success of arms control negotiations and the reduction in US-Soviet tensions, it cannot be said to be the primary driver.

SUMMING UP

In sum, the Soviet reaction to Reagan's statements of resolve is generally in keeping with the theory regarding the impact of security in office presented in Chapter 1. Throughout the 1981–1987 period analyzed, Soviet leaders paid close attention to Reagan's statements and viewed them as genuine indications of his resolve to confront and undermine the Soviet Union. They recognized that Reagan's ability to follow through on his resolved statements was enhanced by strong US military capabilities and the presence of at least somewhat hawkish veto players. However, Soviet leaders initially hoped that insecurity in office due to the need to maintain public approval and win reelection would constrain Reagan's ability to follow through on his statements of resolve in the long term. As increased evidence of Reagan's security in office became available, Soviet leaders began to accept that Reagan was unlikely to ever be forced to back down from his statements of resolve. In response to this realization as well as other pressures, the Soviet Union began to modify its own negotiating position.

8

Vietnam War

In Chapters 6 and 7, I showed how US presidential statements of resolve, coupled with the ability to follow through, helped the United States achieve favorable outcomes in the Cuban Missile Crisis and in arms control negotiations with the Soviet Union under the Reagan administration. In the Cuban Missile Crisis case, the hawkishness of President Kennedy's veto players was an important factor that made his statements more effective. In the Reagan administration case, Soviet leaders became more responsive to the president's resolved statements when Reagan had greater public support and security in office. In this chapter, I will turn to a case in which US presidents had neither very hawkish veto players nor great security in office – the Vietnam War. I will show that North Vietnamese leaders were well aware of the political impediments that US presidents faced to following through on their statements of resolve and that this caused them to largely ignore US statements.

The Vietnam War was the most significant military failure for the United States during the Cold War. The United States entered the war in order to demonstrate its commitment to contain the spread of communism worldwide. However, after over two decades of involvement in Vietnam (including eight years in an active combat role), over 58,000 US deaths, and up to two million Vietnamese deaths (LaFeber 1994, 668), the United States was unable to prevail over North Vietnamese and Viet Cong forces. The United States signed a peace treaty in 1973 that fell far short of its original objectives and then stood by as North Vietnam (also known as the Democratic Republic of Vietnam, or DRV) conquered South Vietnam in 1975.

Throughout the war, US presidents Lyndon Johnson and Richard Nixon struggled to successfully convey US resolve to the North Vietnamese. Expressing his frustration with this, President Johnson said in 1967, "I so much wish that it were within my power to assure that all those in Hanoi could hear one simple message–America is committed to the defense of South Vietnam until an honorable peace can be negotiated. If this one communication gets through and its rational implications are drawn, we should be at the [negotiating] table tomorrow" (March 15, 1967, quoted in Peters and Woolley 2016).

However, US statements of resolve for the most part seemed to fall on deaf ears in North Vietnam. I will show that the most important factor undermining the credibility of US statements of resolve, particularly in the later years of the war, was North Vietnamese awareness of domestic political limitations on the US ability to follow through on its stated commitments. I will also show that after Nixon's political ability to follow through increased slightly in 1972, the North Vietnamese became slightly more willing to compromise.

BACKGROUND

US involvement in Vietnam began in the 1950s, when the United States supported French forces fighting to retain colonial rule over Vietnam. After France withdrew from Vietnam, separate governments were established in the north and south. However, capitalist South Vietnam failed to hold free elections as promised, and communist North Vietnam began to organize and support an insurgent force in the South, commonly referred to as the Viet Cong. As insurgent activities increased, President Kennedy sent 16,000 military advisors to aid South Vietnam in 1961 (Hook and Spanier 2013, 91–92). US involvement further escalated under President Johnson. In 1964, Johnson alleged that North Vietnam had attacked a US naval vessel in the Gulf of Tonkin. This spurred Congress to pass the Gulf of Tonkin Resolution, officially authorizing US military operations in Vietnam. In March 1965, Johnson initiated Operation Rolling Thunder, a campaign of continuous airstrikes on North Vietnam (Thies 1980, 84). Johnson also gradually raised the number of US troops in Vietnam and increased their combat role. By 1969, over 500,000 troops were fighting there (Hook and Spanier 2013, 91–92). The North Vietnamese also escalated their activities in South Vietnam, sending in regular army forces as well as continuing to support and direct the activities of the Viet Cong (Duiker 1996, 274).

The fighting in Vietnam did not go well for the United States, as US military strategy was not well suited for combatting guerilla warfare, and US tactics alienated the local population. In spring 1968, North Vietnamese and Viet Cong forces launched a major military operation, known as the Tet Offensive. While the offensive did not achieve its military goals, it demonstrated that communist forces in Vietnam were still strong. Shortly after the Tet Offensive, President Johnson announced that he would scale back the bombing of North Vietnam and not run for reelection. In response to this, the North Vietnamese agreed to begin negotiations on ending the war (Asselin 2012, 575).

Negotiations continued under President Nixon, both in public and in private. However, little progress was made toward compromise. As an alternate path toward ending the war, Nixon pursued a strategy of "Vietnamization," which involved giving aid to South Vietnamese forces in the hope that they would become capable of defending the country themselves. Nixon's stated aim was to slowly withdraw US forces as South Vietnamese forces became stronger (Kimball 1998, 137–139). In 1972, the North Vietnamese negotiating strategy became slightly more compromising (Asselin 2011), for reasons discussed later in this chapter. This allowed a peace agreement to be signed in January 1973, which ended US fighting in Vietnam.

The agreement fell short of North Vietnam's long-held goal of total victory because it left the South Vietnamese government in place. However, it also fell far short of the US goal of leaving South Vietnam in a secure position, since it even allowed North Vietnamese troops to remain inside South Vietnam (Kimball 1998, 367). Despite the peace agreement and US withdrawal, fighting continued between North and South Vietnam, and the North experienced increasing success. In 1975, Northern forces conquered all of South Vietnam with no US intervention. Vietnam became a unified country under a communist government, the exact outcome that the United States had sought to prevent.

Thus, the United States was involved in Vietnam for over two decades. To make my analysis more manageable, I will begin my examination of US presidential statements of resolve and the North Vietnamese reaction to them beginning in August 1964, the month in which the Gulf of Tonkin incident took place. My analysis will end with the signing of the peace agreement which ended US involvement in the war in January 1973.

US PRESIDENTIAL STATEMENTS OF RESOLVE DURING THE WAR

Both President Johnson and President Nixon made a steady stream of statements of resolve during the Vietnam War. Figure 8.1 shows the level of US presidential statements of resolve made in every month of the war, beginning in August 1964. If this figure is compared to Figure 7.2 in the previous chapter, it is apparent that both Johnson and Nixon made fewer resolved statements targeting the North Vietnamese than Reagan made targeting the Soviet Union, even though the United States was actually involved in a "hot" war with North Vietnam. When compared to all other militarized interstate disputes, the normalized statement score for the Vietnam War is in the 84th percentile. This is not as high as we might expect given the importance of the conflict in US history, but this mostly reflects the length of the conflict and the fact that presidents generally made fewer statements of resolve before the late 1970s. Compared to other disputes that ended in 1973 or earlier, the statement score for the Vietnam War ranks in the 94th percentile.

Figure 8.1 shows that both presidents made similar levels of resolved statements, although Nixon made slightly less. Although there was substantial monthly variation in the level of statements made by both Johnson and Nixon, there is no strong increasing or decreasing trend over time. The regression lines for both presidents plotted in Figure 8.1 are nearly flat. The month with the

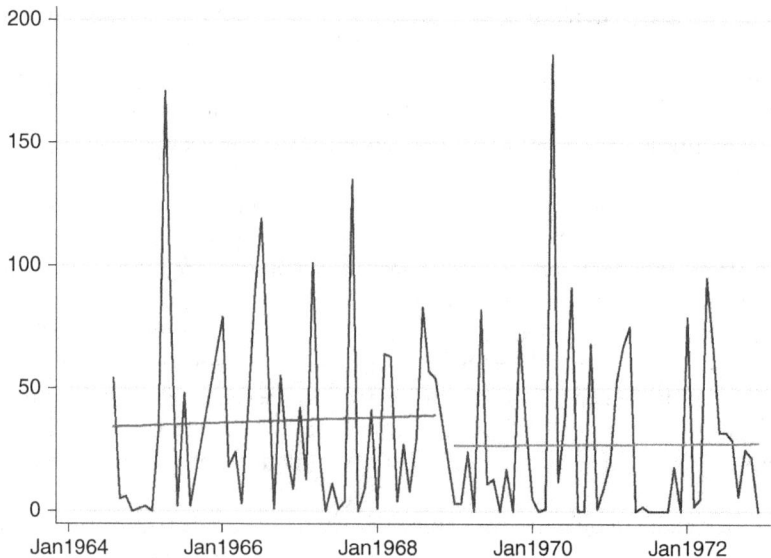

FIGURE 8.1 Monthly Scores for US Presidential Statements Targeting North Vietnam
Note: This figure shows the monthly score for resolved statements directed at North Vietnam, measured using the main dictionary used in previous chapters. The flatter lines are regression lines for the level of statements over time, under both Johnson and Nixon.

highest statement score is April 1970, when Nixon made two televised addresses to the nation regarding the war.

In terms of the content of the statements, President Johnson accused the North Vietnamese of aggression and expressed a commitment to assist South Vietnam for as long as necessary. For example on March 20, 1965, he stated, "It is and it will remain the policy of the United States to furnish assistance to support South Viet-Nam for as long as is required to bring Communist aggression and terrorism under control." In a policy address at Johns Hopkins University on April 7, 1965, he portrayed the Vietnam War as necessary for preserving the US reputation for credibility and preventing communism from spreading further. He said that the United States would do "everything necessary" to protect the independence of South Vietnam, but wanted nothing for itself. As the war progressed, Johnson continued to reiterate this same reasoning for why America must fight in Vietnam and to reassure the world that America was committed. For example, on June 18, 1966, he said the United States was "fully committed" and "determined to see this through" (Peters and Woolley 2016).

In 1969, President Nixon came to office determined to put an end to the Vietnam War. To appeal to the domestic public, he frequently emphasized this goal and spoke to the public about his plans to reduce US forces in Vietnam.

However, like Johnson, he also emphasized the importance of maintaining an honorable reputation and stopping the spread of communism for future US national security. Therefore, beginning with his first address to the nation regarding Vietnam, on May 14, 1969, Nixon asserted that it was important "to end this war in a way that would increase our chances to win true and lasting peace in Vietnam, in the Pacific, and in the world" (Peters and Woolley 2016).

Rather than publicly set a deadline for the end of US involvement in Vietnam, Nixon insisted on July 1, 1970, and other occasions, that it was important for the United States to stay involved "long enough for the South Vietnamese to be strong enough to handle their own defense" or until a peace agreement was reached (Peters and Woolley 2016). Nixon preferred to end the war through a peace agreement, but he said any agreement would have to meet certain conditions, including the return of prisoners of war and adequate security for South Vietnam. For example, on August 29, 1972, he said, "We will do what is necessary to assure the return of our POW's and account for our missing in action." He adamantly refused North Vietnamese demands for the United States to depose the present government of South Vietnam, an action which he said, on July 27, 1972, would be "the height of immorality." Nixon often referred to the type of peace agreement he wanted as "peace with honor," which he contrasted with defeat or surrender. For example, he said on April 25, 1972, "My fellow Americans, let us therefore unite as a nation in a firm and wise policy of real peace – not the peace of surrender, but peace with honor" (Peters and Woolley 2016). Therefore, even though Nixon was eager to end the Vietnam War, his public statements expressed resolve to either achieve certain conditions in negotiations or stay until the South Vietnamese reached an adequate level of military capabilities.

THE SELECTION QUESTION: WHY WERE STATEMENTS OF RESOLVE MADE?

As in the previous case studies, before turning to how presidential statements were perceived by the adversary, I will explore the question of why they were made. This is intended to address concerns raised earlier in the book about statistical bias due to the fact that presidents might make more statements when they already expect to win. In this particular case, given the protracted and ultimately unsuccessful nature of the conflict, Johnson and Nixon would have to have been significantly out of touch with reality if they made statements of resolve due to confidence in victory.

The evidence indicates that Johnson and Nixon were not so unrealistic. By the end of 1965, there were already signs that the Johnson administration recognized the conflict was going poorly. Secretary of Defense Robert McNamara returned from a visit to Vietnam in November 1965 with a prediction that significantly more troops and bombing would be required and that even this "will not guarantee success." The next month, McNamara admitted that the administration's initial predictions had been "too optimistic," and Johnson himself expressed concern that there was no clear sign of victory (Hunt 1996, 109). Nixon entered office with the expectation that he could end the war within a few months, but by October 1969 he believed victory would take up to two more years (Nixon 1978, 349, 404–405). By August 1972, Nixon privately admitted that "South Vietnam probably is never gonna survive," and National Security Advisor Henry Kissinger suggested privately that the US goal should be lowered to finding "some formula that holds the thing together a year or two, after which ... no one will give a damn" (Nixon and Kissinger 1972). However, despite the increasing pessimism about the outcome of the war under both presidents, Figure 8.1 shows no clear decline in the level of resolved statements that they made over time. If Johnson and Nixon did not make statements because they expected a sure victory, why then did they make them?

There is some evidence that both President Johnson and President Nixon thought that their statements of resolve would influence North Vietnamese beliefs about their intentions and improve their chances of winning, in keeping with my theory and other theories of signaling. For example, when Johnson called North Vietnamese interference in South Vietnam "a dangerous game" on February 21, 1964, he told his press secretary that this was intended to be a warning to North Vietnam that the United States might attack the DRV directly if it did not modify its behavior (Thies 1980, 24). There is also evidence that Nixon believed his statements could be influential to the North Vietnamese. Nixon allegedly told his chief of staff that his reputation as a die-hard Cold Warrior would make his threats credible to the North Vietnamese, saying, "They'll believe any threat of force that Nixon makes because it's Nixon" (Haldeman and DiMona 1978, 82–83).

Another motive for Johnson's and Nixon's statements of resolve was probably to rally the US population in support of the war, despite its uncertain prospects for success. There is evidence that Nixon, in particular, pursued this strategy deliberately. In 1969, Nixon began a public relations campaign intended to boost domestic support for a more prolonged war (Kimball 1998, 173–174). In the words of Nixon's chief of staff, it was decided that it was time to "take on" the doves (Haldeman 1994, 96). In a resolved speech to the nation on November 3, 1969, Nixon criticized the "vocal minority" protesting against the war and appealed for the support of the "silent majority" of Americans, arguing that greater national unity would lead to swifter victory in Vietnam (Peters and Woolley 2016). Nixon spent a long time preparing for this speech and closely monitored the domestic reaction to it (Johns 2010, 268–272). Later speeches by Nixon, which combined resolved statements with announcements about troop withdrawals and negotiation status, were also targeted at undermining the antiwar movement (Kimball 1998, 292).

In sum, there is evidence that US presidents made statements of resolve during the Vietnam War to influence the North Vietnamese and also to unite the domestic population around their cause, which they also hoped would contribute to convincing the North Vietnamese to back down. It also appears that Johnson's and Nixon's statements reflected genuine resolve. Johnson had no intention of backing down in Vietnam, and while Nixon was not genuinely committed to the long-term security of South Vietnam, he was firmly committed to obtaining peace terms that would let him claim an "honorable" exit. However, there is no evidence that statements of resolve were made because Johnson or Nixon thought victory would be easy. Therefore, it still seems unlikely that the previous statistical results might be driven by reverse causation.

NORTH VIETNAMESE REACTION TO US STATEMENTS

There is no doubt that the North Vietnamese government heard all or most US presidential statements of resolve. The North Vietnamese leadership closely observed all aspects of US politics and carefully studied the positions of many relevant US political actors (Ang 2004; Asselin 2002; Nguyen 2012). Therefore, they could not ignore statements by the most powerful US actor, the president. We know that the North Vietnamese heard US presidential statements because they directly responded to them on several occasions. *Nhan Dan*, the official newspaper of the North Vietnamese Communist Party, responded specifically to President Johnson's address about the war at Johns Hopkins University on April 7, 1965. The article declared, "We will fight to the end!" (Smith 1991, 89). Similarly, when Johnson made a speech to the Association of American Editorial Cartoonists on May 13, 1965, reiterating the US commitment to South Vietnam (Peters and Woolley 2016), *Nhan Dan* published a rebuttal to the speech (Smith 1991, 132), and Radio Hanoi called the speech a "contemptible trick" (Thies 1980, 96). This represents a strong response to a speech that was not even made in a forum that was intended to elicit a great deal of attention.

The North Vietnamese government also directly responded to several of Nixon's statements about Vietnam. It responded to a major speech by Nixon in May 1969 by rejecting the peace terms discussed in it and deriding Nixon's concept of Vietnamization as a plan to "replace the war of aggression fought by U.S. troops with a war of aggression fought by the puppet army of the United States" (Johns 2010, 256). Furthermore, after Nixon gave a speech making a new peace proposal public on October 7, 1970, the North Vietnamese Foreign Ministry issued a rejection of the proposal, which was published in *Nhan Dan* (Nguyen 2012, 190). As a final example, when Nixon made a speech which revealed the existence of private negotiations and publicized a peace plan that the United States had offered in these talks on January 25, 1972, Hanoi's reaction was "livid" (Nguyen 2012, 237). The North Vietnamese government responded six days later by publicizing its own proposal, arguing that the United States was to blame for the impasse at the talks, and accusing the United States of trying to deceive the public (Kimball 1998, 290; Luthi 2009, 78).

There is evidence that US presidential statements were not only publicly rebutted but were also privately discussed among North Vietnamese officials as evidence of US intentions. An April 1968 Politburo cable to the communist command in South Vietnam stated, "In his 31 March 1968 speech, Johnson's tone was softer and not as arrogant and deceitful," and assessed that "Johnson realized that the U.S. cannot win in Vietnam and that, on the contrary, the U.S. might lose" (Politburo 1968). Indeed, according to my system for scoring statements of resolve, the televised speech referred to in this cable conveyed less than half as much resolve as Johnson's previous television address.[1] A later report presented at a Communist Party Central Committee meeting noted, "The Americans constantly boasted of their economic and military strength, and in early 1968 Johnson and the US generals issued propaganda statements saying that the situation in South Vietnam was very good and that in 1969 US troops might be able to start coming home." However, the report went on to note, the 1968 Tet Offensive had undermined these claims (Communist Party 1968). As another example, November 1971 instructions from Hanoi to North Vietnamese negotiators noted that "through his 12 November statement, Nixon appeared very stubborn" (Ang 2004, 84; Nguyen 2012, 226), suggesting that North Vietnamese officials inferred Nixon's resolve from his statements. According to my measure, Nixon did express more resolve in his November 12 press conference than in any previous remarks in the last six months.

Although there is evidence that North Vietnamese decision-makers heard and analyzed US presidential statements of resolve, it does not appear that the statements substantially influenced North Vietnamese beliefs about the probability that the United States would follow through on its commitment to South Vietnam. As shown in the preceding discussion, the public statements by US presidents were promptly rebutted or dismissed by the North Vietnamese. At least until 1972, the North Vietnamese negotiating position continued to be premised on the belief that they could achieve total victory over the United States (Asselin 2011). Even in the one case noted previously in which the North Vietnamese concluded based on Nixon's statements that he was resolved or "stubborn," it did not prompt them to back down. Rather, they decided to place more emphasis on their military efforts, since they believed there was little immediate prospect of progress in negotiations (Nguyen 2012, 226).

As in the other cases, the United States was sending other signals of resolve in addition to statements. All of the money and human lives that the United States

---

[1] In this speech, Johnson announced a unilateral reduction in the bombing of North Vietnam and his decision not to run for reelection.

was expending in the Vietnam War constituted a very large sunk cost signal of US resolve. It cannot be said that the North Vietnamese were indifferent to the US use of force because it directly hurt them. However, the use of force was ineffective as a *signal of resolve* because, as shown in the subsequent section, it did not cause the North Vietnamese to believe that the United States was truly committed to fighting for as long as it took to win. Why were US statements of resolve – in addition to other resolved actions, including the use of force – so ineffective at convincing the North Vietnamese to back down?

REASONS FOR DISCOUNTING US STATEMENTS OF RESOLVE

This section will make the case that an inability to follow through on statements of resolve due to both presidential insecurity in office and dovish veto players rendered US presidential statements ineffective. When US combat troops were first sent to Vietnam, the war had fairly robust public and congressional support. In fact, the 1964 Gulf of Tonkin Resolution authorizing US involvement in the war passed unanimously in the House and was opposed by only two members of the Senate. However, it did not take long for this support to dissipate. As shown in Figure 8.2, public approval for the war

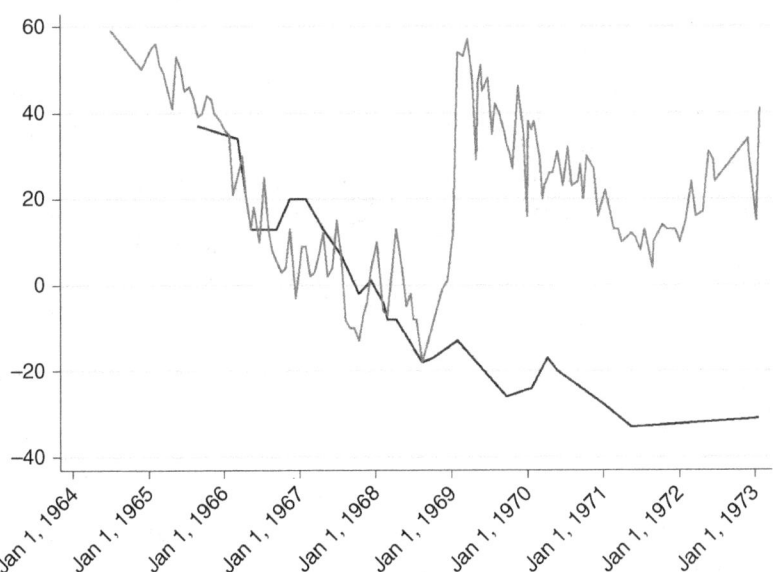

FIGURE 8.2 Effect of the War on Public Opinion
Note: The black line represents net support for the Vietnam War, i.e., the percentage of survey respondents believing the war was not a mistake minus the percentage believing it was (Gillespie 2010). The gray line represents net presidential approval, measured the same way as in the previous chapters (Peters and Woolley 2016).

dropped almost continuously as the war dragged on and casualties rose. By early 1968, net support for the war had fallen below zero, meaning that more Americans believed the war was a mistake than a worthwhile endeavor. By the end of the war, net war support had fallen below −30 percentage points. Opposition to the war was visible not only in the polls but also in the streets, as protests by the domestic antiwar movement grew in size.

The unpopularity of the war also translated into unpopularity for the president, which negatively affected presidential security in office. Figure 8.2 shows that President Johnson's popularity dropped fairly steadily between 1965 and 1968, with his net approval rating eventually falling from nearly 60 percentage points in summer 1964 to −18 percentage points by the time he left office. Demonstrating the importance of public opinion regarding the war to presidential security in office, Johnson's unpopularity eventually forced him to announce that he would not run for reelection. This decision resulted in a temporary boost in his popularity, but afterward his popularity continued to plummet until the transfer of power to President Nixon. While Nixon started off with a high approval rating, his popularity also declined fairly steadily between 1969 and 1971. During this time period, Nixon was well aware that he needed to show progress toward ending the war in order to retain enough public support for reelection (Kimball 1998, 286–287).

As the war became less popular, Congress also began to turn against it. Democrats controlled both houses of Congress throughout the period under consideration, and they increasingly opposed the war, especially after Johnson left office (Johns 2010, 249). In the first major act of congressional opposition, Senator William Fulbright held televised hearings on the shortcomings of US policy in Vietnam in 1966. Although the Republican Party generally remained more supportive of the war, even some Republican members of Congress began to question it. In September 1969, Republican senator Charles Goodell introduced a bill requiring the withdrawal of all US troops from Vietnam by December 1970. Although this bill never came close to passing, it was the first of many similar bills to be introduced. In December 1969, Congress passed an amendment which banned funding for military operations in Laos or Thailand. In June 1970, the Senate passed an amendment that also banned funding for operations in Cambodia. A weaker version of this amendment was passed by the full Congress in December 1970. During the same year, Senators Mark Hatfield and George McGovern proposed another amendment requiring the full withdrawal of US forces from Vietnam, which was voted down. In 1971, Senator Mike Mansfield began introducing amendments to various pieces of legislation requiring a US withdrawal from Vietnam within nine months. Two nonbinding versions of these amendments were passed by the full Congress in the fall (Belasco et al. 2007; Zelizer 2007). Therefore, it seemed increasingly likely that Congress might eventually pass binding legislation blocking the president's ability to continue the war.

North Vietnamese leaders were well aware of the domestic constraints on Johnson's and Nixon's ability to follow through on their stated commitments to fight until an honorable peace was achieved. As early as 1956, Le Duan, who would soon become secretary general of the North Vietnamese Communist Party, wrote a report analyzing US intentions in which he observed that "even the people of an imperialist warlike country like the U.S. want peace" (Shore 2014, 225). Analysis by North Vietnamese officials at a Central Committee meeting, on December 27, 1965, stated that even though the United States was economically and militarily strong, it was politically weak due to the constraints of domestic and international public opinion. The North Vietnamese therefore believed that the United States would not bring its full military power to bear in Vietnam (Ang 2002, 103).

As the war dragged on, the North Vietnamese followed domestic developments in the United States closely. According to the memoirs of Bui Tin (2002, 43), a colonel in the North Vietnamese army, DRV officials paid a great deal of attention to criticism of the Vietnam War by American politicians, journalists, intellectuals, and cultural figures. Speeches and documents produced by officials in the North Vietnamese government show further evidence of this. For example, Ho Chi Minh, the president of North Vietnam, observed in 1966 that domestic opposition to the war was a key weakness of the United States. His speech to Communist Party members noted the existence of youth protests and the civil rights movement in the United States (Shore 2014, 143). As another example, a 1968 cable from the North Vietnamese Politburo to the communist command in South Vietnam listed factors limiting the ability of the United States to continue the fight in Vietnam, including the value of the dollar and cost of living in the United States, statements by presidential candidates and other political opponents of Johnson, Robert Kennedy's presidential candidacy, demonstrations against the war, and riots in response to the assassination of Martin Luther King, Jr. (Politburo 1968).

The DRV leadership was aware of how the growing opposition to the war and other developments in the United States weakened Johnson's security in office, and they deliberately sought to further undermine his security. The North Vietnamese Politburo took into account the 1968 presidential election in making its decision to launch the Tet Offensive, saying a "strategic opportunity had arrived" (Asselin 2012, 573). Johnson's decision not to run for reelection in the aftermath of the offensive convinced the North Vietnamese that if their strategy could bring down the president of the United States, then the United States must be ready to give up in the Vietnam War (Bui Tin 2002, 61–66). Johnson might have hoped that removing reelection pressure from himself would make his ability to follow through in Vietnam more credible to the North Vietnamese. However, North Vietnamese leaders continued to maintain a tough line based on the belief that Johnson would want to make concessions in order to help the prospects of Democratic presidential candidate Hubert Humphrey (Asselin 2002, 8–9).[2]

The North Vietnamese followed developments in Congress closely as well. Ho Chi Minh's 1966 address to the Communist Party directly quoted a statement opposing the war by a US senator (Shore 2014, 143). The DRV leadership understood that if Congress were to succeed in passing a binding version of legislation requiring the withdrawal of troops, it would end the president's ability to follow through in Vietnam. After a nonbinding version of Mansfield's amendment requiring withdrawal passed in the House of Representatives, a North Vietnamese diplomat said that if a binding version had been passed, the North Vietnamese would have known exactly what Nixon's constraints were and seen little need to negotiate a ceasefire (Ang 2004, 72–73).

Therefore, it is clear that both increasing public disapproval for the war and the president and increasingly dovish views in Congress were undermining the president's ability to successfully convey resolve to the North Vietnamese. As the Communist Party Central Committee concluded at a meeting in late 1965, "The American imperialists are the strongest economic and military power in the imperialist camp. The general world situation and the domestic situation in the United States, however, will not allow them to fully utilize their economic and military power in their war of aggression. Politics has always been the enemy's weak point" (Military History Institute of Vietnam 2002, 171). Given this point of view, it is not surprising that US statements of resolve failed to persuade the North Vietnamese to back down. However, the North Vietnamese strategy began to shift slightly in 1972 due to changes in Nixon's ability to follow through.

SHIFT IN 1972

The North Vietnamese initially viewed 1972 as a crucial year during which Nixon would be particularly domestically vulnerable due to the presidential election scheduled in November, which was believed to be a "decisive moment" (Asselin 2011, 119). Many historians attribute the launching of the "Easter Offensive" in late March 1972 to a desire to drive Nixon out of office at election time (Duiker 1996, 318; Luthi 2009, 107). According to a Soviet diplomat, the North Vietnamese leadership drew an explicit parallel to the 1968 Tet Offensive, boasting, "We will overthrow Nixon, like we have overthrown Johnson" (Luthi 2009, 62). Given this belief that they could end Nixon's ability to follow through by driving him out of office, the North Vietnamese clearly had no incentive to pay attention to Nixon's statements of resolve or make any concessions in negotiations at this point.

---

[2] This fits with my assertion in Chapter 4 that domestic public opinion can affect adversary perceptions of the ability to follow through even when the president is not running for reelection.

Over the next few months, however, the North Vietnamese began to reconsider their position. There are several reasons for this. First, the Easter Offensive was not a military success, and Nixon responded to it with increased bombing and the mining of North Vietnamese ports. Second, the DRV was receiving increasing pressure from its Soviet and Chinese allies to reach a negotiated settlement (Asselin 2011, 119–123; Karnow 1997, 661–662; Nguyen 2012, 259–260). Third, and of greater relevance to Nixon's security in office, the North Vietnamese believed that Nixon's policy of détente with the Soviet Union and China was enhancing his domestic prestige and his security in office. The official newspaper of the DRV's Communist Party complained that Moscow's and Beijing's hosting of Nixon was like "throwing life preservers to a drowning pirate" (Porter 1975, 113). The North Vietnamese Politburo referred to warming relations between the United States and China as a "torpedo" against North Vietnamese policies and believed that détente had superseded the Vietnam War as an important issue in the US election, thus helping Nixon's reelection chances (Luthi 2009, 68). The North Vietnamese leadership also believed that the enhancement of Nixon's prestige due to détente led to a "weakening of the struggle of the American people against the war in Vietnam" (Asselin 2011, 118). The public opinion data shown previously in Figure 8.2 confirm that Nixon's popularity with the American people was indeed increasing in 1972, even though most people still thought the Vietnam War was a mistake.

After realizing that Nixon's domestic position was probably strong enough for him to win reelection and continue to follow through on his statements of resolve, the North Vietnamese became highly motivated to reach a deal with him prior to the election. The DRV leadership understood that the months of July–November were important in the US election cycle and believed that the opportunity for reaching an agreement was highest during these months (Ang 2004, 102–107). They hoped that Nixon would be eager to reach a deal to strengthen his security in office before the election (Luthi 2009, 65). The North Vietnamese foreign minister wrote that due to the pacifist statements of Democratic candidate George McGovern, "We now have more ways to exploit the contradictions between the two U.S. parties and to force Nixon to offer a settlement favorable to us" (Nguyen 2012, 264). Another North Vietnamese official told a French diplomat, "We can hope that the momentum that supports him [McGovern] might compel President Nixon, who worries above all about securing a second mandate, to soften at once his attitude" (Asselin 2011, 124).

The North Vietnamese eagerness to secure a deal with Nixon was driven not only by the hope that he would feel insecure in office and be willing to compromise prior to the election but also by the realization that Nixon ultimately had a good chance of winning reelection and would be more secure in office than ever after he did so. In August, North Vietnamese leaders set a goal to reach a peace agreement before the election because they "envisaged a difficult time ahead" if Nixon was reelected (Ang 2004, 107). In late September, the DRV leadership reaffirmed this decision after concluding that Nixon might not only be more resistant to concessions after reelection but might even renege on previous concessions (Ang 2004, 110). Although the North Vietnamese were eager to reach a deal before Nixon's security in office increased further, they did not want to weaken their negotiating position by revealing this to the United States. The North Vietnamese Politburo instructed its negotiators, "Do not let Nixon think that we are afraid of failing to negotiate a settlement when it is really him who is afraid that he won't be able to resolve Vietnam before the elections" (Nguyen 2012, 266).

Despite their reluctance to appear overly eager, the North Vietnamese did make several concessions to the United States in 1972. First, the North Vietnamese leadership decided in June 1972 to switch from "a strategy of war to a strategy of peace," as phrased in a Vietnamese historical account (Asselin 2011, 124). This meant that for the first time, the North Vietnamese would seriously pursue a compromise agreement with the United States rather than holding out for total victory. After several more months of deliberations, on October 8, North Vietnam gave up its long-standing demand that the United States remove President Thieu as the leader of South Vietnam (Asselin 2011, 127). Based on this concession, the United States and North Vietnam were able to negotiate a tentative peace deal by mid-October.

To the disappointment of both parties, the tentative deal collapsed due to South Vietnamese objections. This led the United States to make additional demands of North Vietnam. Since it now seemed quite certain that Nixon would win reelection regardless of the agreement, the DRV had less leverage, but it decided to show a tough face and delayed the resumption of negotiations until after the election (Nguyen 2012, 286). Nixon won the November 1972 presidential election by a landslide. At this point, it seemed undeniable that Nixon was quite secure in office. He had widespread popular support and would never have to run for reelection again, meaning that he could follow through on his statements of resolve with less risk to his political future. Still, the North Vietnamese decided to stand firm and resist additional concessions. To understand why, it is helpful to explore the role of a second factor related to the ability to follow through on statements of resolve – the dovishness of Congress, a key veto player.

As noted earlier, Congress had become increasingly dovish between 1966 and 1971. This trend continued in 1972, as the Senate for the first time passed a binding amendment cutting off funding for the war. Although the amendment did not pass in the House, it was the furthest that any binding measure to end the war had gone (Zelizer 2007). Clearly, momentum was building for Congress to force an end to the war, which undermined Nixon's negotiating position. On July 27, 1972, Nixon complained, "When you put yourself in the position of the enemy, and then they hear that the Congress of the United States says, in effect, 'We will give you what you want regardless of what the President has offered,' why not wait? This is the problem" (Peters and Woolley 2016). This problem had only gotten worse after the November 1972 elections, as many observers speculated that the new Congress to be seated in January would oppose Nixon at least as strongly on the Vietnam War as the previous Congress and might finally succeed in passing binding legislation to end the war (Gwertzman 1972; Reston 1972; Weaver 1972). The North Vietnamese could reasonably hope that Congress would soon make it impossible for Nixon to continue to follow through on his commitments in Vietnam (Asselin 2011, 130). Therefore, the absence of hawkish veto players probably undermined Nixon's ability to persuade the North Vietnamese to back down, even though he had increased security in office. This fits with the results in Chapter 5, which showed that a low enough value of any one factor associated with the ability to follow through can undermine the impact of the others.

In response to North Vietnam's continued refusal to make concessions, Nixon launched a bombing campaign, known as the "Christmas Bombing" because it took place in late December. Not only was the bombing highly destructive, but the North Vietnamese were disappointed with the reaction to the bombing, both internationally and within the United States (Asselin 2011, 131–132). Within the United States, there were many condemnations of the Christmas Bombing among journalists and public figures, and antiwar protests intensified. However, only 51 percent of the American public actually opposed the bombing, according to a poll (Harris Survey 1973). The negativity of the US domestic reaction evidently did not live up to North Vietnamese hopes. According to two separate accounts in diplomatic records, the North Vietnamese "saw no serious [domestic] opposition to the President's recent initiatives" and believed that "American opinion generally remained remarkably passive in the face of ongoing massive bombardments of North Vietnam" (Asselin 2011, 131). The limited outcry gave the North Vietnamese less reason to hope that domestic pressure would constrain Nixon's ability to follow through in the immediate future.

In response to this turn of events, the North Vietnamese agreed on December 26 to resume negotiations in exchange for a halt to the bombing. When negotiations resumed on January 8, the North Vietnamese made more concessions than the United States (Kimball 1998, 367; Luthi 2009, 105). An agreement was reached within days, and the final Paris Peace Accords were signed on January 27. One of the most significant North Vietnamese concessions was agreeing to US language on the demilitarized zone between North and South Vietnam, which the North Vietnamese had long resisted because it suggested that the zone was a border between two states. Another significant concession was allowing US military advisers to remain in South Vietnam, an acknowledgment that US influence in Vietnam would not completely end (Asselin 2011, 132–133).

These additional North Vietnamese concessions allowed the United States to save face, but it was truly the United States that backed down the most from its original war aims. Although the United States had fought to allow South Vietnam to remain independent and noncommunist, the United States ultimately left South Vietnam in an insecure position, making it unlikely that the country could successfully defend its independence in the long term. This fact was privately acknowledged by the Nixon administration (Nixon and Kissinger 1972). Nixon was unable to hold out for a better deal because his ability to follow through was still limited in January 1973. The new Congress had just convened with a vote by the House Democratic Caucus to pursue a policy of ending the war "immediately" and a vow by the Senate Democratic leader to "bring about complete disinvolvement [*sic*]" in Vietnam (Naughton 1973a; Naughton 1973b). It is unclear if or how quickly Congress could have succeeded in cutting off funding for the war, but Nixon did not want to find out and was glad to sign the peace agreement (Kimball 1998, 356).

In sum, the negotiation of the peace agreement that ended US involvement in the Vietnam War was a complicated affair in which both sides backed down to some extent. The United States backed down the most from its original war aims, due to the limitations on the ability to follow through that had plagued the United States throughout the war. However, the North Vietnamese also made nontrivial concessions, giving in to enough key US demands to allow Nixon to avoid openly backing down from his statements of resolve. The aforementioned evidence suggests that the North Vietnamese concessions were motivated in large part by a perceived increase in Nixon's security in office and ability to follow through as a result of Nixon's successful electoral campaign and the relatively small amount of domestic opposition to the Christmas Bombing. As of early 1973, the dovishness of Congress made it unclear exactly how long Nixon could continue to follow through in Vietnam, but both sides preferred to be cautious and sign a peace agreement before things could get any worse for them.

There was no substantial increase or decrease in Nixon's statements of resolve in 1972 compared to previous years. However, while the North Vietnamese were unmoved by hearing US presidential statements of resolve throughout most of the war, when Nixon's ability to follow through increased in 1972, they became willing to concede to what Nixon had been demanding in his statements all along. The most important concession that North Vietnam made, which was to allow the South Vietnamese government to remain in power for the present, was also the demand that Nixon had emphasized most in his statements of resolve.

ALTERNATE EXPLANATIONS

The preceding account provides convincing evidence that lack of an ability to follow through on statements of resolve due to presidential insecurity in office and dovish veto players in Congress rendered US presidential statements of resolve ineffective for most of the war. However, it is possible that additional factors also contributed to the failure of US statements to convince the North Vietnamese to back down. This section will consider the role of three alternate factors that might also influence the effectiveness of resolved statements: military strength, domestic audience costs, and international reputation.

With regard to military strength, the military balance in the Vietnam War clearly favored the United States. It is true that the United States did not excel at combatting guerilla warfare, and the North Vietnamese noted this as a limitation of the United States (Shore 2014, 140). However, military power was not viewed as the main impediment to the US ability to follow through on its statements. The North Vietnamese Politburo acknowledged the United States as "the strongest economic and military power in the imperialist camp," but said that politics was the "weak point" of the United States (Military History Institute 2002, 171). Indeed, the US government placed limits on its military activities in Vietnam due to concerns about public opinion. For example, in 1969, Nixon considered a major escalation of US military operations in Vietnam, known as Operation "Duck Hook," but rejected it for fear of how much it would divide US society (Kimball 1998, 158–169). When the United States did bring more of its military strength to bear, such as during Nixon's two major bombing campaigns in 1972, there is evidence that this put pressure on the North Vietnamese government to make concessions (Asselin 2011, 131–132; Nguyen 2012, 258–260). However, for the most part the North Vietnamese correctly understood that domestic political constraints would limit the US ability to utilize its full military capabilities. Therefore, the absence of hawkish veto players and security in office undermined the impact of US military strength during the war.

Another potential influence on the effectiveness of resolved statements is domestic audience costs. The evidence suggests that domestic audience costs were small for much of the Vietnam War because the US president would not have faced much domestic political punishment for backing down from previous resolved statements. Johnson did initially believe that backing down in Vietnam would hurt him domestically. He told biographer Doris Kearns (1976, 252–253) that losing Vietnam to communism would result in "an endless national debate – a mean and destructive debate – that would shatter my Presidency, kill my administration, and damage our democracy." However, as public opinion turned against the war, there was less probability of punishment for backing down. In fact, Nixon sometimes asserted in public that it would be easier for him to back down. On April 30, 1970, he said that attacking Cambodia might make him a one-term president, but added, "I would rather be a one-term President and do what I believe is right." On May 8, 1972 Nixon said, "From a political standpoint, this [an immediate withdrawal] would be a very easy choice for me to accept. After all, I did not send over one-half million Americans to Vietnam" (Peters and Woolley 2016). Nixon may have exaggerated the purity of his own motives, but his characterization of the political risks he faced in continuing the war were not entirely off-base.

This case therefore demonstrates that there are not always significant domestic audience costs for backing down from resolved statements. It is possible that the absence of high domestic audience costs also contributed to the ineffectiveness of presidential statements of resolve during the Vietnam War, having a complementary effect with the inability to follow through on statements. However, whereas the previous sections showed direct evidence that the North Vietnamese considered the US ability to follow through, I found no evidence that they explicitly considered the president's domestic costs for backing down. Furthermore, domestic audience cost theory would have difficulty explaining the final concessions made by the North Vietnamese after Nixon had been reelected and faced even lower potential audience costs. Therefore, my theory of the ability to follow through provides a stronger explanation for North Vietnamese behavior than audience cost theory.

The final explanation to consider for the North Vietnamese reaction to US statements of resolve is international reputation. This explanation is important to examine because on the US side, the war was fought in large part as an effort to maintain the US reputation for both toughness and credibility. Johnson told an aide that he wanted to prevent China and the Soviet Union from thinking "we're yellow and don't mean what we say" (Hunt 1996, 79). He later told a biographer, "Everything I knew about history told me that if I got out of Vietnam and let Ho Chi Minh run through the streets of Saigon, then I'd be doing exactly what Chamberlain did in World War II. I'd be giving a big fat reward to aggression" (Kearns 1976, 252–253). In public, Johnson said on April 1, 1965, that if the United States violated its commitment to South Vietnam made under the SEATO Treaty, "we might as well tear up all the treaties we are party to" (Peters and Woolley 2016). Nixon also apparently believed that there would be negative international reputational consequences for the United States if it backed down completely in Vietnam. For example, on May 8, 1972, he said, "An American defeat in Vietnam would encourage this kind of aggression all over the world." In addition, Nixon stated, on August 29, 1972, that accepting defeat in Vietnam would lead to "the destruction of the ability of the United States to conduct foreign policy in a responsible way" (Peters and Woolley 2016). Therefore, both Johnson and Nixon seemed to care about maintaining a reputation for keeping commitments as well as being tough against communism. This is in keeping with the theory of international reputational costs.

However, the real questions for this theory are whether the North Vietnamese understood the US desire to maintain a credible reputation and whether this made US statements of resolve more influential to the North Vietnamese. There is some evidence that the North Vietnamese were aware of US reputational concerns. For example, in 1962, Le Duan wrote of presenting "limited demands" in order to allow the United States to "lose at a level which they can accept" (Shore 2014, 118, 227). As another example, in November 1972, the North Vietnamese assessed that Nixon would not back down due to "strategic reasons having to do with the Cold War" (Asselin 2011, 129). In general, however, reputation does not appear to have been a major theme in North Vietnamese discussions of the United States. Furthermore, if the North Vietnamese were highly influenced by beliefs about US reputational costs, then they probably would have been more inclined to back down since it was clear that the United States had staked a large part of its reputation on the outcome of the war. Instead, the DRV leadership seemed to believe that domestic limitations on the ability to follow through would override the US desire to preserve its international reputation.

SUMMING UP

On the whole, the Vietnam War was a failure for the United States. Despite the concessions that the North Vietnamese made in October 1972 and January 1973, the United States made a greater number of concessions than the North Vietnamese over the duration of the conflict, and the war outcome for the United States was far short of original US goals. While the Paris Peace Accords allowed Nixon to avoid backing down from his public commitment not to negotiate away the independence of South Vietnam, the security measures included in the accords were not strong enough to preserve South Vietnam's independence in the long term.

There are many reasons why the US strategy in Vietnam was unsuccessful, but one important reason was the inability of US presidents to credibly convey resolve to the North Vietnamese. Presidents Johnson and Nixon did repeatedly attempt to convey resolve to the DRV with their statements, and there is evidence that the North Vietnamese leadership heard and analyzed the statements. However, at least between 1964 and 1971, the statements failed to convince the North Vietnamese that the United States would truly follow through on its commitment to defend South Vietnam for as long as necessary. It is clear that the main reason for North Vietnamese disbelief that the United States would honor this commitment was domestic obstacles to the continued ability to follow through. The North Vietnamese closely observed US politics and saw that Presidents Johnson and Nixon were insecure in office as a result of the war and faced increasing opposition from Congress. Therefore, they had valid reasons to hope that the president would end the war due to the risk of losing office or be forced to withdraw by veto players in Congress.

In 1972, there were hints that Nixon's security in office was improving, as he looked increasingly likely to win reelection. This spurred the North Vietnamese to begin to make some concessions, and they made further concessions after Nixon's landslide reelection and minimal public and congressional opposition to his December bombing campaign. Thus, a slight improvement in Nixon's perceived ability to follow through led the North Vietnamese to back down slightly and move closer toward the positions that Nixon had committed to in his statements of resolve. However, limitations on the US ability to follow through still remained due to the dovishness of Congress. In the peace agreement that was ultimately negotiated, both sides made concessions, but the United States backed down more from its original war aims.

To conclude, this case provides support for the importance of the ability to follow through as a factor impacting the effectiveness of resolved statements. In particular, this case demonstrates the importance of the political conditions associated with the ability to follow through, namely, hawkish veto players and security in office. Whereas the previous case studies of the Cuban Missile Crisis and the Cold War under Reagan showed how having these conditions makes statements of resolve more effective, this case illustrates how the absence of these conditions renders statements ineffective. Despite the great desire of Presidents Johnson and Nixon to convey resolve and their apparently genuine conviction that the US reputation was at stake, the North Vietnamese dismissed the statements that they heard. They did this because their analysis of US politics indicated that as much as US presidents might want to follow through, they would be politically unable to do so indefinitely.

Conclusion

This book began by asking why the statements of resolve that President Obama made toward the Islamic State beginning in 2014 were ineffective at altering the terrorist organization's behavior. Certainly, particular characteristics of ISIL itself may play a role in answering this question. However, the conflict with ISIL is not an entirely new phenomenon. Throughout its history, the United States has been involved in international disputes in which it has attempted to persuade its adversary to back down. This book has established that in many of these disputes in the post–World War II era, the US president has used public statements of resolve to convey US willingness to fight or continue fighting, seeking to intimidate adversaries. Therefore, understanding what has made statements of resolve effective in the past can help us understand why statements may or may not be effective in more recent conflicts, such as the confrontation with ISIL.

This book has emphasized a new condition that is important for understanding the effectiveness of resolved statements, namely, the ability to follow through on the statements. Statistical and case study evidence indicates that the ability to follow through has been a crucial predictor of the effectiveness of US statements of resolve in past conflicts. Having explored what the ability to follow through includes and how it matters throughout the preceding chapters, we are now in a better position to understand how President Obama lacked a clear ability to follow through against the Islamic State from 2014 onward.

First, despite a massive US advantage in military capabilities over ISIL, US military tactics are not as effective at targeting terrorists or solving the problem of failed states as at traditional military conflict. Therefore, a permanent military defeat of the Islamic State would require a long and costly effort. Second, although Obama was secure in office in the sense that he would not face another reelection campaign, he may have still been sensitive to the fact that he had only limited public support from a highly polarized electorate that was weary of war. Third, Obama's veto players do not seem to have been very hawkish. Although information on internal deliberations within the Obama administration on ISIL is still minimal, it seems that most of Obama's advisors favored a cautious policy that would avoid getting drawn too deeply into conflict with ISIL. In Congress, opinions on the best approach toward ISIL were highly divided, and Congress failed to pass an official authorization to use force against ISIL requested by Obama. This situation was a far cry from the uniform support of hawkish veto players that Kennedy had during the Cuban Missile Crisis or the popularity that Reagan benefited from when negotiating with the Soviet Union. Therefore, under my theory, it is not surprising that Obama was unable to influence the Islamic State with his statements of resolve, even leaving aside the fact that ISIL might be a particularly stubborn adversary and possible weaknesses in Obama's signaling strategy.[1]

As of this writing, President Trump has recently entered office, having vowed to take a tougher line against ISIL. Although Trump's exact plans for dealing with ISIL remain unclear, his public statements convey a high degree of resolve. However, this might be another case in which the inability to follow through reduces the relevance of the president's personal level of resolve. Trump faces the same military constraints as Obama, and although he has more hawkish veto players than Obama, most members of his national security team are more moderate than Trump himself. Therefore, they may discourage a great escalation of military efforts against ISIL. Secretary of Defense Jim Mattis already convinced Trump to step back from his pledge to torture suspected terrorists (Diamond 2017). Furthermore, although Republicans control both houses of Congress, there would still be congressional resistance to sending a large number of ground troops to Iraq and Syria. Trump's already weak approval ratings should also be viewed as a significant constraint on his ability to follow through. Even if Trump himself pays little attention to opinion polls, his weak approval will probably further limit his ability to influence other actors in the government. Thus, while the United States will continue to take limited actions against ISIL under Trump and probably further erode its territorial control, an all-out military effort leading to the complete and permanent defeat of ISIL still appears unlikely. Given this, ISIL leaders will probably continue to hold out hope that they can outlast US efforts in the long term.

SUMMARY OF CONTRIBUTIONS

The example of ISIL again illustrates that statements of resolve are unlikely to persuade an adversary to back down unless a leader has the clear ability to follow through on them. Emphasizing the importance of the ability to follow

---

[1] Although Obama used a lot of resolved phrases, his statements also contained a lot of caveats about things the United States was not willing to do, such as send in combat troops or act unilaterally. This may have weakened the signal of resolve.

through and detailing how various aspects of the ability to follow through influence the effectiveness of statements has been the key theoretical contribution of this book. It is not necessarily controversial to assert that statements of resolve are unlikely to be effective when the ability to follow through is absent, and some previous research has acknowledged this, particularly by examining the effect of military capabilities on the success or failure of threats. However, the ability to follow through consists of more than just military capabilities. This book has sought to develop a more comprehensive theory of what the ability to follow through includes and how it varies among leaders. As I define it, the ability to follow through consists of both an absence of major obstacles to following through and an absence of unacceptable risks to following through.

In many cases, leaders do face considerable risks and obstacles to following through on their statements of resolve. Some risks and obstacles are physical, such as the risk of high casualties in fighting or the inability to carry out a threat because of the lack of military technology. Other risks and obstacles are political. One domestic political obstacle that almost all leaders face is the ability of veto players to block their ability to follow through. Leaders also face the risk of unpopularity and even removal from office if they pursue a military conflict that goes poorly. These political risks and obstacles may be harder to observe than physical ones, but they can create ambiguity about the ability to follow through. If adversaries doubt that a leader has the ability to follow through on statements of resolve, then the statements will be less effective at influencing the adversary to back down.

I proposed several factors that can mitigate these risks and obstacles and give leaders the observable ability to follow through on statements of resolve, thus rendering their statements more effective. The first factor is military strength. If a country has greater military capabilities relative to its adversary, it will face fewer physical obstacles and risks to following through. The second factor is the hawkishness of domestic veto players. If domestic veto players are more hawkish, adversaries will realize that they are less likely to block a leader's decision to follow through. The third factor is security in office. Leaders who are more secure in office have a greater ability to follow through because they are likely to have more leverage over veto players and more freedom to initiate or continue military conflict without the risk of being removed. My theory therefore predicts that when adversaries hear a resolved statement from a leader who is in a strong military position, has hawkish veto players, and is secure in office, they will take the statement seriously because they know that the leader can follow through on it. In contrast, if one or more of the conditions associated with the ability to follow through is absent, adversaries will be more inclined to disregard resolved statements, even if they know that it might damage the leader's domestic or international standing to back down from them.

The empirical chapters in this book tested the impact of the three factors listed in the preceding paragraph as well as other conditions associated with previous theories regarding the effectiveness of resolved statements. Chapter 2 introduced original data, which quantitatively code the level of statements of resolve made by US presidents. This represents the first attempt to code real-world statements of resolve systematically for the purpose of studying their effect over a large number of instances. In Chapter 2, I also performed an initial exploration of the data, focusing on when statements of resolve are likely to be made. I found that the level of statements observed was influenced more by international events than by domestic conditions and that statements are more likely to be made in times of higher tension. Based on this finding, the remainder of the statistical chapters tested the effect of resolved statements in instances of international conflict.

Chapter 3 used the data on US statements of resolve to test the general effectiveness of statements in militarized interstate disputes (MIDs). I found that a higher level of resolved statements was associated with a greater chance of a more favorable MID outcome. This result was both statistically and substantively significant and was robust to a wide variety of adjustments to the statistical model. The findings in this chapter provide the first direct statistical evidence that statements of resolve are effective at credibly conveying resolve and thus persuading adversaries to back down in conflict.

Chapter 4 built on the statistical models in Chapter 3 to investigate the conditions under which statements of resolve are most effective. In keeping with my theory regarding the ability to follow through, I found strong evidence that US presidential statements are more effective when the United States is more powerful relative to its adversary, when US veto players are more hawkish, and when the US president is more secure in office. This chapter also tested hypotheses derived from domestic audience cost theory and international reputational cost theory. I found some evidence that international reputational costs also influence the effectiveness of statements, but no evidence that domestic audience costs have an impact.

Chapter 5 concluded the statistical analysis by exploring the *joint* impact of the conditions that influence the effectiveness of statements. I found that all of the factors related to the ability to follow through enhance each other's impact on statements' effectiveness for the most part, although they can begin to crowd out each other's impact when the ability to follow through is very high. I also found that the factors related to the ability to follow through have a greater impact when the United States has a more credible international reputation. On the other hand, I found that domestic partisan politics have little impact on the effectiveness of statements, since more Republicans in Congress make resolved statements more effective under both Republican and Democratic presidents.

In addition to the statistical analysis, I also examined the conditions for effectiveness of resolved statements using historical case studies. As in the statistical chapters, I found considerable support for my theory regarding the importance of the ability to follow through. In Chapter 6, I examined the Cuban Missile Crisis. I presented evidence that Soviet leaders took President Kennedy's statements of resolve seriously from the beginning, but became even more concerned that he would follow through on them with military action as the crisis developed. The historical record shows that the primary reason for their increasing concern was additional information about the hawkishness of the veto players surrounding Kennedy. As a result of their increasing fear, Soviet leaders eventually conceded to the demand in Kennedy's statements of resolve.

Chapter 7 discussed US-Soviet tensions under Ronald Reagan. It described how Soviet leaders paid a great deal of attention to Reagan's statements and took them as a genuine signal of resolve and even aggression. However, Soviet leaders did not immediately back down in response to the statements in large part because they hoped that Reagan's need to maintain security in office would restrain his behavior. The historical record shows that as Soviet leaders increasingly realized that Reagan had adequate security in office to continue to follow through on his resolved statements, Soviet policy became more accommodating. Soviet leaders backed down from some of their previous positions in arms control negotiations, conceding to key demands that Reagan had made in his statements of resolve.

Finally, Chapter 8 discussed the Vietnam War. In this case, Presidents Johnson and Nixon lacked both hawkish veto players and security in office during much of the war. Therefore, although there is evidence that the North Vietnamese leadership heard US presidential statements of resolve and analyzed them for insight into the president's intentions, they were not influenced to back down because they believed that the United States lacked the ability to follow through in Vietnam over the long term. Eventually, an improvement in Nixon's security in office in 1972 helped to persuade the North Vietnamese to make some concessions, but dovish veto players still constrained the US president, and the United States was forced to back down from many of its original goals in Vietnam.

IMPLICATIONS FOR THEORY

These findings have important implications, both theoretical and practical. The broadest theoretical implication is regarding the relative importance of the ability to follow through on resolved statements versus the costs of backing down from them. The evidence in this book clearly demonstrates that in order to understand and be able to predict the effectiveness of statements of resolve, we must consider the risks and obstacles associated with following through on them. This point has been somewhat neglected in other recent scholarly work, which has primarily focused on the costs of backing down from signals of resolve or, in some cases, on the costs of making the signals. Of course, the costs of making or backing down from a signal are important because they help to explain why statements of resolve are informative and why they are not made indiscriminately. My own theory is compatible with the existence of such costs, and my statistical analysis yielded evidence that international reputational costs are indeed paid when the United States backs down from its statements. However, this book makes the case that such costs are not the only, or even the primary, factors creating variation in the effectiveness of resolved statements. My statistical results and case studies indicate that factors related to the ability to follow through probably play a bigger role in explaining the effectiveness of statements than the costs of backing down. This suggests that future research which seeks to analyze conflict bargaining dynamics should consider the role of the ability to follow through and exactly what this ability consists of in more detail.

The findings in this book also have more specific implications for the existing literature regarding the role of security in office. Ever since Fearon (1994a) introduced the concept of domestic audience costs, it has been widely believed that more insecure leaders can make more effective signals of resolve. However, rather than finding that insecurity makes statements of resolve more effective, I find that more insecure US presidents make *less* effective statements. At a minimum, this finding suggests that researchers should not simply incorporate the idea that greater insecurity contributes to more effective signaling as an untested assumption.

This finding also has implications for the concept of democratic credibility. Since democratic leaders are typically more insecure than autocrats, the belief that insecurity contributes to effective signaling has led to the expectation that democracies have greater credibility in conflict bargaining and other international bargaining situations. According to Downes and Sechser (2012, 458), books and articles advocating the idea of greater democratic credibility have been cited over 1,000 times. However, if my finding that insecurity undermines the effectiveness of resolved statements can be applied to other countries, this may suggest that the concept of democratic credibility is misguided. My findings may even suggest that dictators, and particularly personalistic dictators, will be able to make more effective statements because they have fewer political restrictions on their ability to follow through. For example, it is hard to find evidence that US policymakers ever doubted the ability to follow through of Iraq's Saddam Hussein or even most Soviet leaders. This fits with the findings of Downes and Sechser (2012), who show using a dataset of militarized compellent threats that democracy has a negative, though insignificant, impact on threat success.

On the other hand, if dictators also face fewer costs of backing down or are viewed as being less competent in the military realm (Weeks 2014), this could cancel out their higher political ability to follow through and undermine the effectiveness of their statements. For example, the apparent lack of domestic constraints on North Korea's Kim Jung-un appears to be a double-edged sword for the credibility of North Korean threats. On one hand, there is no evidence that Kim Jung-un faces domestic audience costs or cares about the international reputational costs for failing to follow through on threatening statements. This seemingly complete lack of costs for backing down (which could never exist for a US president) makes his statements less credible. On the other hand, since there is so little to prevent him from following through on the statements, observers still worry that one day he will do so. Given these competing effects of autocracy, further empirical testing with data on resolved statements is necessary to determine whether it is possible to make generalizations about how regime type impacts the effectiveness of statements.

It might be the case that making such broad generalizations is not even appropriate. My findings show a great deal of variation in the effectiveness of resolved statements made by a single country, the United States. Even though the democracy level of the United States remained constant over the period under examination, more subtle factors, including approval for the president and the composition of Congress, greatly impacted the effectiveness of statements. This suggests that it might be fruitful to analyze the internal dynamics of other countries in more detail in order to understand which conditions give their leaders' ability to follow through on resolved statements, rather than relying on generalizations regarding the impact of regime type.

The basic concepts associated with my theory, including military strength, hawkish veto players, and security in office, can be used to analyze the ability to follow through in any country, but they might be observed somewhat differently in different regimes. Clearly, most countries in the world are much less militarily powerful than the United States. It should not be impossible for countries that are weaker than the United States to make effective statements of resolve, so long as the statements target adversaries who are not significantly more powerful than they are. Still, this is likely to mean that weaker countries can make effective statements in a smaller range of situations.

Differences in domestic political systems might also mean that the political ability to follow through operates differently in different countries. In parliamentary regimes, there might be less potential for military action to be vetoed because the same coalition controls both the executive and legislative branches of government. In addition, security in office might be more difficult to observe because elections are not necessarily held on a regular schedule. If security in office and the hawkishness of veto players are harder to observe in parliamentary systems, then these factors might have a weaker impact on the effectiveness of statements. In less democratic regimes, the hawkishness of veto players and security in office might be even harder to observe because most political maneuvering takes place outside the public eye. Therefore, variation in these factors might have a smaller impact on the effectiveness of statements of resolve by non-democracies as well.

Aside from extending the theoretical framework to different countries, another direction for future research might be to extend it outside the context of international conflict and to other situations in which leaders seek to make credible commitments but face costs or risks in following through on them. This might include negotiations on international issues outside the military realm, such as over the recent Greek debt crisis, or even domestic situations in which leaders seek to make long-term commitments. As an example from the realm of domestic political economy, leaders would typically like to commit to a low inflation rate for the long term, but often face incentives to let inflation rise in the short term to boost employment. Applying my theory to this situation, it could be argued that secure leaders will have a greater ability to follow through on their commitment to low inflation because they will not face as much electoral pressure to boost employment.

The findings presented in this book also have implications for other types of signaling. It is important to remember that statements of resolve are not the only signals of resolve. I have made the case that statements are a particularly helpful signal because of the specificity they can convey, and I have attempted to show that statements have an effect that is distinct from other signals of resolve by controlling for other signals in my regressions and analyzing the perceptions of US adversaries in case studies. However, statements are often used in conjunction with other signals of resolve and because equally nuanced data on other signals is not available, it is impossible to rule out that the effect of statements observed in the statistical regressions might also partially reflect the impact of other signals. Indeed, it would be logical to expect statements of resolve and other signals of resolve to complement each other's ability to influence the beliefs of adversaries. Therefore, future research could attempt to create more nuanced data on other signals of resolve and explore this relationship in more detail. It is likely that the ability to follow through also has a similar impact on the effectiveness of other expressions of resolve.

A final possible extension of this research agenda might be to delve more deeply into how a leader's own personal characteristics or life experience impacts the effectiveness of resolved statements. This book has focused on how external characteristics of the domestic situation influence a leader's ability to follow through and the effectiveness of the leader's statements. The only individual characteristic of presidents that was examined – their political party – proved not to have much impact. However, there is an emerging literature on how the personal characteristics of leaders themselves affect international interactions. As one prominent example, Horowitz, Stam, and Ellis (2015) study how leaders' life experience affects their propensity to use force. If leaders with certain life experiences tend to be more resolved on average, and adversaries recognize this, then the resolved statements of leaders with these particular life experiences are likely to be more effective. In addition, if data on a leader's life experiences can help approximate the leader's underlying level of resolve, then this could help to sort out the distinct effects of resolve itself versus statements of resolve. However, the theory presented in this book suggests that statements should have an impact even after controlling for life experiences that contribute to resolve because resolve is still likely to vary somewhat among disputes, creating an information gap that statements can fill. It is difficult to test the role of leaders' life experiences using my dataset, which includes only 12 US presidents, but it could be tested with a broader dataset in the future.

FOREIGN POLICY IMPLICATIONS

The findings in this book also have practical implications for policymakers. Because the empirical chapters focus on US presidential statements, the results can speak most directly to the decision-making of US presidents who are considering making a statement of resolve. As noted in the introduction, the United States is currently entering an era in which the ability to use statements of resolve effectively is particularly important. The United States faces a variety of challenges throughout the world, particularly in the Middle East, and the rise of China and an increasingly antagonistic relationship with Russia may pose further challenges in the future. At the same time, the US public is weary of war, and many have argued that US defense spending needs to be reduced over the long term in order to lower budget deficits. In this type of situation, it would be a boon for the United States to be able to signal its resolve effectively and persuade adversaries to back down without using military force.

This book suggests some particular conditions under which US presidents can expect that their statements will be more effective. First, my results indicate that US statements of resolve are more effective when the United States has greater military power relative to its adversary. This is generally good news for the US president because the United States presently has unparalleled military power, and it does not currently face any adversary as powerful as the Soviet Union was during the Cold War. This suggests that a shortfall in military power is unlikely to pose an obstacle to the effectiveness of US statements in the near future. However, this could change in the long term if the United States significantly cuts its defense budget and China continues to expand its military power. Another caveat is that even though the United States is militarily powerful, it is still in the process of adapting its military equipment and strategies to fight new types of enemies, such as the Islamic State. The findings in this book suggest that further improving the ability to fight all types of adversaries could improve the effectiveness of resolved statements.

Second, my results show that Republican veto players, particularly in Congress, make statements of resolve more effective. Interestingly, this is true for both Republican and Democratic presidents, which suggests a silver lining in the foreign policy sphere for Democratic presidents whose domestic ambitions may be thwarted by a Republican Congress. However, an important caveat to this is that my analysis does not extend far into the Tea Party era. The Tea Party, a libertarian-leaning grassroots movement with ties to the Republican Party, rose to prominence shortly after President Obama entered office in 2009. Republican members of Congress affiliated with the Tea Party, such as Rand

Paul, have advocated an isolationist rather than a hawkish foreign policy. Even President Trump (2016), despite some hawkish positions, has expressed a desire to scale back some US security commitments to allies. If the Tea Party ideology continues to be influential in the Republican Party, it may no longer be safe to assume that the number of Republicans in Congress can serve as a proxy for the number of hawks. It should still be the case that more hawkish members of Congress should make US presidential statements of resolve more effective, but it might be more difficult for both presidents and adversaries to identify the hawkish members without being able to rely as much on party labels.

Finally, the findings in this book suggest that US presidents who are highly popular or who have already been reelected should be able to make more effective statements of resolve because of their greater security in office. This finding should remain relevant for the foreseeable future. However, in today's increasingly polarized political climate, it may be harder for any president to achieve very high levels of popularity. This might mean that we would expect US presidential statements of resolve to become generally less effective. On the other hand, if polarization means that voters are less likely to change their support or opposition to the president based on his or her behavior in office, this might reduce the president's political risks in foreign policy decision-making. This could suggest an increased ability to follow through, which might lead to more effective statements. Thus, it remains to be seen exactly how political polarization will affect the president's ability to follow through or adversaries' interpretations of the president's ability to follow through.

Another important thing to note about security in office is that the case studies show that exactly how secure a president must be before risking military conflict depends to some extent on the attitude of the US public. During the Vietnam War, President Johnson saw his popularity deteriorate substantially due to public dissatisfaction with the conflict, which undermined his security in office and weakened his ability to follow through. In contrast, much of the US public supported the stances of Presidents Kennedy and Reagan against the Soviet Union, meaning that they could continue to stand firm without risking their security in office. Currently, the US public is rather averse to conflict due to negative experiences in Afghanistan and Iraq. If this trend continues, it might suggest that all but the most secure US presidents will hesitate to follow through on their statements of resolve with military action. This is another consideration which suggests that US presidential statements of resolve could be less effective in the future.

Aside from offering specific conditions that presidents or other policymakers might consider when predicting the likely effect of their statements, this book also offers some general reasons to be cautious about making statements of resolve. First, the evidence suggests that there are natural limitations on the president's ability to bluff successfully. The findings in Chapter 5 showed that a low value of just one factor related to the ability to follow through is enough by itself to undermine the effectiveness of statements. Therefore, the ability of statements to be effective is somewhat fragile, and presidents should not assume that their statements will be effective unless their ability to follow through is truly strong in all respects.

Another reason that US presidents should be cautious in making statements of resolve is that backing down from them does appear to have consequences. My results show that when the United States has backed down from more statements of resolve in the recent past, current presidential statements are less effective. This indicates that making statements of resolve without the ability or intention to follow through can squander the ability of the US president to communicate credibility in future disputes, which may be of greater importance.

On the whole, this book shows that statements of resolve can be a powerful tool, allowing presidents to achieve their aims in international conflict by persuading adversaries to back down. However, in order for statements to function effectively, they must be used somewhat sparely. If a president makes a statement of resolve without a clear ability to follow through on it, it is unlikely to be effective at influencing adversaries, and if the president then backs down from the statement, this is likely to harm future US credibility. The implication of this is that presidents should be circumspect in their statement-making and avoid making statements of resolve that they do not have a clear ability and intention to follow through on. If the president's words matter, as this book has found, then it naturally follows that presidents must be careful about what they say.

Being selective about when to make resolved statements might be difficult for presidents because my data show that modern US presidents are highly accustomed to making resolved statements, and the public now expects to hear tough, patriotic language from the president in times of conflict. President Trump's use of Twitter has further increased the expectation that presidents will make tough off-the-cuff remarks in response to many international events. However, attempting to reverse this trend and being more selective about when to make resolved statements would most likely increase the overall effectiveness of presidential statements, particularly in an era in which the ability to follow through has some limitations. The conditions discussed in this book can provide guidelines for presidents and other policymakers in analyzing when their statements are most likely to be effective and thus assist them in being more selective in their decisions to make statements of resolve.

APPENDIX I

Formal Model of the Effect of Veto Players

The logic of how the hawkishness of veto players impacts the ability to follow through and the effectiveness of resolved statements can be illustrated using a formal model. Consider the extensive form game in Figure A1.1. The game is an extension of a simple signaling game presented by Kydd (2015, 165–175). Player 1 is the leader of a country, player 2 is an adversary country (modeled as a unitary actor), and player 3 is a veto player in the same country as player 1. When the game begins, the countries are assumed to already be involved in a dispute, which may or may not already involve military action. At the beginning of the game, player 1 can choose to make a statement threatening to fight or not. Player 2 then has the option to back down or stand firm. If player 2 stands firm, player 1 can choose to fight or back down. Since military conflict may or may not have already been ongoing at the outset of the game, the choice to fight could mean initiating a new military conflict or simply continuing or escalating an existing military conflict. If player 1 chooses to fight, the veto player has the option to approve this decision or not. If player 3 approves of fighting, the outcome of the dispute is decided by war, modeled as a costly lottery.

For players 1 and 2, s_i is the value of each side's satisfaction with winning the issue at stake, and c_i is the cost of war. p is the probability of victory for player 1 in war. All of these parameters can vary from 0 to 1. For player 3, who does not have any very interesting decisions to make, I use even simpler parameters. For player 3, winning the issue at stake gives a utility of 1, and not winning gives a utility of 0. W_3, player 3's war payoff, encompasses the probability of winning in war, the payoff from winning, and the cost of war. W_3 can range from -1 to h_3, where h_3 can range between 0 and infinity. A higher h_3 indicates that the veto player is more hawkish.

a_{1B} represents the domestic audience cost or international reputational cost that ensues if player 1 makes a statement and backs down. Although the cost of failing to carry out a statement is not the theoretical focus of this model, some

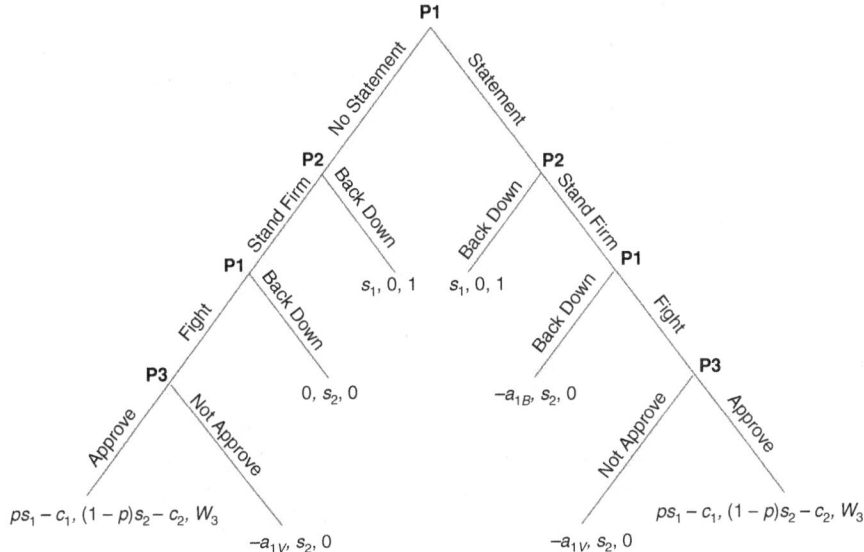

FIGURE A1.1 Veto Player Game Diagram

such cost must exist, or statements would be made indiscriminately. For purposes of this model, I do not take a stand on the exact nature of this cost, since either a domestic audience cost or an international reputational cost could serve the same function and both may exist simultaneously. I also assume that there is some domestic or international reputational cost for player 1 that ensues if player 1 decides to fight but is blocked by the veto player. I call this cost a_{1V}. This cost is likely to exist because being publicly stymied by the veto player is embarrassing, making it apparent to domestic and international audiences that the leader is too weak to control his or her own government. I assume that a_{1V} and a_{1B} can each range between 0 and 1, but that a_{1V} is greater than or equal to a_{1B} since being thwarted by the veto player is likely to create a bigger public spectacle than simply backing down.[1]

If player 2 backs down, it gets nothing, while player 1 gets s_1, and player 3 gets 1. If player 2 stands firm and player 1 backs down, player 1 receives a payoff of 0 if it did not make a statement and a payoff of $-a_{1B}$ if it did. Player 2 receives a payoff of s_2, and player 3 receives a payoff of 0. If player 1 chooses to fight, the game continues and player 3 must decide whether to approve the decision. If it does approve, then every player receives its war payoff. For player 3, this is

[1] The setup of the model assumes that the interaction between player 1 and player 3 is visible to domestic and international audiences. If this interaction were not publicly visible, a_{1V} would be equal to a_{1B} after a statement and equal to 0 in the absence of a statement. However, changing these things does not affect the main prediction of the model.

simply W_3. For players 1 and 2, the war payoff consists of their satisfaction from winning, multiplied by their probability of winning, minus their cost of fighting. If player 3 does not approve the decision to fight, player 2 gets s_2, player 3 gets 0, and player 1 gets $-a_{1V}$.

In order to understand the effect of statements on signaling resolve, I introduce incomplete information about W_3, s_1, and s_2. I assume that s_1 and s_2 are randomly drawn from a uniform distribution ranging from 0 to 1 and that only player i learns the value of s_i at the beginning of the game. I assume that W_3 is randomly drawn from a uniform distribution ranging from -1 to h_3 and that only player 3 learns the value of W_3 at the beginning of the game.[2] However, h_3, which is greater than or equal to 0, is known by all players. Therefore, all of the players know how much of a hawkish bias the veto player has.

The game can be solved by calculating cutpoint values for the unknown parameters. I assume a cutpoint structure in which some types of player 1 will bluff, i.e., make a statement and then back down. There is some theoretical controversy over whether leaders do indeed bluff. Fearon (1997) developed a formal model in which no bluffing can occur in equilibrium. In that model, Fearon assumed that states could generate unlimited levels of audience costs, which is probably not possible in reality. In my model, the audience cost is fixed using the term a_{1B}, so an equilibrium with bluffing can occur. Even Fearon (1997, 83) admits that leaders do bluff in reality, particularly if implicit commitments which are not honored are counted as bluffs.

The cutpoints of interest are shown in Figure A1.2. Player 3's cutpoint is the simplest to comprehend; player 3 will approve action if doing so gives it positive utility and not approve otherwise. The willingness of players 1 and 2 to take risks and bear costs in order to win the issue at stake increases with s_i. Player 1 has three cutpoints, $s_1^\dagger$, s_1^*, and s_1^{**}. The cutpoint s_1^{**} is included for completeness, but it is not of interest for understanding the interaction between the players. All types of player 1 with a value of s_1 above s_1^* will behave the same in practice, making a statement and then fighting if player 2 does not back down. There will never be a situation in which player 1 would fight without making a statement because making a statement has potential benefits and no potential costs for the type that would fight regardless. The cutpoint $s_1^\dagger$ exists because the audience cost, a_{1B}, makes bluffing too risky for some types of player 1. This differentiates the signaling behavior of different types of player 1 and allows player 2 to update its belief about whether player 1 will fight (i.e., whether $s_1 \geq s_1^*$), based on whether player 1 makes a statement. The cutpoint s_2^* divides the types of player 2 between those that care enough about the issue at stake to stand firm after hearing a statement and those that do not. Because the absence of a statement means

---

[2] The model's basic prediction for the effect of h_3 would not change if player 1 also learned the value of W_3 at the beginning of the game, although this would provide an additional advantage to player 1.

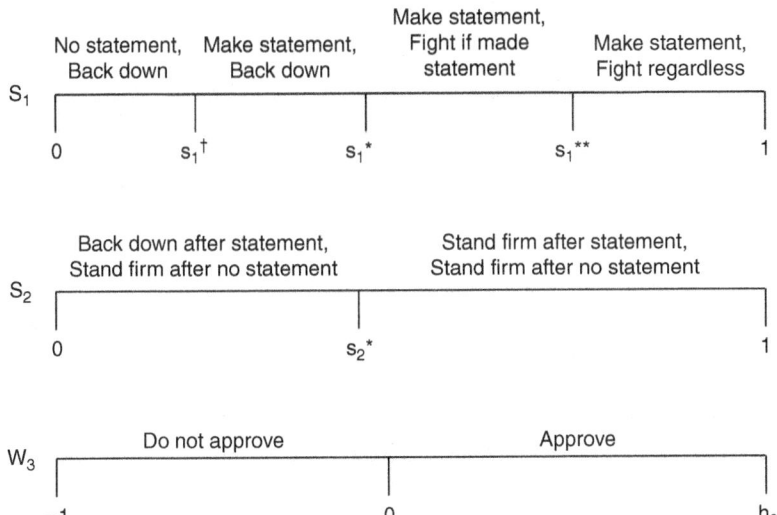

FIGURE A1.2 Cutpoints for the Veto Player Game

that player 1 will certainly back down, player 2 will always stand firm when no statement is made.

In order to determine how the effectiveness of statements varies with the hawkishness of the veto player, it is necessary to calculate the values of the cutpoints. The value of the cutpoint for player 3 is obvious. Player 3 will approve the decision to fight if W_3, its war payoff, is greater than 0, the payoff for not approving. The other cutpoints require more calculations. To calculate s_1^*, we can set equal the expected payoffs for making a statement and selecting to fight and for making a statement and backing down and then solve:

$$\frac{h_3}{h_3 + 1}(ps_1 - c_1) + \left(1 - \frac{h_3}{h_3 + 1}\right)(-a_{1V}) = -a_{1B}$$

$$s_1^* = \frac{\frac{1}{h_3}(a_{1V} - a_{1B}) - a_{1B} + c_1}{p}$$

To calculate $s_1^\dagger$, we can set equal the expected payoffs for making a statement and backing down and for not making a statement and backing down and solve:

$$s_2^*(s_1) + (1 - s_2^*)(-a_{1B}) = 0$$

$$s_1^\dagger = \left(\frac{1}{s_2^*} - 1\right)a_{1B}$$

To calculate s_2^*, we can set equal the expected payoff for standing firm after a statement and the zero payoff for backing down:

$$\left(1 - \frac{1 - s_1^*}{1 - s_1^\dagger}\right)s_2 + \frac{1 - s_1^*}{1 - s_1^\dagger}\left(\frac{h_3}{h_3 + 1}\left((1 - p)s_2 - c_2\right) + \left(1 - \frac{h_3}{h_3 + 1}\right)(s_2)\right) = 0$$

$$s_2^* = \frac{c_2}{\left(\dfrac{1 - s_1^\dagger}{1 - s_1^*}\right)\left(1 + \dfrac{1}{h_3}\right) - p}$$

The expression for s_1^* calculated above already contains only exogenous parameters, but the expressions for $s_1^\dagger$ and s_2^* depend on each other as well as on s_1^*, so further analysis is necessary to fully understand the equilibrium and how a change in h_3 affects it. Solving the equations in terms of exogenous parameters yields the following equilibrium solution:

$$s_1^* = \frac{\dfrac{1}{h_3}(a_{1V} - a_{1B}) - a_{1B} + c_1}{p}$$

$$s_1^\dagger = \left(\frac{h_3 p(1 - p + c_1) + p(a_{1V} + 1)}{h_3[c_2(p - c_1 + a_{1B}) + a_{1B}p] + a_{1B}p - c_2(a_{1V} - a_{1B})} - 1\right)a_{1B}$$

$$s_2^* = \frac{h_3[c_2(p - c_1 + a_{1B}) + a_{1B}p] + a_{1B}p - c_2(a_{1V} - a_{1B})}{h_3 p(1 - p + c_1) + p(a_{1V} + 1)}$$

The crucial question is the effect of h_3, the veto player's hawkishness, on s_2^*, the adversary's probability of backing down. Taking the derivative of s_2^* with respect to h_3 and simplifying yields the following expression:

$$\frac{ds_2^*}{dh_3} = \frac{c_2 + a_{1B}(c_2 + p)}{[h_3 p(1 - p + c_1) + p(a_{1V} + 1)]^2}$$

This expression is always positive, indicating that the expression for s_2^* is increasing in h_3. Therefore, player 2 is more likely to back down in response to a statement when h_3 is higher, meaning that the veto player is more hawkish. This prediction is in keeping with the intuitive logic developed in Chapter 1, which yielded Hypothesis 2.

APPENDIX 2

Formal Model of the Effect of Security in Office

In Chapter 1, I asserted that leaders who are secure in office are likely to have lower costs of backing down as well as lower costs of losing in conflict. In order to better understand how the competing effects of lower costs for backing down and lower costs for fighting balance out, it is helpful to use a formal model. Consider the extensive form game in Figure A2.1. The structure of this game follows the same basic format as the game described in Appendix 1, and the payoffs are also mostly the same. The veto player stage that was included in the previous game has been removed in order to allow exclusive focus on the effect of security in office. Although the joint effect of security in office and hawkish veto players is an important topic, which is discussed in Chapter 5, including both aspects in the same formal model adds unnecessary complexity and reduces tractability.

Aside from the absence of the veto player stage, the key difference between this game and the previous game is the treatment of audience costs. There are two types of audience costs in this game. a_{1L} represents player 1's audience cost for losing in war, and a_{1B} represents player 1's audience cost for backing down from a statement. a_{1L} and a_{1B} can each range from 0 to 1. The audience cost for backing down is standard to include in models of signaling resolve and also appeared in the previous model. The inclusion of an audience cost for losing is an innovation unique to this model. Another innovation is to assume that the size of the audience cost for losing and the size of the audience cost for backing down are related to each other because they are both linked to the leader's vulnerability to removal from office. Therefore, both a_{1L} and a_{1B} are multiplied by v_1, which represents player 1's vulnerability to removal from office. v_1 can range from 0 to 1, with 0 representing a fully secure leader who faces no threat from audience costs and 1 representing the most vulnerable leader imaginable. As vulnerability decreases, the impact of both types of audience costs will decrease, but the impact of whichever cost is bigger will decrease faster. By multiplying the audience cost terms by vulnerability, I am assuming for purposes of this model that the audience cost consists of domestic disapproval for losing or backing down. Of course, international reputational costs for backing down or losing might also exist, but they are not central to this model's goal of exploring the effects of leader security in office.

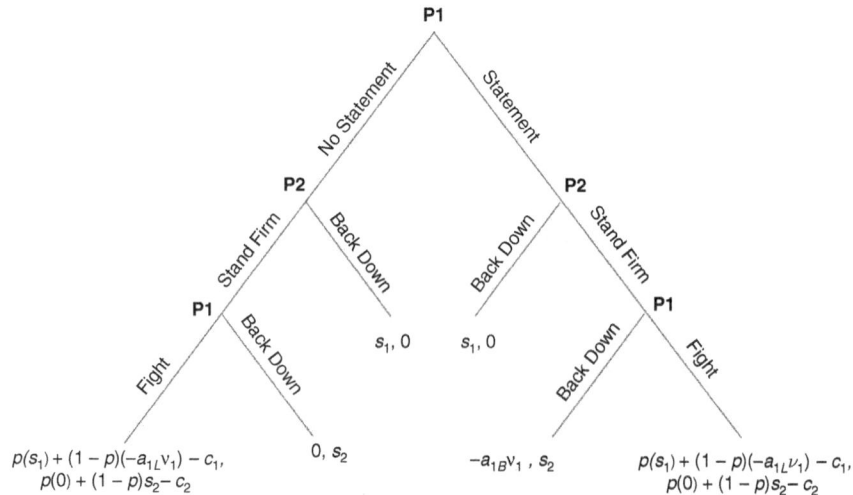

FIGURE A2.1 Leader Vulnerability Game Diagram

As in the previous model, I introduce incomplete information by assuming that s_i is unknown, except by player i, and I solve for the cutpoints shown previously in Figure A1.1. As before, I solve for s_1^* by setting equal the expected payoffs for making a statement and fighting and for making a statement and backing down and simplify:

$$p(s_1) + (1-p)(-a_{1L}v_1) - c_1 = -a_{1B}v_1$$

$$s_1^* = \frac{v_1(a_{1L}(1-p) - a_{1B}) + c_1}{p}$$

To calculate $s_1^\dagger$, we can set equal the expected payoffs for making a statement and backing down and for not making a statement and backing down and solve:

$$(s_2^*)s_1 + (1 - s_2^*)(-a_{1B}v_1) = 0$$

$$s_1^\dagger = \left(\frac{1}{s_2^*} - 1\right)a_{1B}v_1$$

To solve for s_2^*, we can set equal the expected payoff for standing firm after a statement to the zero payoff for backing down and solve:

$$\left(1 - \frac{1 - s_1^*}{1 - s_1^\dagger}\right)s_2 + \frac{1 - s_1^*}{1 - s_1^\dagger}\left((1-p)s_2 - c_2\right) = 0$$

$$s_2^* = \frac{c_2}{\dfrac{1 - s_1^\dagger}{1 - s_1^*} - p}$$

As in the previous model, further analysis is necessary to know the equilibrium values of $s_1^\dagger$ and s_2^* because the expressions for these cutpoint values depend upon each other and upon s_1^*. Solving in terms of exogenous parameters yields the following equilibrium:

$$s_1^* = \frac{v_1\left(a_{1L}(1-p) - a_{1B}\right) + c_1}{p}$$

$$s_1^\dagger = \left(\frac{v_1(a_{1L} - a_{1L}p) + 1 - p + c_1}{v_1\left(\frac{-a_{1L}c_2}{p} + a_{1L}c_2 + \frac{a_{1B}c_2}{p} + a_{1B}\right) - \frac{c_1 c_2}{p} + c_2} - 1\right) a_{1B}v_1$$

$$s_2^* = \frac{v_1\left(\frac{-a_{1L}c_2}{p} + a_{1L}c_2 + \frac{a_{1B}c_2}{p} + a_{1B}\right) - \frac{c_1 c_2}{p} + c_2}{v_1(a_{1L} - a_{1L}p) + 1 - p + c_1}$$

The crucial question is what effect v_1, player 1's vulnerability to removal from office, has on s_2^*, player 2's probability of backing down. My theory would predict that s_2^* will usually be decreasing in v_1, meaning that player 2 would be less likely to back down in response to a statement when player 1 is more vulnerable (and thus more likely to back down when player 1 is more secure in office). Audience cost theory, in contrast, would predict that s_2^* should be increasing in v_1. The effect of v_1 on s_2^* can be determined by taking the derivative, which yields the following long expression (with the numerator taking up two lines):

$$\frac{ds_2^*}{dv_1} = \frac{[v_1(a_{1L} - a_{1L}p) + 1 - p + c_1]\left[\frac{-a_{1L}c_2}{p} + a_{1L}c_2 + \frac{a_{1B}c_2}{p} + a_{1B}\right]}{[v_1(a_{1L} - a_{1L}p) + 1 - p + c_1]^2}$$

This expression is not universally positive or universally negative. Therefore, s_2^* is not *always* increasing in v_1, nor is it *always* decreasing in v_1. However, it can be shown that s_2^* will be decreasing in v_1 if the following expression is true:

$$a_{1L} > \frac{a_{1B}}{1-p}\left((1 - p + c_1)\left(1 + \frac{p}{c_2}\right)\right)$$

To show that it is possible for this expression to be true, Table A2.1 gives examples of parameter values that make it true. Examining the condition that makes the derivative negative tells us that s_2^* is more likely to be decreasing in v_1, as predicted by my theory, when a_{1L} is higher, when a_{1B} is lower, when c_1 is lower, and when c_2 is higher. The impact of p is not entirely clear-cut, but a higher value of p will usually decrease the probability that the derivative is

TABLE A2.1 *Examples of Parameter Values for Which s_2^* Decreases with v_1*

a_{1B}	a_{1L}	c_1	c_2	p	v_1	$\frac{ds_2^*}{dv_1}$	s_1^*	$s_1^\dagger$	s_2^*
0	0.9	0.7	0.6	0.9	0.2	−0.090	0.798	0.000	0.148
0.04	0.14	0.4	0.9	0.6	0.1	−0.006	0.669	0.007	0.374
0.06	0.9	0.2	0.1	0.7	0.6	−0.010	0.466	0.230	0.135
0.1	0.4	0.1	0.4	0.3	0.2	−0.255	0.453	0.052	0.279
0.3	0.5	0.1	0.7	0.2	0.6	−0.142	0.800	0.461	0.281
0.6	0.9	0.05	0.9	0.2	0.1	−0.512	0.310	0.021	0.739
0.8	0.9	0.01	0.7	0.05	0.2	−0.352	0.420	0.160	0.500

negative. Therefore, in substantive terms, the formal model tells us that vulnerability in office is more likely to be harmful (and security is more likely to be helpful) to the effectiveness of statements when the audience cost associated with backing down is lower, the audience cost associated with losing is higher, the probability of winning is lower, the cost of fighting for the country issuing a statement is lower, and the cost of fighting for the adversary is higher.

In the main text of Chapter 1, I make a logical argument that the first three conditions identified by the model (low audience costs for backing down, high audience costs for losing, and a high probability of losing) are likely to be very common and that security in office will therefore most frequently be beneficial to the effectiveness of statements. The latter two conditions (low cost of fighting for the country issuing a statement and high cost of fighting for the adversary) are not as universally applicable, but for the United States, the focus of my empirical analysis, they are likely to be true. This gives us further reason to expect that security in office will have a positive impact on the effectiveness of statements in my sample of observations. Of course, there is no way to prove what the real-world distribution of any of these parameter values is. The only thing that this formal modeling exercise has proved definitively is that it is logically *possible* for security in office to have a beneficial impact on the effectiveness of statements. Whether it commonly does have a beneficial impact is ultimately an empirical question, which is addressed in Chapter 4.

APPENDIX 3

Content Analysis Dictionary

This appendix presents the main three-tiered dictionary and the alternate dictionary with weights ranging from 1 to 10. The dictionary with equal weights is identical to these dictionaries, except each word has a weight of 1. I removed the spaces from the phrases that are included in the dictionary because the *Yoshikoder* content analysis program cannot search for spaces. An asterisk (*) indicates a wildcard. Note that some of these words are typically used in the negative sense. For example, presidents often say, "We will not fail," but almost never say, "We will fail." Therefore, "fail" is considered to be a word associated with resolve.

TABLE A3.1 *Content Analysis Dictionary and Weights*

Word or Phrase	Three-Tiered Dictionary Weight	One-to-Ten Dictionary Weight
notaccept	2	6.75
*notallow	2	5.71
notbeaccept	2	5.75
*notbeallowed	2	5.71
*notbepermitted	2	6.25
*notpermit	2	6.25
*notrule	3	8.33
*notruleout	3	8.33
abandon	2	6
abet*	1	3
abhor*	1	3.71
abus*	1	2.71

(*continued*)

TABLE A3.1 *(continued)*

Word or Phrase	Three-Tiered Dictionary Weight	One-to-Ten Dictionary Weight
accountable	2	6
actionisnecessary	3	8
actionnecessary	3	8.13
actionsarenecessary	3	8.13
actionsnecessary	3	8.13
aggression	1	2.86
aggressor*	1	2.88
alarming	1	2.13
amcommitted	2	5.75
americascommitment*	2	6
amresolved	2	6.25
angry	1	3.38
appeas*	2	6.25
arecommitted	2	5.75
arrogan*	1	2.43
atrocit*	1	3.38
barbaric*	1	3.25
belligerence	1	3.14
blackmail	2	5.5
blatant*	1	2
bloodshed	1	2
brutal*	1	3.71
bully*	1	2.71
callfor	1	2.88
callon	1	3
callous*	1	2.86
callupon	1	2.71
churchill	2	5.14
cleansing	1	3.86
clearandpresent	2	5.25
coercion	1	1
coldblooded*	1	3.43
compel	3	8.13
condemn*	1	4.13
confident	2	5.57

TABLE A3.1 *(continued)*

Word or Phrase	Three-Tiered Dictionary Weight	One-to-Ten Dictionary Weight
consequence*	3	8
crime*	1	2.75
criminal	1	3
cruel*	1	3.29
cynical*	1	2.14
decisive*	3	7.5
defeat*	3	8
defend*	2	7
defiance	1	2.57
defy*	1	2.38
demand*	2	6.38
deplor*	1	3.5
despot*	1	3.13
destabiliz*	1	2
deter	2	7
determination	2	5
determined	2	5.5
disagree*	1	2
disappoint*	1	1.6
disapprov*	1	2
disgust*	1	2.88
disturbed	1	2.33
disturbing	1	2.33
doubt	2	6.5
duty	2	6.25
endanger	1	3.13
endur*	2	5.71
enem*	2	5.88
error	2	7
everythingnecessary	3	8.25
evil*	1	3.86
expansionist	1	2.71
expect	2	4.33
exploit*	1	2.86
fail	2	5.75

(continued)

TABLE A3.1 *(continued)*

Word or Phrase	Three-Tiered Dictionary Weight	One-to-Ten Dictionary Weight
falter	2	5.63
fedup	1	3.38
firm*	2	5.25
flagrant*	1	3.5
flout*	1	2.75
futile	2	7
genocid*	1	3.63
grave	1	3.63
gravity	1	3.13
gross	1	3.29
grounds	1	2.43
guarantee	2	7.25
guilty	1	3.63
harbor*	1	3.38
hitler	1	4.25
horrible	1	2.86
horrif*	1	2.75
hostile	1	2.75
hypocri*	1	2.14
illegal*	1	2.5
illusion*	2	5.63
immoral*	1	2.88
imperial*	1	3.14
implor*	2	4.13
impunity	2	6
inconsistent	1	1.6
inhuman*	1	2.88
insidious	1	3
insist*	2	5.5
intimidat*	2	5.5
intolerable	1	4.75
intransigen*	1	2.75
invader*	1	1
irresponsible	1	2
itistime	2	5

TABLE A3.1 (*continued*)

Word or Phrase	Three-Tiered Dictionary Weight	One-to-Ten Dictionary Weight
justice	2	3.86
lie*	1	3
liketothink	1	1.33
loathsome	1	3
lying	1	2.75
mad	1	3.29
massacr*	1	3.88
meansarenecessary	3	8.38
meansnecessary	3	8.38
menac*	1	3
misapprehension	2	6.13
miscalculat*	2	6.25
mistake*	2	6.25
misunderstand	2	5.43
moral	2	5.57
murder*	1	3.38
mustact	2	6.5
myresolve	2	6.13
necessaryaction*	3	8.25
necessarymeans	3	8.38
necessaryresponse	3	8
necessarysteps	3	7.88
neverallow	2	5.71
neverpermit	2	6.25
noncompliance	1	3
nonegotiation*	2	7.5
nonnegotiable	2	7.25
notgoingtoallow	2	5.71
notgoingtopermit	2	6.25
notgoingtorule	3	8.33
notintendtoallow	2	5.71
notintendtopermit	2	6.25
notnegotia*	2	6.88
notruled	3	8.33
notruledout	3	8.33

(*continued*)

TABLE A3.1 (*continued*)

Word or Phrase	Three-Tiered Dictionary Weight	One-to-Ten Dictionary Weight
notruling	3	8.33
notrulingout	3	8.33
obligat*	2	5.25
obstruct*	1	2.88
oppress*	1	3.25
ourcommitment*	2	6
ourresolve	2	6.13
outlaw	1	3.14
outrage*	1	3
peril	3	7
persecut*	1	3.13
persevere	2	5.13
persist	2	5.57
pledge*	2	5.57
preparedtoact	3	7.38
preparedtouseforce	3	10
prevail	2	6.63
prevent	2	7.13
price	3	7.25
promise*	2	6.63
provoca*	1	3.13
rape	1	3.71
raping	1	3.71
readytoact	2	7.57
readytouseforce	3	10
reaffirm	2	5.75
reckless*	1	2.75
regret*	1	1.63
reject*	2	5.75
repel	3	8
repress*	1	3.38
resist	2	6.63
resolute	2	6.38
responseisnecessary	3	8.38
revulsion	1	3.25

TABLE A3.1 (*continued*)

Word or Phrase	Three-Tiered Dictionary Weight	One-to-Ten Dictionary Weight
rogue	1	2
rulednothing	3	8.33
ruledout	3	8.33
rulenothing	3	8.33
ruleout	3	8.33
rulingnothing	3	8.33
rulingout	3	8.33
runningout	2	6.07
ruthless*	1	2
sanctuar*	1	3.71
savage*	1	3.38
scorn*	1	2.43
shelter*	1	3.25
shocked	1	3.13
shocking	1	3.13
slaughter*	1	3.75
stake*	2	4.75
stand	2	6.5
staythecourse	2	6.13
stead*	2	5.63
stepsarenecessary	3	7.86
stepsnecessary	3	7.86
strength*	2	5.63
strong*	2	5.5
subjugat*	1	3.25
subver*	1	2.63
supress*	1	3.13
takeaction	3	8.38
takemilitaryaction	3	9.88
terrible	1	2.75
terroriz*	1	3
threat	1	4.75
threaten*	1	4
timeisathand	2	6.5
timeisup	3	7.88

(*continued*)

TABLE A3.1 (*continued*)

Word or Phrase	Three-Tiered Dictionary Weight	One-to-Ten Dictionary Weight
tolerate*	2	5.5
totalitarian*	1	2.75
tragedy	1	3.63
troubled	1	2.38
troubling	1	2.13
tyran*	1	2.75
unacceptable	2	4.88
unambiguous*	2	5.63
uncivilized	1	3.25
unconscionable	1	3.75
underanycircumstances	2	6.88
underestimate	2	6.13
unequivocal*	2	6
unfortunate	1	2.14
unitedstatescommitment*	2	6
unjustifi*	1	3.13
unprovoked	1	3.38
unrelenting	2	5.38
unscrupulous	1	3
unshakable	2	6
unswerving	2	5.71
unwarranted	1	3.38
unwavering	2	5.88
unyielding	2	6
upset*	1	1.63
urge	2	3.88
vicious*	1	3.25
vigilan*	2	5.13
violat*	1	3
violen*	1	3.38
vitalinterest*	2	5.43
walkaway	2	6
wanton	1	3.63
warn*	2	6.38
whateveraction*	3	8.75

TABLE A3.1 (*continued*)

Word or Phrase	Three-Tiered Dictionary Weight	One-to-Ten Dictionary Weight
whateverisnecessary	3	9
whateverisneeded	3	9
whateverisrequired	3	9
whateverittakes	3	9
whatevermeans	3	9
whatevermust	3	9
willfight	3	10

References

Aldrich, John, Christopher Gelpi, Peter Feaver, Jason Reifler, and Kristin Thompson Sharp. 2006. "Foreign Policy and the Electoral Connection." *Annual Review of Political Science* 9:477–502.

Allison, Graham T. 1969. "Conceptual Models and the Cuban Missile Crisis." *American Political Science Review* 63(3):689–718.

Anderson, Martin, and Annelise Anderson. 2009. *Reagan's Secret War: The Untold Story of His Fight to Save the World from Nuclear Disaster*. New York: Crown Publishers.

Ang, Cheng Guan. 2002. *The Vietnam War from the Other Side: The Vietnamese Communists' Perspective*. New York: Routledge.

2004. *Ending the Vietnam War: The Vietnamese Communists' Perspective*. New York: Routledge.

Arena, Philip, and Glenn Palmer. 2009. "Politics or the Economy: Domestic Correlates of Dispute Involvement in Developed Democracies." *International Studies Quarterly* 53 (4):955–975.

Asselin, Pierre. 2002. *A Bitter Peace: Washington, Hanoi, and the Making of the Paris Agreement*. Chapel Hill, NC: University of North Carolina Press.

2011. "Revisionism Triumphant: Hanoi's Diplomatic Strategy in the Nixon Era." *Journal of Cold War Studies* 13(4):101–137.

2012. "'We Don't Want a Munich': Hanoi's Diplomatic Strategy, 1965–1968." *Diplomatic History* 36(3):547–581.

Baum, Matthew A. 2004. "Going Private: Public Opinion, Presidential Rhetoric, and the Domestic Politics of Audience Costs in U.S. Foreign Policy Crises." *Journal of Conflict Resolution* 48(5):603–631.

BBC. 2014. "Islamic State: 'Baghdadi Message' Issued by Jihadists." November 13. www.bbc.com/news/world-middle-east-30041257 (April 26, 2016).

Belasco, Amy, Lynn J. Cunningham, Hannah Fischer, and Larry A. Niksch. 2007. "Congressional Restrictions on U.S. Military Operations in Vietnam, Cambodia, Laos, Somalia, and Kosovo: Funding and Non-Funding Approaches." Congressional Research Service Report for Congress, January 16. www.fas.org/sgp/crs/natsec/RL33803.pdf (December 11, 2013).

Beschloss, Michael R. 1991. *The Crisis Years: Kennedy and Khrushchev 1960–1963*. New York: Edward Burlingame Books.

Besheer, Margaret. 2014. "Ukraine Fears Russian Invasion." Voice of America, April 25. www.voanews.com/content/ukraine-fears-russian-invasion-/1901612.html (November 24, 2014).

Blake, Aaron, and Sean Sullivan. 2013. "Syria Resolution Is No Sure Thing in the Senate. Here's Why." *Washington Post*, September 10. www.washingtonpost.com/blogs/the-fix/wp/2013/09/10/syria-resolution-is-no-cinch-in-the-senate/ (June 10, 2015).

Brace, Paul, and Barbara Hinckley. 1992. *Follow the Leader: Opinion Polls and the Modern Presidents*. New York: Basic Books.

Braumoeller, Bear F. 2004. "Hypothesis Testing and Multiplicative Interaction Terms." *International Organization* 58(4):807–820.

Brooks, Stephen G., and William C. Wohlforth. 2000/2001. "Power, Globalization, and the End of the Cold War: Reevaluating a Landmark Case for Ideas." *International Security* 25(3):5–52.

Brown, Archie. 1996. *The Gorbachev Factor*. Oxford: Oxford University Press.

Brumfield, Ben. 2014. "Ukraine's President Vows to Defend Territory 'No Matter What.'" CNN, June 7. www.cnn.com/2014/06/07/world/europe/ukraine-president-inauguration/ (November 24, 2014).

Bueno de Mesquita, Bruce, James D. Morrow, Randolph M. Siverson, and Alastair Smith. 1999. "An Institutional Explanation of the Democratic Peace." *American Political Science Review* 93(4):791–807.

Bueno de Mesquita, Bruce, and Randolph M. Siverson. 1995. "War and the Survival of Political Leaders: A Comparative Study of Regime Types and Political Accountability." *American Political Science Review* 89(4):841–855.

Bui, Tin. 2002. *From Enemy to Friend: A North Vietnamese Perspective on the War*. Annapolis, MD: Naval Institute Press.

Byman, Daniel. 2013. "Mr. Obama, Don't Draw That Red Line." *New York Times*, May 4. www.nytimes.com/2013/05/05/opinion/sunday/dont-draw-that-red-line.html?pagewanted=all (June 2, 2013).

Campagna, Anthony S. 1994. *The Economy in the Reagan Years: The Economic Consequences of the Reagan Administrations*. Westport, CT: Greenwood Publishing Group.

Canes-Wrone, Brandice, and Scott de Marchi. 2002. "Presidential Approval and Legislative Success." *Journal of Politics* 64(2):491–509.

Carroll, Royce, Jeff Lewis, James Lo, Nolan McCarty, Keith Poole, and Howard Rosenthal. 2011. "DW-NOMINATE Scores with Bootstrapped Standard Errors." http://voteview.com/dwnominate.asp (November 15, 2012).

Charles, Elizabeth C. 2015. "Gorbachev and the Decision to Decouple the Arms Control Package: How the Breakdown of the Reykjavik Summit Led to the Elimination of the Euromissiles." In *The Euromissile Crisis and the End of the Cold War*, ed. Leopoldo Nuti, Frederic Bozo, Marie-Pierre Rey, and Bernd Rother. Washington, DC: Woodrow Wilson Center Press, 66–84.

Carter, Bill. 1994. "Networks Held Back the News That Invasion Planes Were Headed for Haiti." *New York Times*, September 20, A12.

Chaudoin, Stephen. 2014. "Promises or Policies? An Experimental Analysis of International Agreements and Audience Reactions." *International Organization* 68(1):235–256.

Chernyaev, Anatoly S. [1993] 2000. *My Six Years with Gorbachev*. Trans. Robert D. English and Elizabeth Tucker. University Park, PA: Pennsylvania State University Press.

Chiozza, Giacomo. 2017. "Presidents on the Cycle: Elections, Audience Costs, and Coercive Diplomacy." *Conflict Management and Peace Science* 34(1):3–26.

Chiozza, Giacomo, and H. E. Goemans. 2004. "International Conflict and the Tenure of Leaders: Is War Still Ex Post Inefficient?" *American Journal of Political Science* 48(3):604–619.

Clare, Joe. 2014. "Hawks, Doves, and International Cooperation." *Journal of Conflict Resolution* 58(7):1311–1337.

CNN. 2012. "America's Choice 2012 Races and Results: Exit Polls." www.cnn.com/election/2012/results/race/president (May 25, 2013).

Communist Party of Vietnam Central Committee. 1968. "Report Presented to the 15 Plenum of the Communist Party of Vietnam Central Committee." August 29. History and Public Policy Program Digital Archive, Archive of the Party Central Committee, Hanoi. Translated for WIHP by Merle Pribbenow. http://digitalarchive.wilsoncenter.org/document/113979 (May 15, 2015).

Croco, Sarah E. 2011. "The Decider's Dilemma: Leader Culpability, War Outcomes, and Domestic Punishment." *American Political Science Review* 103(3):457–477.

Croco, Sarah E., and Jessica L.P. Weeks. 2015. "Willing and Able: Culpability, Vulnerability and Leaders' Sensitivity to War Outcomes." Working paper.

Dafoe, Allan, Jonathan Renshon, and Paul Huth. 2014. "Reputation and Status as Motives for War." *Annual Review of Political Science* 17:371–393.

Danilovic, Vesna. 2002. *When the Stakes Are High: Deterrence and Conflict among Major Powers*. Ann Arbor: University of Michigan Press.

De Groot, Michael. 2011. "Ronald Reagan's 10 Best Quotes." *Deseret News*, February 7. www.deseretnews.com/top/103/5/We-begin-bombing-in-five-minutes-Ronald-Reagans-10-best-quotes.html (December 23, 2013).

Debs, Alexandre, and H.E. Goemans. 2010. "Regime Type, the Fate of Leaders, and War." *American Political Science Review* 104:430–445.

Debs, Alexandre, and Jessica Chen Weiss. 2015. "Circumstances, Domestic Audiences, and Reputational Incentives in International Crisis Bargaining." *Journal of Conflict Resolution* 60(30):403–433.

Department of State. 1962. *Department of State Bulletin* XLVII(1213):450. https://ia700506.us.archive.org/5/items/departmentofstat471962unit/departmentofstat471962unit.pdf (July 1, 2015).

Diamond, Jeremy. 2017. "Trump: Defense Secretary Mattis Can 'Override' Me on Torture." *CNN*. www.cnn.com/2017/01/27/politics/donald-trump-defense-secretary-override-on-torture/ (March 19, 2017).

Dobbs, Michael. 2008. *One Minute to Midnight: Kennedy, Khrushchev, and Castro on the Brink of Nuclear War*. New York: Vintage Books. Paperback edition.

Dobrynin, Anatoly. 1995. *In Confidence: Moscow's Ambassador to America's Six Cold War Presidents*. New York: Times Books. Paperback edition.

Downs, George W., and David M. Rocke. 1994. "Conflict, Agency, and Gambling for Resurrection: The Principal-Agent Problem Goes to War." *American Journal of Political Science* 38(2):362–380.

Downes, Alexander B., and Todd S. Sechser. 2012. "The Illusion of Democratic Credibility." *International Organization* 66(3):457–489.

Doyle, Michael. 1983. "Kant, Liberal Legacies, and Foreign Affairs, Part I." *Philosophy and Public Affairs* 12(3):205–235.

Drew, Elizabeth. 2007. *Richard M. Nixon: The American Presidents Series: The 37th President, 1969–1974*. New York: Times Books.

Dueck, Colin. 2010. *Hard Line: The Republican Party and US Foreign Policy since World War II*. Princeton, NJ: Princeton University Press.

Duiker, William J. 1996. *The Communist Road to Power in Vietnam: Second Edition*. Boulder: Westview Press.

Edwards, George C. III. 2003. *On Deaf Ears: The Limits of the Bully Pulpit*. New Haven, CT: Yale University Press.

English, Robert D. 2000. *Russia and the Idea of the West*. New York: Columbia University Press.

Eyerman, Joe, and Robert A. Hart Jr. 1996. "An Empirical Test of the Audience Cost Proposition: Democracy Speaks Louder than Words." *Journal of Conflict Resolution* 40(4):597–616.

Fearon, James D. 1994a. "Domestic Political Audiences and the Escalation of International Disputes." *American Political Science Review* 88(3):577–592.

1994b. "Signaling versus the Balance of Power and Interests: An Empirical Test of a Crisis Bargaining Model." *Journal of Conflict Resolution* 38(2):236–269.

1995. "Rationalist Explanations for War." *International Organization* 49(3): 379–414.

1997. "Signaling Foreign Policy Interests: Tying Hands versus Sinking Costs." *Journal of Conflict Resolution* 41(1):68–90.

Fischer, Beth A. 1997. *The Reagan Reversal: Foreign Policy and the End of the Cold War*. Columbia, MO: University of Missouri Press.

Frankel, Max. 2004. *High Noon in the Cold War: Kennedy, Khrushchev, and the Cuban Missile Crisis*. New York: Ballantine Books.

Fursenko, Aleksandr, and Timothy Naftali. 1997. *One Hell of a Gamble: Khrushchev, Castro, and Kennedy, 1958–1964*. New York: W. W. Norton & Company. Paperback edition.

2006. *Khrushchev's Cold War: The Inside Story of an American Adversary*. New York: W. W. Norton & Company. Paperback edition.

Garthoff, Raymond L. 1994. *The Great Transition: American-Soviet Relations and the End of the Cold War*. Washington, DC: The Brookings Institution.

Gartzke, Erik. 2006. "The Affinity of Nations Index, 1946–2002." Version 4. http://dss.ucsd.edu/~egartzke/datasets.htm (November 9, 2011).

Gearan, Anne. 2012. "Netanyahu Calls for a 'Red Line' to Stop Iran from Developing Weapon." *Washington Post*, September 28, A4.

Gearan, Anne, Ed O'Keefe, and William Branigin. 2013. "Senate Committee Approves Resolution Authorizing U.S. Strike on Syria." *Washington Post*, September 4. www.washingtonpost.com/world/national-security/officials-press-lawmakers-to-approve-syria-strike-obama-invokes-congresss-credibility/2013/09/04/4c93a858-155c-11e3-804b-d3a1a3a18f2c_story.html (June 10, 2015).

Gelpi, Christopher F. 1997. "Crime and Punishment: The Role of Norms in Crisis Bargaining." *American Political Science Review* 91(2):339–360.

Gelpi, Christopher F., and Michael Griesdorf. 2001. "Winners or Losers? Democracies in International Crisis, 1918–94." *American Political Science Review* 95:633–647.

George, Lloyd. 1911. "Speech on the International Situation Delivered at the Mansion House, July 21, 1911." In *Life of David Lloyd George: Volume IV Speechs*, ed.

Herbert Du Parcq. London: Caxton Publishing Company, 789–792. Available https://archive.org/details/lifeofdavidlloyd04dupauoft (May 30, 2015).

Gibler, Douglas M. 2009. *International Military Alliances, 1648–2008*. Washington, DC: CQ Press.

Gillespie, Mark. 2010. "Americans Look Back at Vietnam War." Gallup Polls, November 17. www.gallup.com/poll/2299/americans-look-back-vietnam-war.aspx. (May 27, 2015).

Goemans, H.E. 2000. *War and Punishment: the Causes of War Termination and the First World War*. Princeton, NJ: Princeton University Press.

Golby, James Thomas. 2011. *Duty, Honor . . . Party? Ideology, Institutions, and the Use of Military Force*. Dissertation, Stanford University.

Goldstein, Joshua S. 1992. "A Conflict-Cooperation Scale for WEIS Events Data." *Journal of Conflict Resolution* 36(2):369–385.

Gorbachev, Mikhail. [1995] 1997. *Memoirs*. Trans. Georges Peronansky and Tatjana Varsavsky. New York: Bantam Books.

Gottfried, Matthew S., and Robert F. Trager. 2016. "A Preference for War: How Fairness and Rhetoric Influence Leadership Incentives in Crises." *International Studies Quarterly* 60(2):243–257.

Grachev, Andrei. 2008. *Gorbachev's Gamble: Soviet Foreign Policy and the End of the Cold War*. Malden, MA: Polity Press.

Graebner, Norman A., Richard Dean Burns, and Joseph M. Siracusa. 2008. *Reagan, Bush, Gorbachev: Revisiting the End of the Cold War*. Westport, CT: Praeger Security International.

Granger, C. W. J. 1969. "Investigating Causal Relations by Econometric Models and Cross-spectral Methods." *Econometrica* 37(3):424–438.

Grimmer, Justin, and Brandon M. Stewart. 2013. "Text as Data: The Promise and Pitfalls of Automatic Content Analysis Methods for Political Texts." *Political Analysis* 21:267–297.

Gromyko, Andrei. 1984. "Information of Comrade A. A. Gromyko on International Questions." March 28, History and Public Policy Program Digital Archive, Mongolian Foreign Ministry Archive: fond 2, dans 1, kh/n 489, khuu 46–49. Obtained and translated by Sergey Radchenko. http://digitalarchive.wilsoncenter.org/document/119908 (April 4, 2015).

    1989. *Memories*. Trans. Harold Shukman. New York: Doubleday.

Guisinger, Alexandra, and Alastair Smith. 2002. "Honest Threats: The Interaction of Reputation and Political Institutions in International Crises." *Journal of Conflict Resolution* 46(2):75–200.

Gwertzman, Bernard. 1972. "No U.S. Comment on Thieu's Speech; But Officials Make it Clear White House Is Annoyed." *New York Times*, December 13. http://query.nytimes.com/gst/abstract.html?res=9C05E5DA1631E63BBC4B52DFB4678389669EDE (May 27, 2015).

Haig, Alexander. 1981. Quoted in "Major Points from Appearance by Haig before Senate Committee." *New York Times*, January 10. www.nytimes.com/1981/01/10/us/major-points-from-appearance-by-haig-before-senate-committee.html (July 4, 2015).

Haldeman, H.R. 1994. *The Haldeman Diaries: Inside the Nixon White House*. New York: Berkley Books.

Haldeman, H.R., with Joseph DiMona. 1978. *The Ends of Power*. New York: Times Books.

Hanmer, Michael J., and Kerem Ozan Kalkan. 2013. "Behind the Curve: Clarifying the Best Approach to Calculating Predicted Probabilities and Marginal Effects from Limited Dependent Variable Models." *American Journal of Political Science* 57(1):263–277.

Harris Survey. 1973. January 14–17. Retrieved December 12, 2013 from the iPOLL Databank, The Roper Center for Public Opinion Research, University of Connecticut.

　1983. April. Retrieved December 27, 2013 from the iPOLL Databank, The Roper Center for Public Opinion Research, University of Connecticut.

　1983–1984. Polls between December 1983 and November 1984. Retrieved December 27, 2013 from the iPOLL Databank, The Roper Center for Public Opinion Research, University of Connecticut.

Haslam, Jonathan. 2011. *Russia's Cold War: From the October Revolution to the Fall of the Wall*. New Haven, CT: Yale University Press.

Holloway, David. 2015. "The Dynamics of the Euromissile Crisis, 1977–1983." In *The Euromissile Crisis and the End of the Cold War*, ed. Leopoldo Nuti, Frederic Bozo, Marie-Pierre Rey, and Bernd Rother. Washington, DC: Woodrow Wilson Center Press, 11–30.

Hook, Steven W., and John Spanier. 2013. *American Foreign Policy since World War II*. 19th ed. Los Angeles: Sage Publications.

Horowitz, Michael C., Allan C. Stam, and Cali M. Ellis. 2015. *Why Leaders Fight*. New York: Cambridge University Press.

Howell, William G., and Jon C. Pevehouse. 2007. *While Dangers Gather: Congressional Checks on Presidential War Powers*. Princeton, NJ: Princeton University Press.

Hunt, Michael H. 1996. *Lyndon Johnson's War: America's Cold War Crusade in Vietnam, 1945–1968*. New York: Hill and Wang.

Huth, Paul, and Bruce Russett. 1984. "What Makes Deterrence Work? Cases from 1900 to 1980." *World Politics* 36(4):496–526.

Huth, Paul K. 1988. *Extended Deterrence and the Prevention of War*. New Haven, CT: Yale University Press.

　1997. "Reputations and Deterrence: A Theoretical and Empirical Assessment." *Security Studies* 7(1):72–99.

Huth, Paul K., and Todd L. Allee. 2002. *The Democratic Peace and Territorial Conflict in the Twentieth Century*. New York: Cambridge University Press.

Iacus, Stefano M., Gary King, and Giuseppe Porro. 2012. "Causal Inference without Balance Checking: Coarsened Exact Matching. *Political Analysis* 20(1):1–24.

Ignatius, David. 2012. "The 'Red Line' Herring." *Washington Post*, September 16, A23.

James, Patrick, and Jean Sébastien Rioux. 1998. "International Crises and Linkage Politics: The Experiences of the United States, 1953–1994." *Political Research Quarterly* 51(3):781–812.

Johns, Andrew L. 2010. *Vietnam's Second Front: Domestic Politics, the Republican Party, and the War*. Lexington, KY: University Press of Kentucky.

Johnson, Jesse C., Brett Ashley Leeds, and Ahra Wu. 2015. "Capability, Credibility, and Extended General Deterrence." *International Interactions* 41(2):309–336.

Karnow, Stanley. 1997. *Vietnam: A History*. New York: Penguin Books.

Kearns, Doris. 1976. *Lyndon Johnson and the American Dream*. New York: Harper & Row.

Kershner, Isabel. 2009. "Israel's Labor Party Votes to Join Netanyahu Coalition." *New York Times*, March 24. www.nytimes.com/2009/03/25/world/middleeast/25mideast.html?_r=0 (May 30, 2016).

Kertzer, Joshua D., and Ryan Brutger. 2015. "Decomposing Audience Costs: Bringing the Audience Back into Audience Cost Theory." *American Journal of Political Science* 60(1):234–249.

Khrushchev, Nikita. 2007. *Memoirs of Nikita Khrushchev, Volume 3: Statesman 1953–1964.* ed. Sergei Khrushchev. Trans. George Shriver. University Park, PA: Pennsylvania State University Press.

Khrushchev, Sergei N. 2000. *Nikita Khrushchev and the Creation of a Superpower.* Trans. Shirley Benson. University Park, PA: Pennsylvania State University Press.

Kimball, Daryl G. 2004. "Looking Back: The Nuclear Arms Control Legacy of Ronald Reagan." *Arms Control Today*, July/August. www.armscontrol.org/act/2004_07–08/Reagan (December 22, 2013).

Kimball, Jeffrey. 1998. *Nixon's Vietnam War.* Lawrence, KS: University Press of Kansas.

King, Gary, and Will Lowe. 2003. "An Automated Information Extraction Tool for International Conflict Data with Performance as Good as Human Coders: A Rare Events Evaluation Design." *International Organization* 57:617–642.

Koch, Michael T., and Patricia Sullivan. 2010. "Partisanship, Approval, and the Duration of Major Power Democratic Military Interventions." *Journal of Politics* 72(3):616–629.

Krebs, Ronald R. 2015. *Narrative and the Making of US National Security.* New York: Cambridge University Press.

Kurizaki, Shuhei. 2007. "Efficient Secrecy: Public versus Private Threats in Crisis Diplomacy." *American Political Science Review* 101(3):543–558.

Kydd, Andrew H. 2015. *International Relations Theory: The Game Theoretic Approach.* New York: Cambridge University Press.

LaFeber, Walter. 1994. *The American Age: U.S. Foreign Policy at Home and Abroad, 1750 to the Present.* New York: W.W. Norton and Company.

Levendusky, Matthew S., and Michael C. Horowitz. 2012. "When Backing Down Is the Right Decision: Partisanship, New Information, and Audience Costs." *Journal of Politics* 74(2):323–338.

Leventoglu, Bahar, and Ahmer Tarar. 2005. "Prenegotiation Public Commitment in Domestic and International Bargaining." *American Political Science Review* 99(3):419–433.

Levy, Jack S. 1989. "The Diversionary Theory of War." In *The Handbook of War Studies*, ed. Manus Midlarsky. Boston: Unwin Hyman, 259–288.

Levy, Jack S., and William F. Mabe, Jr. 2004. "Politically Motivated Opposition to War." *International Studies Review* 6(4):65–83.

Luthi, Lorenz M. 2009. "Beyond Betrayal: Beijing, Moscow, and the Paris Negotiations, 1971–1973." *Journal of Cold War Studies* 11(1):57–107.

MacAskill, Ewen. 2013. "US Warns North Korea of Increased Isolation if Threats Escalate Further." *The Guardian*, March 29. www.theguardian.com/world/2013/mar/29/us-condemns-north-korea-threats (November 24, 2014).

Maoz, Zeev. 2005. Dyadic MID Dataset (Version 2.0). http://psfaculty.ucdavis.edu/zmaoz/dyadmid.html (June 15, 2011).

Marshall, Monty G., Keith Jaggers, and Ted Robert Gurr. 2010. "Polity IV Project: Political Regime Characteristics and Transitions, 1800–2010." www.systemicpeace.org/inscr/inscr.htm (September 6, 2011).

Mastny, Vojtech. 2009. "How Able Was 'Able Archer'? Nuclear Trigger and Intelligence in Perspective." *Journal of Cold War Studies* 11(1):108–123.

Matlock, Jack F, Jr. 1995. *Autopsy on an Empire: The American Ambassador's Account of the Collapse of the Soviet Union.* New York: Random House.

2004. *Reagan and Gorbachev: How the Cold War Ended.* New York: Random House.

Matray, James I. 2002. "Dean Acheson's Press Club Speech Reexamined." *Journal of Conflict Studies* 22(1). http://journals.hil.unb.ca/index.php/jcs/article/view/366/578 (June 2, 2013).

McClelland, Charles A. 1978. *World Event/Interaction Survey (WEIS) Project, 1966–1978.* Third ICPSR Edition. Ann Arbor, MI: Inter-University Consortium for Political and Social Research.

Mearsheimer, John J. 1983. *Conventional Deterrence.* Ithaca: Cornell University Press.

"Memorandum of Conversation Between Secretary of the Interior Udall and Chairman Khrushchev." September 6, 1962. *Foreign Relations of the United States, 1961–1963.* Volume XV, Berlin Crisis, 1962–1963, Document 112.

Mercer, Jonathan 1996. *Reputation and International Politics.* Ithaca: Cornell University Press.

Milenkoski, Mile, and Jove Talevski. 2001. "Delineation of the State Border between the Republic of Macedonia and the Federal Republic of Yugoslavia." *IBRU Boundary and Security Bulletin* 9(2):93–98.

Military History Institute of Vietnam. 2002. *Victory in Vietnam: The Official History of the People's Army of Vietnam, 1954–1975.* Trans. Merle L. Pribbenow. Lawrence, KS: University Press of Kansas.

Miller, Gregory D. 2011. *The Shadow of the Past: Reputation and Military Alliances before the First World War.* Ithaca: Cornell University Press.

Miller, Ross A. 2015. "You've Got to Know When to Fold 'Em: International and Domestic Consequences of Capitulation, 1919–1999." *International Interactions* 41(4):674–698.

Morgan, Clifton T., Navin A. Bapat, and Yoshiharu Kobayashi. 2013. Threat and Imposition of Sanctions (TIES) Data 4.0 Users Manual. www.unc.edu/~bapat/TIES .htm (January 21, 2014).

Naughton, James M. 1973a. "Congress Critics of War Threaten to Fight Funding." *New York Times*, January 3. http://query.nytimes.com/gst/abstract.html?res=9504E6DE13 3BE53ABC4B53DFB7668388669EDE (May 27, 2015).

1973b. "Pullout Sought." *New York Times*, January 4. http://query.nytimes.com/gst/ abstract.html?res=9906E2DF1531EF34BC4C53DFB7668388669EDE (May 27, 2015).

Netanyahu, Benjamin. 2012. Speech to the United Nations General Assembly, September 27. Quoted in *Reuters*, "Key Portions of Israeli PM Netanyahu's U.N. Speech on Iran." www.reuters.com/article/2012/09/27/us-un-assembly-israel-text-idUSBRE88Q1RR20120927 (October 4, 2012).

Neuendorf, Kimberly A. 2002. *The Content Analysis Guidebook.* Thousand Oaks, CA: Sage Publications.

Neustadt, Richard E. 1976. *Presidential Power: The Politics of Leadership with Reflections on Johnson and Nixon.* New York: John Wiley and Sons.

Nguyen, Lien-Hang T. 2012. *Hanoi's War: An International History of the War for Peace in Vietnam.* Chapel Hill, NC: University of North Carolina Press.

Nixon, Richard. 1978. *RN: The Memoirs of Richard Nixon*. New York: Simon and Schuster.

1986. "Memorandum on Conversation with General Secretary Gorbachev at the Kremlin, July 18, 1986." Richard Nixon Library and Museum, Ronald Reagan Post-Presidential Correspondence Collection.

Nixon, Richard, and Henry Kissinger. 1972. "Nixon, Kissinger, and the 'Decent Interval,'" August 3. Audio transcript available from the Miller Center. http://millercenter.org/presidentialclassroom/exhibits/nixon-kissinger-and-the-decent-interval (May 13, 2015).

Obama, Barack. 2012. "Obama to Iran and Israel: 'As President of the United States, I Don't Bluff.'" Interview by Jeffrey Goldberg. *Atlantic*, March 2. www.theatlantic.com/international/archive/2012/03/obama-to-iran-and-israel-as-president-of-the-united-states-i-dont-bluff/253875/ (October 5, 2012).

Ostrom, Charles W. Jr., and Dennis M. Simon. 1985. "Promise and Performance: A Dynamic Model of Presidential Popularity." *American Political Science Review* 79(2):334–358.

Palmer, Glenn, Vito D'Orazio, Michael Kenwick, and Matthew Lane. 2015. "The MID4 Dataset, 2002–2010: Procedures, Coding Rules and Description." *Conflict Management and Peace Science* 32(2):222–242.

Palmer, Glenn, Tamar R. London, and Patrick M. Regan. 2004. "What's Stopping You?: The Sources of Political Constraints on International Conflict Behavior in Parliamentary Democracies." *International Interactions* 30(1):1–24.

Parent, Joseph M., and Paul K. MacDonald. 2011. "The Wisdom of Retrenchment: America Must Cut Back to Move Forward." *Foreign Affairs* 90(6):32–47.

Partell, Peter J., and Glenn Palmer. 1999. "Audience Costs and Interstate Crises: An Empirical Assessment of Fearon's Model of Dispute Outcomes." *International Studies Quarterly* 43(2):389–405.

Paterson, Thomas G., and William J. Brophy. 1986. "October Missiles and November Elections: The Cuban Missile Crisis and American Politics, 1962." *Journal of American History* 73(1):87–119.

Peters, Gerhard, and John Woolley. 2016. *American Presidency Project*, University of California, Santa Barbara. www.presidency.ucsb.edu (June 18, 2011–April 26, 2016).

Peters, Jeremy. 2014. "Senate Panel Approves Limited Fight Against ISIS, Reopening War Powers Debate." *New York Times*, December 11. www.nytimes.com/2014/12/12/us/politics/senate-panel-approves-limited-fight-against-isis-reopening-war-powers-debate.html (June 20, 2015).

Pipes, Richard. 1977. "Why the Soviet Union Thinks It Could Fight and Win a Nuclear War." *Commentary* 64(1):21–34.

Politburo. 1962. "Minutes # 60a of October 22, 1962." Kremlin Decision-Making Project, Miller Center of Public Affairs. http://web1.millercenter.org/kremlin/62_10_22.pdf (June 20, 2015).

Politburo. 1968. "Secret North Vietnam Politburo Cable." April 8. History and Public Policy Program Digital Archive, Archive of the Party Central Committee, Hanoi. Translated for CWIHP by Merle Pribbenow. http://digitalarchive.wilsoncenter.org/document/113978 (May 15, 2015).

Politburo. 1983. "Meeting Minutes of the Politburo of the CC CPSU, Regarding Western Plans for Deployment of New Nuclear Weapons in Europe." May 31. History and

Public Policy Program Digital Archive, TsKhSD, F. 89, Op. 42, D. 53, Ll. 1–14. http://digitalarchive.wilsoncenter.org/document/115981 (April 4, 2015).

Politburo. 1986a. "Meeting Minutes of the Politburo of the CC CPSU, Regarding the Aftermath of the Reykjavik US Soviet summit." October 22. History and Public Policy Program Digital Archive, TsKhSD, F. 89, Op. 42, D. 53, Ll. 1–14. http://digitalarchive.wilsoncenter.org/document/115984 (May 1, 2015).

Politburo. 1986b. "USSR CC CPSU Politburo Session on Results of the Reykjavik Summit, October 14, 1986." In *The Reykjavik File: Previously Secret Documents from U.S. and Soviet Archives on the 1986 Reagan-Gorbachev Summit*, ed. Svetlana Savranskaya and Thomas Blanton. The National Security Archive, George Washington University, Washington DC. http://nsarchive.gwu.edu/NSAEBB/NSAEBB203/ (July 4, 2015).

Porter, Gareth. 1975. *A Peace Denied: The United States, Vietnam, and the Paris Agreement*. Bloomington, IN: Indiana University Press.

Powell, Robert. 2004. "Bargaining and Learning while Fighting." *American Journal of Political Science* 48(2):344–361.

Press, Daryl G. 2005. *Calculating Credibility: How Leaders Assess Military Threats*. Ithaca: Cornell University Press.

Ramsay, Kristopher W. 2004. "Politics at the Water's Edge: Crisis Bargaining and Electoral Competition." *Journal of Conflict Resolution* 48(4):459–486.

Reiter, Dan, and Allan C. Stam III. 1998. "Democracy, War Initiation, and Victory." *American Political Science Review* 92(2):377–389.

Renshon, Jonathan, Allan Dafoe, and Paul Huth. 2015. "To Whom Do Reputations Adhere? Experimental Evidence on Influence-Specific Reputations." Working Paper.

Reston, James. 1972. "President Nixon's Trump Cards." *New York Times*, December 3. http://query.nytimes.com/gst/abstract.html?res=9904E3DD143DE53ABC4B53DFB4678389669EDE (May 27, 2015).

Risse-Kappen, Thomas. 1991. "Did 'Peace through Strength' End the Cold War? Lessons from INF." *International Security* 16(1):162–188.

Rivers, Douglas, and Nancy L. Rose. 1985. "Passing the President's Program: Public Opinion and Presidential Influence in Congress." *American Journal of Political Science* 29(2):183–196

Roe, Patrick C. 2000. *The Dragon Strikes: China and the Korean War, June–December 1950*. New York: Presidio Press.

Roosevelt, Theodore. 1901. *The Strenuous Life: Essays and Addresses by Theodore Roosevelt*. New York: The Century Company.

Roper Report. 1984. Report 84–88, August. Retrieved December 27, 2013 from the iPOLL Databank, The Roper Center for Public Opinion Research, University of Connecticut.

Sanders, Jerry Wayne. 1983. *Peddlers of Crisis: The Committee on the Present Danger and the Politics of Containment*. Cambridge, MA: South End Press.

Sartori, Anne E. 2005. *Deterrence by Diplomacy*. Princeton, NJ: Princeton University Press.

Saunders, Elizabeth N. 2015. "War and the Inner Circle: Democratic Elites and the Politics of Using Force." *Security Studies* 24(3):466–501.

Schelling, Thomas C. 1960. *The Strategy of Conflict*. Cambridge: Harvard University Press.

1966. *Arms and Influence*. New Haven, CT: Yale University Press.

Schmemann, Serge. 1983. "Gromyko News Conference: A 'Virtuoso Performance.'" *New York Times*, April 4. www.nytimes.com/1983/04/04/world/gromyko-news-conference-a-virtuoso-performance.html (July 21, 2015).

Schultz, Kenneth A. 1998. "Domestic Opposition and Signaling in International Crises." *American Political Science Review* 92(4):829–844.

1999. "Do Democratic Institutions Constrain or Inform? Contrasting Two Institutional Perspectives on Democracy and War." *International Organization* 53(2):233–266.

2001. "Looking for Audience Costs." *Journal of Conflict Resolution* 40(1):16–40.

2005. "The Politics of Risking Peace: Do Hawks or Doves Deliver the Olive Branch?" *International Organization* 59(1):1–38.

Schwartz, Andrew H., and Lyle H. Ungar. 2015. "Content Analysis of Social Media: A Systematic Overview of Automated Methods." *Annals of the American Academy of Political and Social Science* 659(1):78–94.

Sciutto, Jim, Barbara Starr, and Kevin Liptak. 2016. "ISIS Fighters in Libya Surge as Group Suffers Setbacks in Syria, Iraq." CNN, February 4. www.cnn.com/2016/02/04/politics/isis-fighters-libya-syria-iraq/ (April 26, 2016).

Sechser, Todd S. 2011. "Militarized Compellent Threats, 1918–2001." *Conflict Management and Peace Science* 28(4):377–410.

Shea, Patrick, Terence K. Teo, and Jack S. Levy. 2014. "Opposition Politics and International Crises: A Formal Model." *International Studies Quarterly* 58:741–751.

Shore, Zachary. 2014. *A Sense of the Enemy: The High-Stakes History of Reading your Rival's Mind*. New York: Oxford University Press.

Simmons, Beth A., and Daniel J. Hopkins. 2005. "The Constraining Power of International Treaties: Theory and Method." *American Political Science Review* 99(4):623–631.

Singer, David J., Stuart Bremer, and John Stuckey. 1972. "Capability Distribution, Uncertainty, and Major Power War, 1820–1965." In *Peace, War, and Numbers, ed.* Bruce Russett. Beverly Hills: Sage Publications, 19–48. Version 4.0 used directly, Version 3.0 used by EUGene for weighting *Alliance Similarity*.

Slantchev, Branislav L. 2003. "The Principle of Convergence in Wartime Negotiations." *American Political Science Review* 97(3):621–632.

2006. "Politicians, the Media, and Domestic Audience Costs." *International Studies Quarterly* 50:445–477.

2010. "Feigning Weakness." *International Organization* 64:357–388.

Smith, Alastair. 1996. "International Crises and Domestic Politics." *American Political Science Review* 92(3):623–638.

Smith, Ralph B. 1991. *An International History of the Vietnam War, Volume III: The Making of a Limited War, 1965–1966*. New York: St. Martin's Press.

Snyder, Jack, and Erica Borghard. 2011. "The Cost of Empty Threats: A Penny, Not a Pound." *American Political Science Review* 105(3):437–456.

Stern, Sheldon M. 2005. *The Week the World Stood Still: Inside the Secret Cuban Missile Crisis*. Stanford, CA: Stanford University Press.

Taubman, William. 2003. *Khrushchev: The Man and His Era*. New York: W.W. Norton and Company.

Thies, Wallace J. 1980. *When Governments Collide: Coercion and Diplomacy in the Vietnam Conflict 1964–1968.* Berkeley: University of California Press.

Thompson, William R. 2001. "Identifying Rivals and Rivalries in World Politics." *International Studies Quarterly* 45(4):557–586.

Thucydides. 400 B.C.E. [2006]. *The History of the Peloponnesian War.* Trans. Richard Crawley and revised by Donald Lateiner. New York: Barnes and Noble Classics.

Thyne, Clayton L. 2010. "Supporter of Stability or Agent of Agitation? The Effect of US Foreign Policy on Coups in Latin America, 1960–1999." *Journal of Peace Research* 47(4):449–461. Online appendix. www.uky.edu/~clthyn2/ (May 12, 2012).

Tomlinson, Rodney G. 1993. "World Event/Interaction Survey (WEIS) Coding Manual." Manuscript, United States Naval Academy.

Tomz, Michael. 2007. "Domestic Audience Costs in International Relations: An Experimental Approach." *International Organization* 61:821–840.

Trachtenberg, Marc. 2012. "Audience Costs: An Historical Analysis." *Security Studies* 21(1):3–42.

Trager, Robert F. 2010. "Diplomatic Calculus in Anarchy: How Communication Matters." *American Political Science Review* 104(2):347–368.

2013. "How the Scope of a Demand Conveys Resolve." *International Theory* 5(3):414–445.

2015. "Diplomatic Signaling among Multiple States." *Journal of Politics* 77(3):635–647.

Trager, Robert F., and Lynn Vavreck. 2011. "The Political Costs of Crisis Bargaining: Presidential Rhetoric and the Role of Party." *American Journal of Political Science* 55(3):526–545.

Trump, Donald. 2016. "Transcript: Donald Trump Expounds on His Foreign Policy Views." *New York Times*, March 26. www.nytimes.com/2016/03/27/us/politics/donald-trump-transcript.html (May 29, 2016).

US House of Representatives Office of the Clerk. 2014. "Party Divisions of the House of Representatives (1789 to Present)." http://artandhistory.house.gov/house_history/partyDiv.aspx (March 1, 2014).

US Senate Historical Office. 2014. "Party Division in the Senate, 1789-Present." www .senate.gov/pagelayout/history/one_item_and_teasers/partydiv.htm (March 1, 2014).

Voeten, Erik, and Adis Merdzanovic. 2009. "United Nations General Assembly Voting Data." http://thedata.harvard.edu/dvn/dv/Voeten/faces/study/StudyPage .xhtml?studyId=38311&versionNumber=1 (February 25, 2014).

Wagner, R. Harrison. 2000. "Bargaining and War." *American Journal of Political Science* 44(3):469–484.

Walt, Stephen. 2011. "WikiLeaks, April Glaspie, and Saddam Hussein." *Foreign Policy*, January 9. http://foreignpolicy.com/2011/01/09/wikileaks-april-glaspie-and-sadd am-hussein/ (May 14, 2016).

Waltz, Kenneth N. 1979. *Theory of International Politics.* New York: McGraw-Hill.

Washington Post Editorial Board. 2013. "Iran Heeds Israel's Warning of Uranium 'Red Line.'" April 8. http://articles.washingtonpost.com/2013–04-08/opinions/383714 92_1_uranium-red-line-iran-s (June 2, 2013).

Weaver, Wrren [Warren] Jr. 1972. "Democrats Gain 2 Seats And Have 57–43 Majority." *New York Times*, November 9. http://query.nytimes.com/gst/abstract .html?res=9E02E7D7113DEF34BC4153DFB7678389669EDE (May 27, 2015).

Weeks, Jessica L. 2008. "Autocratic Audience Costs: Regime Type and Signaling Resolve." *International Organization* 62(1):35–64.

2012. "Strongmen and Straw Men: Authoritarian Regimes and the Initiation of International Conflict." *American Political Science Review* 106(2):326–347.

2014. *Dictators at War and Peace*. Ithaca: Cornell University Press.

Weisbrot, Robert. 2001. *Maximum Danger: Kennedy, the Missiles, and the Crisis of American Confidence*. Chicago: Ivan R. Dee.

Weisiger, Alex, and Keren Yarhi-Milo. 2015. "Revisiting Reputation: How Past Actions Matter in International Politics." *International Organization* 69(2):473–495.

Williams, Richard. 2006. "Generalized Ordered Logit/Partial Proportional Odds Models for Ordinal Dependent Variables." *Stata Journal* 6(1):58–82.

Wilson, James Graham. 2014. *The Triumph of Improvisation: Gorbachev's Adaptability, Reagan's Engagement, and the End of the Cold War*. Ithaca: Cornell University Press.

Wittner, Lawrence S. 2010. "The Nuclear Freeze and Its Impact." Arms Control Association, December 5. www.armscontrol.org/act/2010_12/LookingBack (April 11, 2015).

Wood, B. Dan. 2012. *Presidential Saber Rattling: Causes and Consequences*. New York: Cambridge University Press.

Wolford, Scott. 2012. "Incumbents, Successors, and Crisis Bargaining: Leadership Turnover as a Commitment Problem." *Journal of Peace Research* 49(4):517–530.

Woodward, Bob. 2004. *Plan of Attack*. New York: Simon and Schuster

Zagare, Frank C., and D. Marc Kilgour. 2000. *Perfect Deterrence*. New York: Cambridge University Press.

Zaitchik, Alexander. 2013. "Inescapable, Apocalyptic Dread: The Terrifying Nuclear Autumn of 1983." *Salon*, September 29. www.salon.com/2013/09/29/inescapable_apocalyptic_dread_the_terrifying_nuclear_autumn_of_1983/ (April 11, 2015).

Zakaria, Fareed. 2012. "The Folly of a 'Red Line.'" *Washington Post*, September 14, A19.

Zelizer, Julian. 2007. "How Congress Helped End the Vietnam War." *The American Prospect*, February 6. http://prospect.org/article/how-congress-helped-end-vietnam-war (November 29, 2013).

Zubok, Vladislav M. 2007. *A Failed Empire: The Soviet Union in the Cold War from Stalin to Gorbachev*. Chapel Hill, NC: University of North Carolina Press.

Index

Note: Page numbers in italics represent figures or tables.